19.99
333.703
AF791542

A-Z of the Environment

Covering [illegible] and legal issues facing all types of organisation

Jeremy Stranks

THOROGOOD

Thorogood Publishing Ltd
10-12 Rivington Street
London EC2A 3DU
Telephone: 020 7749 4748
Fax: 020 7729 6110
Email: info@thorogoodpublishing.co.uk
Web: www.thorogoodpublishing.co.uk

© Jeremy Stranks 2008

All rights reserved. No part of this publication may be reproduced, stored in a retrieval system or transmitted in any form or by any means, electronic, photocopying, recording or otherwise, without the prior permission of the publisher.

This book is sold subject to the condition that it shall not, by way of trade or otherwise, be lent, re-sold, hired out or otherwise circulated without the publisher's prior consent in any form of binding or cover other than in which it is published and without a similar condition including this condition being imposed upon the subsequent purchaser.

No responsibility for loss occasioned to any person acting or refraining from action as a result of any material in this publication can be accepted by the author or publisher.

A CIP catalogue record for this book is available from the British Library.

ISBN: RB: 1 85418 420 2/978-185418420-7
PB: 1 85418 415 6/978-185418415-3

Book designed and typeset by Driftdesign

Printed in the UK by Ashford Colour Press

Special discounts for bulk quantities of Thorogood books are available to corporations, institutions, associations and other organizations. For more information contact Thorogood by telephone on **020 7749 4748**, by fax on **020 7729 6110**, or e-mail us: **info@thorogoodpublishing.co.uk**

Preface

The environment and the problems of environmental pollution are not new. The Industrial Revolution, whilst bringing prosperity to Great Britain, could be said to be the starting point for the increasing concern over environmental pollution. Early public health legislation, such as the Public Health and Clean Air Acts, endeavoured to regulate pollution to some extent, but it wasn't until the Environmental Protection Act 1990 that any major strides were made in controlling emissions to the environmental media: air, water and land.

The environment is a vast area of study embracing many disciplines, such as ecology, law, physics, chemistry, biology, environmental health, toxicology, genetic engineering and radiology. Moreover, the continuing emphasis on climate change, greenhouse gas emissions and the need to conserve energy are matters of continuing international significance with the majority of countries seeking solutions to secure the health of future generations.

The subject of the environment is now universally topical and employers and operators of businesses need to be aware of the main issues and legal requirements, together with the scientific, economic and legal terminology involved, in order to make decisions that may have an effect on the environment. The law, in particular, has moved forward at a great pace in the last decade, covering subjects as diverse as that relating to the incineration of wastes, the control of landfill sites and of ozone-depleting substances.

This book reviews the principal terminology, current legal requirements, the offences and the role of the statutory authorities together with the principal environmental issues. Its aim is to provide those who use it with a ready reference to these matters and to the action they need to take in certain cases.

Jeremy Stranks
2008

List of figures and abbreviations

Figures

List of abbreviations

ACOP	Approved Code of Practice
BAT	Best Available Techniques
BATNEEC	Best Available Techniques Not Entailing Excessive Cost
BOD	Biochemical Oxygen Demand
BPEO	Best Practicable Environmental Option
BS	British Standard
CFC	Chlorofluorocarbon
CHIP	Chemicals (Hazard Information and Packaging for Supply) Regulations
CHP	Combined Heat and Power
COD	Chemical Oxygen Demand
COMAH	Control of Major Accident Hazards Regulations
COSHH	Control of Substances Hazardous to Health Regulations
DEFRA	Department of Environment, Food and Rural Affairs
EA	Environment Agency
ECJ	European Court of Justice
EEA	European Environment Agency
EIA	Environmental Impact Assessment
ELV	Exposure Limit Value
EMAS	(European) Eco-Management and Audit Scheme
EMS	Environmental Management System
EPA	Environmental Protection Act
EU	European Union
GHS	Globally Harmonised System
GMO	Genetically Modified Organism
HCFC	Hydrochlorofluorocarbon
HMIP	Her Majesty's Inspectorate of Pollution
HSE	Health and Safety Executive
ILO	International Labour Organisation
IPC	Integrated Pollution Control

IPPC	Integrated Pollution Prevention and Control
LAPC	Local Air Pollution Control
LAAPC	Local Authority Air Pollution Control
LCA	Life Cycle Analysis (Assessment)
LEAV	Low Exposure Action Value
LEV	Local Exhaust Ventilation
LPA	Local Planning Authority
MDI	Mean Daily Intake
mSv	microSievert
nm	nanometre
NPA	National Parks Authority
NRA	National Rivers Authority
PCB	Polychlorinated biphenyls
PPE	Personal Protective Equipment
PPC	Pollution Prevention and Control
PPGN	Planning Policy Guidance Note
REACH	Registration, Evaluation, Authorisation and Restriction of Chemicals
SGV	Soil Guidance Value
TCOW	True Cost of Waste
TCPA	Town and Country Planning Act
TDI	Tolerable Daily Intake
TDSI	Tolerable Daily Soil Intake
TPO	Tree Preservation Order
UEAV	Upper Exposure Action Value
URGENT	Urban Regeneration and the Environment
VOC	Volatile Organic Compound
WCA	Waste Control Authority
WDA	Waste Disposal Authority
WEL	Workplace Exposure Limit
WHO	World Health Organisation
WRA	Waste Regulation Authority

Contents

A

B

C

D

F

G

H

I

K

L

M

N

O

R

S

T

U

V

W

A

Abandoned mines

Abandoned mines can be a serious source of water pollution. The Environment Act 1996 lays down specific requirements in respect of water pollution from abandoned mines by way of a system of consents and the requirement for mine owners to give the Environment Agency at least six months notice prior to abandoning a mine.

Environment Act 1995

Abatement

The process of reducing the degree or intensity of, or eliminating, pollution.

The process of eliminating or controlling, in particular, statutory nuisances.

Under the common law, abatement is known as the "self-help" remedy whereby an occupier of land affected may take action to abate the damage.

Abatement Notice

Noise and Statutory Nuisances Act 1993

Noise nuisance

Nuisance

Powers of inspectors

Private actions

Private nuisances

Public nuisance

Statutory nuisances

Abatement Notice

Section 80 of the EPA outlines the summary proceedings for statutory nuisances.

Where a local authority is satisfied that a statutory nuisance exists or is likely to occur or recur in the area of the authority, the authority shall serve an Abatement Notice imposing all or any of the following requirements:

(a) requiring the abatement of the nuisance or prohibiting or restricting its occurrence or recurrence;

(b) requiring the execution of such works, and the taking of such other steps, as may be necessary for any of those purposes, and the Notice shall specify the time or times within which the requirements of the Notice are to be complied with.

The Abatement Notice shall be served:

(a) except in the case of (b) and (c) below, on the person responsible for the nuisance;

(b) where the nuisance arises from any defect of a structural character, on the owner of the premises;

(c) where the person responsible for the nuisance cannot be found or the nuisance has not yet occurred, on the owner or occupier of the premises.

A person served with an Abatement Notice may appeal to a Magistrates' Court within 21 days beginning with the date on which he was served with the Notice.

If a person on whom an Abatement Notice is served, without reasonable cause, contravenes or fails to comply with any requirement or prohibition imposed by the Notice, he shall be guilty of an offence.

Failure to comply with an Abatement Notice can result in the defendant being subjected to a fine not exceeding level 5 on the standard scale together with a further fine of an amount equal to one-tenth of that level for each day the offence continues after conviction. A person who commits an offence on industrial, trade or business premises, however, shall be liable to a fine not exceeding £20,000. It is a defence to prove that best practicable means were used to prevent, or to counteract the effects of, the nuisance.

Action in default

"Best practicable means"

Environmental Protection Act 1990

Offences

Powers of inspectors

Statutory nuisances

Abatement Order

Section 82 of the EPA makes separate provision for 'aggrieved persons' to formally complain to a Magistrates' Court in respect of statutory nuisances. Thus, a Magistrates' Court may act under this Section on complaint made by any person on the ground that he is aggrieved by the existence of a statutory nuisance. Where the court is satisfied that the alleged nuisance exists, or that, although abated, it is likely to recur on the same premises, the court may make an Order (Abatement Order) for either or both of the following purposes:

(a) requiring the defendant to abate the nuisance, within a time specified in the Order, and execute any works necessary for that purpose;

(b) prohibiting a recurrence of the nuisance and requiring the defendant, within a time specified in that Order, to execute any works necessary to prevent the recurrence,

and may also impose on the defendant a fine not exceeding level 5 on the standard scale.

Where a court is satisfied that the nuisance exists and is such as, in the opinion of the court, to render premises unfit for human habitation, an Order may be made prohibiting the use of the premises for human habitation until the premises are, to the satisfaction of the court, rendered fit for that purpose.

Complaint to a Magistrates' Court

Environmental Protection Act 1990

Statutory nuisances

Absolute duties

Where a risk to the environment is inevitable if legal requirements are not followed, a statutory duty may well be strict or absolute. Absolute duties are qualified by the terms "shall" or must" and there is little or no defence available when charged with such an offence.

Most of the duties under the Environmental Protection Act 1990 and Regulations made under the Act are of a strict or absolute nature. Similar provisions are incorporated in health and safety legislation, such as the Management of Health and Safety at Work Regulations 1999 and the Workplace (Health, Safety and Welfare) Regulations 1992.

Acidification

The process of a medium, such as soil, increasing its acidity, below a pH of 6.

Acid rain

Acid rain

Acid rain is a term which describes the acidity of wet and dry deposition. This includes acidity falling as rain, snow, sleet, hail, mist, fog (wet deposition) and the dry deposition of gases and particles.

Rain water is naturally acidic as a result of carbon dioxide dissolved in water and from volcanic emissions of sulphur. However, the chemical conversion of sulphur and nitrogen emissions from power stations, factories, vehicles and domestic premises, where fossil fuels are burnt, is generally associated with acid rain.

Acid rain is created by the release into the atmosphere of certain gases, such as sulphur dioxide, nitric oxide and nitrogen dioxide. Other chemicals, such as ammonia, ozone and various hydrocarbons are also implicated in the formation of acid rain. These pollutants can be converted through a series of complex chemical reactions into sulphuric acid, nitric acid or hydrochloric acid, increasing the acidity of the rain or other type of precipitation.

Carbon dioxide + water = Carbonic acid (weak)

Sulphur dioxide + water = Sulphuric acid

Nitrogen oxides + water = Nitric acid

Rainfall acidity is based on pH, a scale which ranges from 0 to 14, 0 being the most acid, 7 being neutral and 14 the most alkaline.

Air pollution

Ammonia

Carbon dioxide

Fossil fuels

Nitrogen oxides

Sulphur oxides

Action in default

Section 81 of the EPA gives the local authority power, where an Abatement Notice has not been complied with, and whether or not they have already taken proceedings, to abate the nuisance and do whatever may be necessary in execution of that Notice. Any expenses reasonably incurred may be recovered by them from the person by whose act or default the nuisance was caused or apportioned among several persons accordingly.

This Section also gives power to a local authority, where proceedings for an offence would afford an inadequate remedy in the case of any statutory nuisance, to take proceedings in the High Court for the purpose of securing the abatement, prohibition or restriction of the nuisance, and the proceedings shall be maintainable notwithstanding the local authority have suffered no damage from the nuisance.

Abatement Notice

Environmental Protection Act 1990

Statutory nuisances

Aerobic digestion

The decomposition of organic matter by micro-organisms in the presence of oxygen.

Anaerobic digestion

Agricultural nitrate pollution

Nitrates are salts of nitric acid and have an important function in enhancing plant growth. However, the quantity of nitrates sufficient to permit plants to reach full growth is limited so it is necessary for those in agriculture to add further nitrate-based products to land to achieve the maximum yield from a crop. These may include organic manures and inorganic fertilisers.

However, not all sources of nitrates are accounted for. In many cases the quantity of nitrates applied is greater than the crop requires. As a result, excess nitrates may leach into the ground and surface waters bringing about an increase in nitrate levels. This release of nitrates into the water environment is a matter for great concern as nitrate pollution can contribute to eutrophication.

Agriculture is a major source of water pollution and a significant source of air pollution. According to the Report by the Policy Commission on Food and Farming (2002):

- over 70% of nitrates and 40% of phosphates in English waters originate from agricultural land;
- up to a half of England's bathing waters are affected by short-term contamination by agricultural pollution, mainly by microbes from livestock manure being washed off farm land after rain;

- the majority of silt loads to English rivers and lakes is derived from heavy soil erosion from agricultural land; this alters the composition of gravel sediments, reducing water clarity and causing serious risks to the life of fish, plants and insects;
- pesticides are contaminating drinking water sources, requiring extensive additional treatment at water works to remove pesticides before this water can be supplied to consumers.

Recent legislation, such as the Action Programme for Nitrate Vulnerable Zones (England and Wales) Regulations 1998, together with the Nitrate Vulnerable Zones (Additional Designations) (England) (No.2) Regulations 2002, was brought in as an attempt to remedy this situation.

Bathing Waters (Classification) Regulations 1991

Diffuse pollution

Eutrophication

Nitrate Vulnerable Zone

Pesticide

Soil erosion

Agricultural waste

This term is not defined in law but comes within the general definition of "waste". Similarly, agricultural wastes are not specified, but can include all forms of waste encountered in agricultural activities such as packaging waste, building waste, animal health products and their packaging, empty chemical containers and various forms of hazardous waste, such as agrochemical concentrates, oils and brake fluids.

Where an agricultural business produces more than 500 kg (1100 lbs) or 500 litres (110 gallons) of hazardous waste a year, they must register with the Environment Agency.

Agricultural waste must be stored and disposed of in accordance with the Waste Management (England and Wales) Regulations 2006.

Environmental Protection (Duty of Care) Regulations 1991

Waste

Waste Management (England and Wales) Regulations 2006

Air

Air extends to the limits of the atmosphere and should be taken to include the air within buildings and other natural and man-made structures above or below the ground.

[Environmental Information Regulations 1992]

Airborne particulates

Air pollution

Release into the air: substances

Airborne particulates

Particulates are a collection of particles, each of which is an aggregation of many molecules. As aerosols, they take a number of forms and can be classified as:

Dusts

Dust is an aerosol composed of solid inanimate particles. (ILO). Dusts are solid airborne particles, often created by operations such as grinding, crushing, milling, sanding and demolition. Two of the principal dusts encountered in industry are asbestos and silica.

Dusts may be:

(a) *fibrogenic* – they cause fibrotic changes to lung tissue, e.g. silica, cement dust, coal dust and certain metals;

(b) *toxic* – they eventually poison the body systems e.g. arsenic, mercury, beryllium, phosphorus and lead.

Mists

A mist comprises airborne liquid droplets, a finely dispersed liquid suspended in air. Mists are mainly created by spraying, foaming, pickling and electro-plating. Danger arises most frequently from acid mist produced in industrial treatment processes e.g. oil mist, chromic acid mist.

Fumes

These are fine solid particulates formed from the gaseous state usually by vaporisation or oxidation of metals e.g. lead fume. Fumes usually form an oxide in contact with air. They are created by industrial processes which involve the heating and melting of metals, such as welding, smelting and arc air gouging. A common fume danger is lead poisoning associated with the inhalation of lead fume.

Gases

These are formless fluids usually produced by chemical processes involving combustion or by the interaction of chemical substances. A gas will normally seek to completely fill the space into which it is liberated. A classic gas encountered in industry is carbon monoxide. Certain gases such as acetylene, hydrogen and methane are particularly flammable.

Vapours

A vapour is the gaseous form of a material normally encountered in a solid or liquid state at normal room temperature and pressure. Typical examples are solvents, such as trichloroethylene, which release vapours when the container is opened. Other liquids produce a vapour on heating, the amount of vapour being directly related to the boiling point of that particular liquid. A vapour contains very minute droplets of the liquid. However, in the case of a **fog**, the liquid droplets are much larger.

Smoke

Smoke is a product of incomplete combustion, mainly of organic materials. It may include fine particles of carbon in the form of ash, soot and grit that are visibly suspended in air.

Contaminant	Particle size range (Microns)	Characteristics
Dust	0.1 – 75	Generated by natural fragmentation or mechanical cutting or crushing of solids e.g. wood, rock, coal, metals, etc. Grit particles, usually considered to be above 75 microns, are unlikely to remain airborne.
Fume	0.001 – 1.0	Small solid particles of condensed vapour, especially metals, as in welding or melting processes. Often agglomerate into larger particles as the smaller particles collide.
Smoke	0.01 – 1.0	Aerosol formed by incomplete combustion of organic matter; does not include ash, e.g. fly ash.
Mist	0.01 – 10.0	Aerosol of droplets formed by condensation from the gaseous state or as dispersion of a liquid state e.g. hot open surface tank, electroplating.
Vapour	0.005	Gaseous state of materials that are liquid or solid at normal room temperature and pressure e.g.solvent vapours
Gas	0.0005	Materials which do not normally exist as liquids or solids at normal room temperature and pressure.

Figure 1: COMPARISON OF TYPES OF AIRBORNE CONTAMINANT

Production of particulates

This is largely brought about as a result of a size reduction process through operations such as pulverisation, grinding, chemical action, transportation, spray drying, sieving, polishing and the associated grading, screening, blending and packing of dusty products. Other particulates may be produced as a result of heat processes.

Aerosol behaviour

All dusts and fumes are potential aerosols and the behaviour of particles is influenced by:

(a) the rate of air movement;

(b) Brownian motion, that is the "joggling" movement or effect imparted to submicron particles by molecular bombardment; and

(c) the size, density and shape of the particle.

Evaluation of airborne particulate hazards

The following factors should be considered:

(a) type of particulate;

(b) source of the particulate;

(c) duration of exposure;

(d) air monitoring system necessary;

(e) existing cleaning/control methods; and

(f) current legal requirements.

Control of airborne particulates

In determining the appropriate controls, the following factors should be considered:

(a) type of particulate – particle size and shape, weight, density, air velocity and toxicity;

(b) the sources of particulate in a particular process e.g. blending, screening;

(c) number of people exposed, duration of exposure (continuous or intermittent) per day, and the number of days per week this exposure takes place;

(d) the methods available for monitoring exposure e.g. static sampling, personal dosimetry, and the results of past monitoring activities;

(e) the efficiency of current cleaning methods; manual methods e.g. sweeping, should be replaced by the use of industrial vacuum cleaners; and

(f) the efficiency of arrestment plant, including the system for examination, maintenance and testing of such plant.

Emphasis should always be placed on control at source by means of efficient control systems (local exhaust ventilation) sooner than the provision and use of respiratory protective equipment.

In workplaces, the requirements of the Control of Substances Hazardous to Health Regulations 2002 should be implemented as most airborne particulates are classified as "substances hazardous to health" under these Regulations.

Air pollution

Carbon monoxide

Chlorine

Control of Substances Hazardous to Health (COSHH) Regulations 2006

Copper

Environmental monitoring in the workplace

Ferrous metals

Grit, dust and fumes

Heavy metal pollution

Lead and lead poisoning

Respiratory diseases

Sulphur oxides

Air pollution

Air pollution arises when harmful substances, such as carbon monoxide, nitrogen dioxide, sulphur dioxide and lead are discharged to the atmosphere. Pollution may take the form of smoke, gases, fumes and dust from a variety of sources, such as ventilation systems, combustion of fuels, incineration of wastes and as a result of certain processes. Pollutants can affect the upper respiratory tract resulting in diseases such as bronchitis. Air pollution caused by substances such as benzene, may also be a factor in the incidence of cancer of the lung, oesophagus and stomach.

Acid rain

Air

Airborne particulates

Clean Air Act 1993

Control of Substances Hazardous to Health (COSHH) Regulations 2006

"Dark smoke"

Dark smoke offences

Emission

Emission limit value

Environmental Protection Act 1990

Fossil fuels

Global warming

Greenhouse effect

Grit, dust and fumes

Incineration

Local exhaust ventilation (LEV) systems

Ozone depletion

Part B activities

Pollution of the environment

Release into the air: substances

Respiratory diseases

Smoke

Smoke Control Areas

Smoke Control Areas (Authorised Fuels) (England) Regulations 2002 – 2006

Smoke-free premises and vehicles

Air Quality Management Area

Local authorities have duties under the Environment Act 1995 for local air quality management. This includes undertaking regular reviews and assessments of air quality against standards and objectives set out in the National Air Quality Strategy and which have been prescribed in Regulations for the purpose of Local Authority Air Quality Management.

An Air Quality Management Area is an area designated by a local authority in which recommended air quality targets are not being, or are unlikely to be, met. In such cases, the local authority must prepare and implement remedial actions to address the problem.

Environment Act 1995

Pollution Prevention and Control (PPC)

Air Quality Standard

An Air Quality Standard is the level of pollutants prescribed by Regulations that must not be exceeded during a given time in a defined area.

The Air Quality Standards Regulations 2007 implemented Directive 2004/107/EC on arsenic, cadmium, mercury, nickel and polycyclic aromatic hydrocarbons in ambient air and the European air quality legislation previously implemented in the Air Quality Limit Values Regulations 2003.

These Regulations require the Secretary of State to divide England into zones for air quality management purposes. They establish:

(a) concentration limit values for Group A pollutants (benzene, carbon monoxide, lead, nitrogen dioxide and oxides of nitrogen, particulate matter (PM_{10}) and sulphur dioxide);

(b) target for Group B pollutants (the content of arsenic, benzo(a)pyrene, cadmium and nickel, and their compounds within the PM_{10} fraction); and

(c) target values and long-term objectives for ozone.

The Secretary of State has the duty to assess the concentration of pollutants in each zone and to take the necessary measures to ensure that the standards are attained. In the case of Group B pollutants, this is through the application of measures not entailing disproportionate costs or best available techniques (BAT) where the pollutants arise from Pollution Prevention and Control (PPC) installations. In certain instances, exceedences of standards for certain pollutants, or the risk of exceedences, require the Secretary of State to draw up and implement improvement plans.

Additional duties are placed on the Secretary of State with respect to the monitoring of specified other air pollutants and the deposition of some Group B pollutants.

Environment Act 1995

Air Quality Management Area

All reasonable precautions and all due diligence

This defence is available under much protective legislation, including that relating to health and safety and food safety. In the majority of cases, it is for a court to decide whether *all* reasonable precautions have been taken and *all* due diligence exercised taking into account the individual circumstances of the case.

Section 118 of the EPA provides that it shall be a defence for a person charged with an offence with respect to the requirements in relation to genetically modified organisms that he took all reasonable precautions and exercised all due diligence to avoid the commission of the offence.

"All reasonable precautions" has been said to be related to those risks of harm reasonably foreseeable when "a prudent and competent person applies his mind seriously to the situation".

On the other hand, an obligation to exercise due diligence has been said to be "indistinguishable from an obligation to exercise reasonable care".

Environmental Protection Act 1990

Harm

Hazard

Offences

Reasonable excuse

Ammonia

Ammonia is a corrosive toxic substance used for a wide range of purposes, as a refrigerant (anhydrous ammonia) in the food industry, and as a cleaning agent when dissolved in water. As a gas, it is colourless with a sharp odour.

The most common route of entry into the body is through inhalation of the gas, resulting in coughing, narrowing of the bronchi, narrowing of the throat causing upper airway obstruction, accumulation of fluid in the lungs, chest pain, impaired vision, headache and dizziness.

Contact with the skin can cause irritation and skin burns depending upon the concentration of the ammonia solution. Exposure to a concentrated vapour or solution may cause the victim to experience pain, redness and blistering of the skin.

Ammonia, even at low concentrations, can irritate the eyes and cause burning, swelling, photophobia and, in some cases, blindness.

The consequences of chronic long-term exposure to ammonia may also include pneumonia, kidney damage, cataracts, glaucoma, ulceration and perforation of the cornea, and blindness.

Acid rain

Hazardous substances: classification

Anaerobic digestion

The breaking down of organic matter in oxygen free conditions.

Aerobic digestion

Animal and vegetable matter and food industries

These scheduled activities are:

Part A(1)

(a) Tanning hides and skins at plant with a treatment capacity of more than 12 tonnes of finished products per day;

(b) Slaughtering animals at plant with a carcass production capacity of more than 50 tonnes per day;

(c) Disposing of or recycling animal carcasses or animal waste, other than by rendering, at plant with a treatment capacity exceeding 10 tonnes per day of animal carcasses or animal waste or, in aggregate, of both;

(d) Treating and processing materials intended for the production of food products from:

 (i) animal raw materials (other than milk) at plant with a finished product production capacity of more than 75 tonnes per day;

 (ii) vegetable raw materials at plant with a finished product production capacity of more than 300 tonnes per day (average value on a quarterly basis);

(e) Treating and processing milk, the quantity of milk received being more than 200 tonnes per day (average value on an annual basis);

(f) Processing, storing or drying by the application of heat of the whole or part of any dead animal or any vegetable matter (other than the treatment of effluent so as to permit its discharge into controlled waters or into a sewer unless the treatment involves the drying of any material with a view to its use as animal feedstuff) if:

   (i) the processing, storing or drying does not fall within another Section of this Schedule or Part A(2) of this Section and is not an exempt activity; and

   (ii) it may result in the release into water of any substance listed in paragraph 13 of Part 2 of this Schedule in a quantity which, in any period of 12 months, is greater than the background quantity by more than the amount specified in relation to the substance in that paragraph.

Part A(2)

(a) Disposing of or recycling animal carcasses or animal waste by rendering at plant with a treatment capacity exceeding 10 tonnes per day of animal carcasses or animal waste, or, in aggregate, of both.

Part B

(a) Processing, storing or drying by the application of heat of the whole or part of any dead animal or any vegetable matter (other than the treatment of effluent so as to permit its discharge into controlled waters or into a sewer unless the treatment involves the drying of any material with a view to its use as animal feedstuff) if:

   (i) the processing, storing or drying does not fall within another Section of this Schedule or Part A(1) or Part A(2) of this Section and is not an exempt activity;

   (ii) the processing, storing or drying may result in the release into the air of a substance described in paragraph 12 of Part 2 of this Schedule or any offensive smell noticeable outside the premises on which the activity is carried out;

(b) Breeding maggots in any case where 5 kg or more of animal matter or of vegetable matter or, in aggregate, of both are introduced into the process in any week.

Animal includes a bird or a fish.

Exempt activity means:

(a) any activity carried on in a farm or agricultural holding other than the manufacture of goods for sale;

(b) the manufacture or preparation of food or drink for human consumption other than:

   (i) the extraction, distillation or purification of animal or vegetable oil or fat otherwise than as an activity incidental to the cooking of food for human consumption;

   (ii) any activity involving the use of green offal or the boiling of blood except the cooking of food (other than tripe) for human consumption;

   (iii) the cooking of tripe for human consumption elsewhere than on premises on which it is consumed.

(c) the fleshing, drying and cleaning of pelts of fur-bearing mammals;

(d) any activity carried on in connection with the operation of a knacker's yard, as defined in article 3(1) of the Animal By-Products Order 1999;

(e) any activity for the manufacture of soap not falling within Part A(1) of Section 4.2 (Inorganic chemicals);

(f) the storage of vegetable matter not falling within any other Section of this Schedule;

(g) the cleaning of shellfish shells;

(h) the manufacture of starch;

(i) the processing of animal or vegetable matter at premises for feeding a recognised pack of hounds registered under article 13 of the Animal By-Products Order 1999;

(j) the salting of hides or skins, unless related to any other activity listed in this Schedule;

(k) any activity for composting animal or vegetable matter or a combination of both, except where that activity is carried out for the purposes of cultivating mushrooms;

(l) any activity for cleaning, and any related activity for drying or dressing, seeds, bulbs, corms or tubers;

(m) the drying of grain or pulses;

(n) any activity for the production of cotton yarn from raw cotton or for the conversion of cotton yarn into cloth.

Food includes:

(a) drink;

(b) articles and substances of no nutritional value which are used for human consumption; and

(c) articles and substances used as ingredients in the preparation of food.

Green offal means the stomach and intestines of any animal, other than poultry, and their contents.

[Schedule 1: Part 1: Pollution Prevention and Control (England and Wales) Regulations 2000]

Animal By-Products Regulations 2005

Composting

Part A activities

Part B activities

Pollution Prevention and Control Act 1999

Pollution Prevention and Control (England and Wales) Regulations 2000

Scheduled activities

Animal by-products

Animal by-products include whole animal carcasses, parts of carcasses or products of animal origin that are not intended for human consumption. In addition to whole carcasses and parts of carcasses, they include manure and intestinal contents, blood, ova, embryos, hides, skins, horns, hooves, shells, feathers, fur, wool, hair and some catering wastes. Generally, catering wastes are excluded from legal controls unless they are to be used as animal feed, or in a biogas or treatment plant, or arise from international transport, i.e ships and aircraft.

Animal by-products are categorised according to their risk to human and animal health or to the environment and there are different rules for the disposal of each category of by-product.

Category 1 – Very high risk material

(a) animals and materials suspected or confirmed as being infected by transmissible spongiform encephalopathies (TSEs) such as scrapie in sheep and bovine spongiform encephalytis (BSE) in cattle;

(b) animals which have been experimented on;

(c) carcasses of zoo and pet animals;

(d) specified risk material, i.e. tissues of cattle, sheep or goats which are, or might be, infected with BSE.

Category 2 – High risk material

(a) diseased animals;

(b) manure or animal by-products that could be contaminated with animals' diseases;

(c) animals that die on farms and do not contain specified risk material.

Category 3 – Low risk material

Material which is fit, but not intended for, human consumption, including:

(a) raw meat and fish from food manufacturers and retailers;

(b) catering waste;

(c) eggs and other by-products that do not show signs of transmissible disease;

(d) raw milk;

(e) fish and other sea animals;

(d) shells.

Animal and vegetable matter and food industries

Animal By-Products Regulations 2005

Pollution Prevention and Control (England and Wales) Regulations 2000

Scheduled activities

Animal By-Products Regulations 2005

These Regulations are concerned with procedures to be followed in the collection, transportation, storage, handling, processing and disposal of animal by-products with particular reference to Categories 1, 2 and 3 materials. They place certain restrictions on access to animal by-products and lay down a regime for the approval of premises by the competent authority. Provisions are made for sampling at processing plants, biogas and composting plants.

Requirements are laid down for the placing on the market of animal by-products and processed products with respect to:

(a) processed animal protein and other processed products that could be used as feed material;

(b) pet food, dog chews and technical products; and

(c) compost or digestion residues for use on agricultural land.

Parts 6 to 8 deal with derogations, record keeping requirements and administration and enforcement respectively.

Animal and vegetable matter and food industries

Animal by-products

Pollution Prevention and Control (England and Wales) Regulations 2000

Scheduled activities

Anti-Pollution Works Regulations 1999

These Regulations are made under the Water Resources Act 1991 and prescribe the contents of anti-pollution Works Notices served under Section 161A, the procedure to be followed in relation to appeals against such Notices and the compensation for rights of entry in connection with anti-pollution works paid under Section 161B of the Act.

Water Resources Act 1991

Works Notice

Appeals

Section 15 of the EPA provides various rights of appeal in relation to all of Part I. In addition, the Environmental Protection (Application, Appeals and Registers) Regulations provide detailed information about the appeals procedure. An appeal must be brought within two months.

A right of appeal lies with the person seeking the authorisation or the authorisation holder against the following:

(a) refusal to grant an authorisation;

(b) the conditions attached to an authorisation;

(c) refusal to grant a variation of an authorisation sought by the authorisation holder under Section 11 (variations of conditions, etc);

(d) revocation of an authorisation; and

(e) a Variation Notice, Enforcement Notice or Prohibition Notice.

Furthermore, Section 22 (Exclusion from registers of certain confidential information) allows a right of appeal concerning exclusion of commercially confidential information from the public register of information.

The Secretary of State has power to take the following action in respect of appeals:

(a) affirm the decision made by HMIP;

(b) where the decision entailed a refusal to grant an authorisation, or a variation of an authorisation, direct HMIP to grant the authorisation or vary it accordingly;

(c) quash all or any of the conditions of an authorisation;

(d) quash a decision to revoke an authorisation;

(e) give directions as to the conditions to be attached to an authorisation; and

(f) quash, affirm or modify a Variation, Enforcement or Prohibition Notice.

Most appeals are dealt with by inspectors who have the same powers as the Secretary of State. The appeal itself may be in writing or may take the form of a hearing which may be held in private.

Enforcement Notice

Environmental Protection Act 1990

Environmental Protection (Duty of Care) Regulations 1991

Offences

Prohibition Notice

Public registers of information (various)

Variation Notice

Water Resources Act 1991

Approved Supply List

This is the list entitled *Information Approved for the Classification and Labelling of Substances and Preparations Dangerous for Supply* approved by the Health and Safety Commission comprising Parts I to VI, together with such notes and explanatory material as are requisite for the use of the list.

Chemicals (Hazard Information and Packaging for Supply) (CHIP) Regulations 1994 – 2002

Hazardous substances: classification

Areas of Outstanding Natural Beauty

These areas designated solely for their landscape qualities for the purpose of conserving and enhancing their natural beauty, which includes landform and geology, plants and animals, landscape features and the rich history of human settlement over the centuries. These areas were introduced under the Countryside and Rights of Way Act 2000 and cover approximately 15% of England.

Countryside and Rights of Way Act 2000

Sites of Special and Scientific Interest

Asbestos

Asbestos is a term given to a group of naturally occurring mineral compounds extracted from mines in, principally, Canada, South Africa and Russia. Asbestos crystals are fibrous in nature and can be woven like cotton fibres, or used in loose form, rather like cotton wool, for insulation purposes. The fibres can be used to reinforce materials such as cement.

There are various forms of asbestos, which differ quite markedly in properties such as fibre strength, resistance to acids and insulating properties. The most commonly encountered are:

(a) *Chrysotile* (white asbestos) which, in the pure form, looks like dirty cotton wool;

(b) *Crocidolite* (blue asbestos) because of its sky blue appearance in the pure form; and

(c) *Amosite,* a dirty grey/brown coloured fibrous material, commonly known as 'brown asbestos'.

Industry	Use
Electricity generating	Thermal lagging of pipes, etc; blue asbestos commonly present
Buildings	Sprayed coatings on girders, etc.; blue asbestos may be present; asbestos reinforced sheeting for roofs
Railway carriages, locomotives	Thermal and sound insulation; blue asbestos used extensively for this purpose
Steel, heavy engineering	Some blue or acid resistant thermal insulation may be found
Ships	Extensively in boiler insulation; blue asbestos commonly used in the past
Heating and ventilating systems Insulating panels Decorative ceiling panels	Mostly white asbestos thermal insulation on ducting, etc; sites include hospitals, schools, domestic and industrial premises

Figure 2: OCCURRENCE OF ASBESTOS

Apart from the more general duties of employers under the Health and Safety at Work Act, employers and others must comply with the requirements of the Control of Asbestos at Work Regulations 2006.

Asbestos: activities involving

Control of Asbestos at Work Regulations 2006

Scheduled activities

Asbestos: activities involving

These scheduled activities are:

Part A(1)

(a) Producing asbestos or manufacturing products based on or containing asbestos;

(b) Stripping asbestos from railway vehicles except:

   (i) in the course of the repair or maintenance of the vehicle;

   (ii) in the course of recovery operations following an accident; or

   (iii) where the asbestos is permanently bonded in cement or in any other material (including plastic, rubber or resin);

(c) Destroying a railway vehicle by burning if asbestos has been incorporated in, or sprayed on to, its structure.

Part A(2)

Nil

Part B

(a) The industrial finishing of any of the following products where not related to any activity falling within Part A(1) of this Section:

asbestos cement	asbestos cement products
asbestos fillers	asbestos filters
asbestos floor coverings	asbestos friction products
asbestos insulating board	asbestos jointing, packaging and reinforcement material
asbestos packing	asbestos paper or card
asbestos textiles	

Asbestos includes any of the following fibrous silicates: actinolite, amosite, anthophyllite, chrysotile, crocidolite and tremolite.

[Schedule 1: Part 1: Pollution Prevention and Control (England and Wales) Regulations 2000]

Control of Asbestos at Work Regulations 2006

Part A activities

Part B activities

Pollution Prevention and Control (England and Wales) Regulations 2000

Scheduled activities

Authorised discharge consent

Section 88 of the EPA provides that a person will not be guilty of an offence under Section 85 (offences of polluting controlled waters) in respect of the entry or discharge of matter into controlled waters, if the entry or discharge is made under and in accordance with a consent provided by the National Rivers Authority (NRA) under the Water Resources Act.

Authorised discharges

Consents: controlled waters

Controlled waters

National Rivers Authority

Water Resources Act 1991

Authorised discharges

Any discharges made into controlled waters which are in compliance with conditions set down by either the NRA or Environment Agency.

Any discharges made under and in accordance with:

(a) a Waste Management Licence granted under Part II of the EPA; there is an exception, however, where the offence is of discharging trade or sewage effluent or where a prohibition is in force;

(c) a licence granted under Part II of the Food and Environment Protection Act 1985 authorising the deposit of waste at sea;

(d) Section 163 of the Water Resources Act 1991 or Section 165 of the Water Industry Act 1991 concerned with discharges for works purposes;

(e) any local statutory provision or statutory order which expressly confers power to discharge effluent into water; and

(f) any prescribed enactment.

Thus, any discharges made into controlled waters which are in compliance with conditions set down by the NRA or Environment Agency are classed as authorised discharges.

Authorised discharge consent

Consents: Controlled waters

National Rivers Authority

Waste Management Licences

Water Resources Act 1991

Authorised fuels

Authorised fuels are defined by the Smoke Control Areas (Authorised Fuels) (England) Regulations 2002-2006.

It is an offence to purchase solid unauthorised fuel for use in a Smoke Control Area, unless for an exempted fireplace (as defined), and to retail unauthorised fuel for unauthorised use in a Smoke Control Area.

[Clean Air Act 1993]

Clean Air Act 1993

Fossil fuels

Smoke Control Areas

Smoke Control Areas (Authorised Fuels)(England) Regulations 2002-2006

Authorised transport purposes

Waste may be transferred to a person for authorised transport purposes. *Authorised transport purposes* are defined in Section 34 of the EPA as:

(a) the transport of controlled waste within the same premises between different places in those premises;

(b) the transport to a place in Great Britain of controlled waste which has been brought from a country or territory outside Great Britain not having been landed in Great Britain until it arrives at that place; and

(c) the transport by air or sea of controlled waste from a place in Great Britain to a place outside Great Britain.

Environmental Protection Act 1990

Controlled waste

Waste

Waste offences

Waste transfer

B

Background quantity

In relation to the release of a substance resulting from an activity, means such quantity of that substance as is present in:

(a) water supplied to the site where the activity is carried out;

(b) water abstracted for use in the activity; and

(c) precipitation onto the site on which the activity is carried out.

[Pollution Prevention and Control (England and Wales) Regulations 2000]

Pollution Prevention and Control Act 1999

Pollution Prevention and Control (England and Wales) Regulations 2000

Scheduled activities

Bathing Waters (Classification) Regulations 1991

These Regulations implement the Bathing Waters Directive and prescribe a system for classifying relevant territorial waters, coastal waters and inland waters which are bathing waters.

Coastal waters

Fresh water limit

Inland fresh waters

Water classification

Batteries and accumulators

A source of electrical energy generated by direct conversion of chemical energy and consisting of one or more primary (non-rechargeable) batteries or secondary cells containing:

(a) either:

  (i) more than 25 mg mercury per cell; or

  (ii) in the case of alkaline manganese batteries, more than 0.25% mercury by weight;

(b) more than 0.025% cadmium by weight; or

(c) more than 0.4% lead by weight.

[Batteries and Accumulators (Containing Dangerous Substances) Regulations 1994-2001]

Batteries and Accumulators (Containing Dangerous Substances) Regulations 1994 – 2001

Batteries and Accumulators (Containing Dangerous Substances) Regulations 1994-2001

These Regulations ban the marketing of a *'prohibited battery'*, namely

(a) an alkaline manganese battery which contains more than 0.025% of mercury by weight;

(b) in the case of an alkaline manganese battery for prolonged use in extreme conditions, which contains more than 0.05% of mercury by weight,

but in the case of either (a) or (b) above excludes alkaline manganese button cells or batteries composed of button cells.

Reference to *extreme conditions* above includes, but without prejudice to the generality of the expression, temperatures below 0°C or above 50°C or where the battery is likely to be exposed to shocks.

Manufacturers of batteries and accumulators are required to:

(a) print on a battery or accumulator a separate collection mark and a mark indicating the relevant metal content or, as the case may be, on the packaging for that battery or accumulator;

(b) in relation to an appliance into which a battery or accumulator is or, as the case may be, is to be incorporated, the manufacturer of that appliance shall ensure that the battery or accumulator can be readily removed, when spent, by the consumer.

Where a battery or accumulator is not marked correctly, the Secretary of State may give notice to the manufacturer specifying marking requirements to be met within a period specified in the notice.

Batteries and accumulators

Best Available Techniques (BAT)

The most effective and advanced stage in the development of activities and their methods of operation which indicates the practical suitability of particular techniques for providing, in principle, the basis for emission limit values designed to prevent and, where that is not practicable, generally to reduce emissions and the impact on the environment as a whole.

For the purpose of this definition:

(a) *available techniques* means those techniques which have been developed on a scale which allows implementation in the relevant industrial sector, under economically and technically viable conditions, taking into consideration the cost and advantages whether or not the techniques are used or produced inside the United Kingdom, as long as they are reasonably accessible to the operator;

(b) *best* means, in relation to techniques, the most effective in achieving a high general level of protection of the environment as a whole; and

(c) *techniques* include both the technology used and the way in which the installation is designed, built, maintained, operated and decommissioned.

This term is defined under Integrated Pollution Prevention and Control (IPPC). Best Available Techniques has more cost and implementation issues than its predecessor BATNEEC.

Schedule 2 of the Pollution Prevention and Control (England and Wales) Regulations 2000 provides guidance in the determination of Best Available Techniques.

Subject to paragraph 2, in determining Best Available Techniques, special consideration shall be given to the following matters, bearing in mind the likely costs and benefits of a measure and the principles of precaution and prevention:

1. the use of low-waste technology;
2. the use of less hazardous substances;
3. the furthering of recovery and recycling of substances generated and used in the process and of waste, where appropriate;
4. comparable processes, facilities or methods of operation which have been tried with success on an industrial scale;
5. technological advances and changes in scientific knowledge and understanding;
6. the nature, effects and volume of the emissions concerned;
7. the commissioning dates for new or existing installations or mobile plant;
8. the length of time needed to introduce the Best Available Technique;
9. the consumption and nature of raw materials (including water) used in the process and the energy efficiency of the process;
10. the need to prevent or reduce to a minimum the overall impact of the emissions on the environment and the risks to it;
11. the need to prevent accidents and to minimise the consequences for the environment;

12. the information published by the Commission pursuant to Article 16(2) of the Directive or by international organisations.

Sub-paragraphs 1 to 3 and 9 to 12 shall not apply for the purposes of determining Best Available Techniques in relation to Part B installations and Part B mobile plant.

[Schedule 2: Pollution Prevention and Control (England and Wales) Regulations 2000]

Best Available Techniques Not Entailing Excessive Cost (BATNEEC)

Environmental Protection Act 1990

Integrated Pollution Prevention and Control (IPPC)

Pollution Prevention and Control Act 1990

Pollution Prevention and Control (England and Wales) Regulations 2000

Scheduled activities

Best Available Techniques Not Entailing Excessive Cost (BATNEEC)

The BATNEEC principle was dealt with in Part 1 of the EPA and was the basis for Integrated Pollution Control (IPC) and Local Authority Air Pollution Control (LAAPC). The Act required BATNEEC to be used by all prescribed processes in order to:

(a) prevent the release of substances prescribed for any environmental medium into that medium or, where that is not practicable by such means for reducing the release of such substances to a minimum and for rendering harmless any such substances which are so released; and

(b) for rendering harmless any other substances which might cause harm if released into any other environmental medium.

Fundamentally, processes subject to Integrated Pollution Control were required to use BATNEEC in order to achieve the best practicable environmental option.

BATNEEC has been replaced by Best Available Techniques (BAT).

Best Available Techniques (BAT)

Environmental Protection Act 1990

Pollution Prevention and Control (England and Wales) Regulations 2000

Scheduled activities

Best Practicable Environmental Option (BPEO)

This is a procedure that took into account the total impact of a process and the technical possibilities for dealing with it. BPEO established the waste management option, or a mix of options, that provides the greatest benefit or the least damage to the environment, at reasonable cost, in both the long-term and the short-term.

This concept was first introduced under Section 7(7) of the EPA as part of the system of Integrated Pollution Control (IPC). This was replaced by Integrated Pollution Prevention and Control (IPPC) under the Pollution Prevention and Control (England and Wales) Regulations 2000.

Best Available Techniques Not Entailing Excessive Cost (BATNEEC)

Environmental Protection Act 1990

Integrated Pollution Prevention and Control (IPPC)

Pollution Prevention and Control Act 1999

Pollution Prevention and Control (England and Wales) Regulations 2000

Scheduled activities

Waste management option

"Best practicable means"

There is no statutory definition of this term which appears in much environmental legislation. Fundamentally, it is a flexible standard which takes account of individual circumstances. "Best practicable means" is available as a defence in relation to certain statutory nuisances and noise-related offences.

To rely on this defence, a defendant must prove that the "best practicable means" were implemented to either prevent or counteract the effects of the nuisance.

In any proceedings for an offence in respect of a statutory nuisance, it is a defence to prove that "best practicable means" were used to prevent, or to counteract the effects of, the nuisance.

This defence is not new to environmental protection legislation. It originally existed under Section 94(5) of the Public Health Act 1936 and was further developed in the Clean Air Act 1956 and the Control of Pollution Act 1974 (CPA). It is defined in Section 79(9) of the EPA thus:

(a) *practicable* means reasonably practicable having regard among other things to local conditions and circumstances, to the current state of technical knowledge and to financial implications;

(b) the means to be employed including the design, installation, maintenance and manner and periods of operation of plant and machinery, and the design, construction and maintenance of buildings and structures;

(c) the test is to apply only so far as compatible with any duty imposed by law;

(d) the test is to apply only so far as compatible with safety and safe working conditions, and with the exigencies of any emergency or unforeseeable circumstances;

and, in circumstances where a Code of Practice under Section 71 of the Control of Pollution Act 1974 (noise minimisation) is applicable, regard shall be had to the guidance given in it.

A "best practicable means" defence is not available:

(a) in the case of a nuisance falling within paragraphs (a), (d), (e), (f) or (g) of Section 79(1) except where the nuisance arises on industrial, trade or business premises;

(b) in the case of a nuisance falling within paragraph (b) except where the smoke is emitted from a chimney; and

(c) in the case of a nuisance falling within paragraphs (c) or (h).

Noise Act 1996

Practicable: definition

Statutory nuisances

Biochemical Oxygen Demand (BOD)

The amount of oxygen required by micro-organisms, usually in polluted water, slurry or industrial effluent for oxidation processes. It is measured as milligrams of oxygen taken up by a sample when incubated at a standard temperature of 20°C for five days.

Biocides

Substances used in a range of industries to control unwanted organisms, such as animals, insects, bacteria, viruses and fungi. They are intended to kill or otherwise exert a controlling effect by chemical or biological means.

Biocompatibility

Biocompatibility

The ability of a material to perform with an appropriate host response to a specific application.

The quality of a substance of not having toxic or injurious effects on biological systems.

Biocides

Biodiversity

Biodegradability

The capability of a material to decompose in nature within a relatively short period of time.

Biodiversity

The range of plant and animal species and communities associated with terrestrial, aquatic and marine habitats.

The total sum of life's variety on Earth, expressed at the genetic, species and ecosystem level. (Holdgate, 1991)

Biocompatibility

Biofuels

These are fuels derived from biological materials (*biomass* or *biomatter*) including living organisms, or their by-products, plants, crops, trees and animal wastes, such as manure.

Agriculturally produced biomass fuels, such as biodiesel, ethanol and bagasse (a by-product of sugar cane cultivation) can be burned in internal combustion engines or boilers.

Biogas, which consists mainly of biologically produced methane, is a biofuel produced through the intermediary stage of anaerobic digestion. Many organic materials release gases due to the metabolisation of organic material by bacteria, the process of anaerobic digestion or fermentation. This gas, created in landfill operations and known as "landfill gas", has to be vented to reduce the potential for explosion. Animal faeces release methane under the influence of anaerobic bacteria. Biogas is readily produced from current waste streams created by processes such as paper and sugar production and from sewage and animal remains.

Liquid biofuels are mainly bioalcohols, such as ethanol, biodiesel and virgin vegetable oils. 5% bioethanol is increasingly being added to petrol. Renewable natural gas is a biogas which has been upgraded to a quality similar to natural gas, making it possible to distribute the gas to the national grid.

Anaerobic digestion

Geothermal energy

Landfill: disposal of waste

Renewable energy

Solar energy

Water power

Wind power

Biological agents

Schedule 9 to the Control of Substances Hazardous to Health (COSHH) Regulations covers the special provisions relating to biological agents. These provisions are, in the majority of cases, additional to the other provisions of the Regulations and are directed at protecting employees against risks to their health, whether immediate or delayed, arising from biological agents.

Classification of biological agents

The Schedule enables the HSC to approve and publish a document entitled *Categorisation of biological agents according to hazard and categories of containment* containing a list of biological agents together with the classification of each agent which it has approved.

Where a biological agent does not have an approved classification, the employer shall provisionally classify that agent in accordance with the classification below, having regard to the nature of the agent and of the properties of which he may reasonably be expected to be aware. The employer shall assign that agent to one of the following Groups according to its level of risk of infection and, if in doubt as to which of the two alternative Groups is the most appropriate, he shall assign it to the higher of the two -

Group 1 – unlikely to cause human diseases;

Group 2 – can cause human disease and may be a hazard to employees; it is unlikely to spread to the community and there is usually effective prophylaxis or treatment available;

Group 3 – can cause severe human disease and may be a serious hazard to employees; it may spread to the community, but there is usually effective prophylaxis or treatment available;

Group 4 – can cause severe human disease and is a serious hazard to employees; it is likely to spread to the community and there is usually no effective prophylaxis or treatment available.

Figure 3: CLASSIFICATION OF BIOLOGICAL AGENTS

Assessment of health risks

Every employer who intends to carry on any work which is liable to expose his employees to any biological agent shall take account of the Group into which that agent is classified when making an assessment of the risks created by that work.

Prevention of exposure to a biological agent

If the nature of the activity so permits, every employer shall ensure that the exposure of his employees to a particular biological agent is prevented by substituting a biological agent which is less hazardous.

Control of exposure to biological agents

Where there is a risk of exposure to a biological agent and it is not otherwise reasonably practicable to prevent that exposure then it shall be adequately controlled, in particular by the following measures which are to be applied in the light of the results of the assessment -

(a) keeping as low as practicable the number of employees exposed or likely to be exposed to the biological agent;

(b) designing work processes and engineering control measures so as to prevent or minimise the release of biological agents into the place of work;

(c) displaying the biohazard sign (see below) and other relevant warning signs;

(d) drawing up plans to deal with accidents involving biological agents;

(e) specifying appropriate decontamination and disinfection procedures;

(f) instituting means for the safe collection, storage and disposal of contaminated waste, including the use of secure and identifiable containers, after suitable treatment where appropriate;

(g) making arrangements for the safe handling and transport of biological agents, or materials that may contain such agents, within the workplace;

(h) specifying procedures for taking, handling and processing samples that may contain biological agents;

(i) providing collective prevention measures and, where exposure cannot be adequately controlled by other means, individual protection measures including, in particular, the supply of appropriate protective clothing or other special clothing;

(j) where appropriate, making available effective vaccines for those employees who are not already immune to the biological agent to which they are exposed or are liable to be exposed;

(k) instituting hygiene measures compatible with the aim of preventing or reducing the accidental transfer or release of a biological agent from the workplace, including, in particular –

   (i) the provision of appropriate and adequate washing and toilet facilities; and

   (ii) the prohibition of eating, drinking, smoking and application of cosmetics in working areas where there is a risk of contamination by biological agents.

In this paragraph, *appropriate* in relation to clothing and hygiene measures means appropriate for the risks involved and the conditions at the place where exposure to the risk may occur.

Special control measures are laid down in the Schedule with respect to:

(a) health and veterinary care facilities; and

(b) laboratories, animal rooms and industrial processes.

Examination and maintenance of personal protective equipment (PPE)

Every employer who provides PPE, including protective clothing, to meet the requirements of these Regulations as they apply to biological agents shall ensure that it is -

(a) properly stored in a well-defined place;

(b) checked and cleaned at suitable intervals; and

(c) when discovered to be defective, repaired or replaced before further use.

PPE which may be contaminated by biological agents shall be -

(a) removed on leaving the working area; and

(b) kept apart from uncontaminated clothing and equipment.

In the above case, the employer shall ensure that the equipment is subsequently decontaminated and cleaned or, if necessary, destroyed.

Other provisions of the Schedule

These include:

(a) a duty on employers to provide written emergency instructions, together with displaying notices, in the event of an accidental release of a biological agent;

(b) a duty on employees to report accidents or incidents which have or may have resulted in an accidental release which could cause severe human disease to the employer;

(c) a duty on employers to inform his employees forthwith of an accidental release, and subsequently, of the causes of the accident and the measures taken or to be taken to rectify the situation;

(d) a duty on employers to maintain a list of employees exposed to a Group 3 or Group 4 biological agent, together with specified details of each exposure, for at least 10 years following the last known exposure;

(e) a duty on employers to notify the HSE in writing at least 30 days in advance prior to the storage and use of biological agents in Groups 2, 3 or 4 at a particular premises; and

(f) a duty on employers to notify the HSE in writing at least 30 days in advance prior to the consignment of biological agents specified in Part V of the Schedule, namely:

   (i) all Group 4 biological agents;

   (ii) rabies virus;

   (iii) Simian herpes B virus;

   (iv) Venezuelan equine encephalitis virus;

   (v) tick-borne encephalitis group viruses in Group 3;

   (vi) monkeypox virus; and

   (vii) Mopeia virus.

Biological matter

Control of Substances Hazardous to Health (COSHH) Regulations 2006

Environmental Protection Act 1990

Biological matter

Biological matter means anything (other than an entity mentioned above) which consists of or includes -

(a) tissue or cells (including gametes or propagules) or subcellular entities, of any kind, capable of replication or of transferring genetic material; or

(b) genes or other genetic material, in any form, which are so capable,

and it is immaterial, in determining if something is or is not an organism or biological matter, whether it is the product of natural or artificial processes of reproduction and, in the case of biological matter, whether it has ever been part of a whole organism.

[Environmental Protection Act 1990]

Biological agents

Biological treatment

Any biological process that changes the properties of waste, e.g. anaerobic digestion, composting. It includes licensed landspreading activities.

Aerobic digestion

Anaerobic digestion

Composting

Landspreading

Biotechnology

The development of biological processes and products i.e. genetic modification.

Genetically modified organism (GMO)

Genetically Modified Organisms (Contained Use) Regulations 2000

Genetic engineering

Breach of Conditions Notice

Conservation Area

Breach of licence conditions

Pollution control is largely exercised through a system of licensing of operators and premises by statutory authorities. 'Conditions' may be attached to a licence and failure to comply with such licence conditions may result in the licence being revoked. In most cases, it is not an offence to pollute one of the three environmental media providing the potentially polluting operations or processes have been authorised by the relevant authority.

It is an offence to contravene the conditions of a Waste Management Licence. Similarly, failure to comply with the conditions attached to a discharge consent, issued by the National Rivers Authority under the Water Resources Act, constitutes an offence.

Consents: controlled waters

Discharge consent

National Rivers Authority

Waste

Waste Management Licences

Waste Management Licensing Regulations 1994-2006

Waste offences

Water Resources Act 1991

Breach of statutory duty

Many environmental statutes which prohibit an activity, or make it a criminal offence, also provide for some degree of civil liability.

In order to bring a civil action for breach of statutory duty, a claimant must establish all of the following:

(a) that the statute creates a duty or obligation;

(b) that the statute permits a breach to give rise to civil liability;

(c) that the harm suffered by the claimant is within the general class of risks at which the statute is directed;

(d) that the claimant is a member of the class of persons to which the statute gives protection;

(e) that the defendant has breached the statute; and

(f) that this breach of statute has caused the harm, damage or loss specified in the claim.

Civil liability

Damages

Duty of care

Negligence

Nuisance at common law

Tort

Breach of statutory duty of care

Breach of a statutory duty of care under the EPA gives rise to criminal liability. This is particularly the case with respect to the handling of waste where all waste holders, irrespective of whether they hold or require a Waste Management Licence, have a statutory duty of care in respect of waste.

Duty of care

Duty of care in respect of waste

Environmental Protection (Duty of Care) Regulations 1991

Waste Management Licences

Brownfield land

Land which has previously been used for industrial or commercial purposes.

BS 8555: Environmental Management Systems

BS 8555 was established in 2003 with the objective of assisting organisations to break down an environmental management system into manageable sections or phases. It allows organisations to implement parts of an environmental management system, or put an environmental management system in place, in line with a standard that can be externally certified at any phase.

BS 8555 was developed and piloted through the Acorn Trust and is now controlled by the Institute of Environmental Management and Assessment (IEMA). The process of installing a formal environmental management system is broken down into five phases with a sixth phase that allows organisations to develop a system with the possibility of seeking recognition against the internationally accepted environmental management standard, ISO 14001 or registering under EMAS.

The six phases of the standard are:

- Commitment and establishing the baseline
- Identifying and ensuring compliance with legal and other requirements
- Developing objectives, targets and programmes
- Implementation and operation of the environmental management system
- Checking, audit and review
- Environmental management system acknowledgement
- Copies of the Standard are available from the British Standards Institution.

Environmental management system (EMS)

ISO 14001: Environmental Management Systems

Building Regulations 2000

These Regulations are made under the Building Act 1984 and impose requirements on people carrying out certain building operations. The Regulations are principally concerned with the various aspects of building control, such as "material change of use" of buildings, and contain provisions directed at:

(a) securing the safety, health and welfare and convenience of people in and about buildings;

(b) furthering the conservation of fuel and power by the use of energy ratings for buildings;

(c) supervision of building work; and

(d) unauthorised building work.

Generally, building work and any material change of use must comply with the "applicable requirements" detailed in Schedule 1. Any building work must be carried out with adequate and proper materials and in "a workmanlike manner". Compliance with the requirements in Parts A to K and N of Schedule 1 does not require anything to be done "beyond what is necessary to secure reasonable standards of health and safety".

Schedule 1 – Requirements

This Schedule incorporates specific requirements with regard to:

- Structure
- Fire safety
- Site preparation and resistance to moisture
- Toxic substances
- Resistance to the passage of sound
- Ventilation
- Hygiene
- Drainage and waste disposal
- Heat producing appliances
- Protection from falling, collision and impact
- Conservation of fuel and power
- Access and facilities for disabled people
- Glazing – safety in relation to impact, opening and cleaning

The specific environmental issues of Schedule 1 are covered below.

Part D – Toxic substances

Cavity insulation

If insulating material is inserted into a cavity in a cavity wall, reasonable precautions shall be taken to prevent the subsequent permeation of any toxic fumes from that material into any part of the building occupied by people.

Part E – Resistance to the passage of sound

Airborne sound (walls)

A wall which:

- separates a dwelling from another building or from another dwelling: or
- separates a habitable room or kitchen within a dwelling from another part of the same building which is not used exclusively as part of the dwelling,
- shall have reasonable resistance to the transmission of airborne sound.

Part F – Ventilation

Means of ventilation

There shall be adequate means of ventilation provided for people in the building.

Part G – Hygiene

Sanitary conveniences and washing facilities

Adequate sanitary conveniences shall be provided in rooms provided for that purpose, or in bathrooms. Any such room or bathroom shall be separated from places where food is prepared.

Adequate washbasins shall be provided in:

- rooms containing water closets; or
- rooms or spaces adjacent to rooms containing water closets.

Any such room or space shall be separated from places where food is prepared.

There shall be a suitable installation for the provision of hot and cold water to washbasins provided in accordance with the above paragraph.

Sanitary conveniences and washbasins to which this paragraph applies shall be designed and installed so as to allow effective cleaning.

Hot water storage

A hot water storage system that has a hot water storage vessel which does not incorporate a vent pipe to the atmosphere shall be installed by a person competent to do so, and there shall be precautions to:

- prevent the temperature of stored water at any time exceeding 10°C; and
- ensure that the hot water discharged from safety devices is safely conveyed to where it is visible but will not cause danger to persons in or about the building.

Part J – Heat producing appliances

Air supply

Heat producing appliances shall be so installed that there is an adequate supply of air to them for combustion and for the efficient working of any flue-pipe or chimney.

Discharge of products of combustion

Heat producing appliances shall have adequate provision for the discharge of the products of combustion to the outside air.

Protection of building

Heat producing appliances and flue-pipes shall be so installed, and fireplaces and chimneys shall be so constructed, as to reduce to a reasonable level the risk of the building catching fire in consequence of their use.

Part M – Access and facilities for disabled people

Interpretation

In this Part "disabled people" means people who have:

- an impairment which limits their ability to walk or which requires them to use a wheelchair for mobility; or
- impaired hearing or sight.

Access and use

Reasonable provision shall be made for disabled people to gain access to and use the building.

Sanitary conveniences

If sanitary conveniences are provided in any building which is not a dwelling, reasonable provision shall be made for disabled people.

Provision shall be made for any windows, skylights or any transparent or translucent walls, ceilings or roofs to be safely accessible for cleaning.

Approved documents

The Secretary of State is empowered by the Building Act 1984 to approve and issue documents containing practical guidance with respect to the requirements contained in these Regulations.

Built environment

Ventilation of buildings

Built environment

This term refers to the man-made surroundings that provide the setting for human activity, ranging from large scale building developments to individual homes. Much of the built environment takes the form of architecture designed for a specific purpose. In urban planning, considerable attention is paid to the impact of the built environment on the health of the population with respect to population density, consumption of resources, disposal of wastes, traffic movements and constructional elements of the built environment.

C

Carbonaceous material

This includes such materials as charcoal, coke, peat, rubber and wood.

[Pollution Prevention and Control (England and Wales) Regulations 2000]

Combustion activities

Carbon activities

These scheduled activities are:

Part A(1)

(a) Producing carbon or hard-burnt coal or electro-graphite by means of incineration or graphitisation.

Part A(2)

Nil

Part B

Nil

[Schedule 1: Part 1: Pollution Prevention and Control (England and Wales) Regulations 2000]

Part A activities

Part B activities

Pollution Prevention and Control Act 1999

Pollution Prevention and Control (England and Wales) Regulations 2000

Scheduled activities

Carbon dioxide

Carbon dioxide is normally present in atmospheric air and may take the form of a gas, liquid and solid. As a gas, it is colourless, odourless and has a biting taste. Prolonged exposure to low concentrations of carbon dioxide may cause headaches and exhaustion.

Exposure to the gas at high concentrations may cause asphyxiation and paralysis of the respiratory function. Inhaling an atmosphere rich in the gas can cause immediate loss of consciousness and rapid death. Symptoms of asphyxiation may include rapid and gasping respiration, rapid fatigue, nausea, vomiting and cyanosis. This ultimately leads to unconsciousness or death from anoxia (oxygen deficiency).

Exposure to the cold gas or solid carbon dioxide can cause cold burns and frost bite.

Climate change

Global warming

Greenhouse effect

Greenhouse gases

Carbon disulphide or ammonia: activities

These scheduled activities are:

Part A(1)

(a) Any manufacturing activity which may result in the release of carbon disulphide into the air;

(b) Any activity for the manufacture of a chemical which involves the use of ammonia or may result in the release of ammonia into the air other than an activity in which ammonia is only used as a refrigerant.

Part A(2)

Nil

Part B

Nil

[Schedule 1: Part 1: Pollution Prevention and Control (England and Wales) Regulations 2000]

Ammonia

Part A activities

Part B activities

Pollution Prevention and Control Act 1999

Pollution Prevention and Control (England and Wales) Regulations 2000

Scheduled activities

Carbon monoxide

This gas is produced as a result of combustion.

It causes death by poisoning due to its ability to deprive the body tissues of oxygen. Its propensity to combine with haemoglobin in the blood is at least 200 times greater than that of oxygen and the victim of carbon monoxide poisoning dies from asphyxiation.

Carbon offsetting

Everyday activities by people, such as the use of heating appliances, driving a vehicle, flying to places and operating machinery and plant, consume energy and produce emissions of carbon dioxide. The concept of carbon offsetting implies compensating for the emissions produced by making an equivalent saving in carbon dioxide. It involves calculating the emissions that could be produced and then purchasing 'credits' from projects which result in emission reductions. On this basis, these projects have prevented or removed an equivalent amount of carbon dioxide.

The philosophy is based on the fact that greenhouse gases mix evenly in the atmosphere and tend to have a long life span. Wherever they are emitted in the world, the effect on climate change is the same. By people and organisations making efforts to reduce carbon emissions, reductions will be achieved in other parts of the world resulting in a zero overall effect.

Carbon dioxide

Climate change

Greenhouse gases

Carcinogens

These are substances and preparations which can cause cancer.

Carcinogen means:

(a) a substance or preparation which is classified in accordance with the classification provided for by Regulation 4 of the CHIP Regulations would be in the category of danger, carcinogenic (category 1) or carcinogenic (category 2) whether or not the substance or preparation would be required to be classified under those Regulations; or

(b) a substance or preparation:

(i) listed in Schedule 1; or

(ii) arising from a process specified in Schedule 1 which is a substance hazardous to health.

[Chemicals (Hazard Information and Packaging for Supply Regulations 1994 - 2002]

Chemicals (Hazard Information and Packaging for Supply) (CHIP) Regulations 1994-2002

Hazardous substances: classification

Carriage of dangerous goods

The Carriage of Dangerous Goods and Use of Transportable Pressure Equipment Regulations 2004 ("the Carriage Regulations") implement:

- the European Agreement concerning the International Carriage of Dangerous Goods by Road 2003 (ADR 2003) with a number of exceptions; and
- the Council Directive 96/49/EEC on the approximation of the laws of the Member States with regard to the transport of dangerous goods by rail (as amended); this Directive applies the Regulations concerning the International Carriage of Dangerous Goods by Rail (RID) which form Annex 1 to Appendix B to the Convention concerning International Carriage by Rail (RID 2003).

ADR 2003 sets out the conditions under which dangerous goods can be carried by road, with detailed requirements incorporated in two Annexes to the Agreement.

The Carriage Regulations also implement a further Directive on transportable pressure equipment and replace twelve previous statutory instruments that regulated the carriage of dangerous goods by road and rail in the United Kingdom. Detailed guidance on the requirements of ADR and the Carriage Regulations is incorporated in the HSE publication *Working with ADR: an introduction to the carriage of dangerous goods by road.*

The scope of the Carriage Regulations is extensive. Part II of the Regulations details the requirements for RID and ADR, including training requirements, the safety obligations of those involved in the carriage of dangerous goods, the functions of safety advisers, reporting procedures for accidents and incidents, emergency plans for marshalling yards, classification of goods and the use, construction and testing of packaging and packages.

The Regulations take account of national derogations agreed with the European Commission in respect of certain transport operations involving local journeys or the movement of dangerous goods in small quantities. They retain the mandatory Emergency Action Code system for placarding certain GB-registered vehicles on journeys in Great Britain. The Regulations will be supported by a number of letters of authorisation allowing time-limited relaxations to some requirements.

The functions of the 'competent authority' are specified in Part III, together with requirements for transportable pressure equipment in Part IV. Additional requirements to RID and ADR are dealt with in Part V.

There are 14 Schedules to the Carriage Regulations, which include detailed requirements for placards, marks and plate marking for carriage within Great Britain.

Causing pollution (offence)

Anyone who causes pollution, such as depositing controlled waste or causing a noxious substance or polluting matter to enter controlled water, commits an offence which carries strict liability. Causing pollution requires some form of positive act but not necessarily intent to actually pollute or be negligent. However, there must be a direct relationship between the actual act of pollution and the offence specified.

Environmental crimes

Environmental Protection Act 1990

Offences

Waste offences

Cement and lime production

These scheduled activities are:

Part A(1)

(a) Producing cement clinker producing and grinding cement clinker;

(b) Producing lime:

(i) in kilns or other furnaces with a production capacity of more than 50 tonnes per day; or

(ii) where the activity is likely to involve the heating in any period of 12 months of 5,000 tonnes or more of calcium carbonate or calcium magnesium carbonate or, in aggregate, both.

Part A(2)

(a) Unless falling within Part A(1) of this Section, grinding cement clinker;

(b) Unless falling within Part A(1) of Section 2.1 or 2.2 (ferrous and non-ferrous metals), grinding metallurgical slag in plant with a grinding capacity or more than 250,000 tonnes in any period of 12 months.

Part B

(a) Storing, loading or unloading cement or cement clinker in bulk prior to further transportation in bulk;

(b) Blending cement in bulk or using cement in bulk other than at a construction site, including the bagging of cement and cement mixtures, the batching of ready-mixed concrete and the manufacture of concrete blocks and other cement products;

(c) Slaking lime for the purpose of making calcium hydroxide or calcium magnesium hydroxide;

(d) Producing lime where the activity is not likely to involve the heating in any period of 12 months of 5,000 tonnes or more of calcium carbonate or calcium magnesium carbonate, or both.

[Schedule 1: Part 1: Pollution Prevention and Control (England and Wales) Regulations 2000 as amended]

Part A activities

Part B activities

Pollution Prevention and Control (England and Wales) Regulations 2000

Scheduled activities

Ceramic production

These scheduled activities are:

Part A(1)

(a) Manufacturing ceramic products (including roofing tiles, bricks, refractory bricks, tiles, stoneware or porcelain) by firing in kilns, where:

(i) the kiln production capacity is more than 75 tonnes per day; or

(ii) the kiln capacity is more than 4 m^3 and the setting density is more than 300 kg/m^3;

and a reducing atmosphere is used other than for the purposes of colouration.

Part A(2)

(a) Unless falling within Part A(1) of this Section, manufacturing ceramic products (including roofing tiles, bricks, refractory bricks, tiles, stoneware or porcelain) by firing in kilns where:

(i) the kiln production capacity is more than 75 tonnes per day; or

(ii) the kiln capacity is more than 4 m^3 and the setting density is more than 300 kg/m^3.

Part B

(a) Unless falling within Part A(1) or A(2) of this Section, firing heavy clay goods or refractory materials (other than heavy clay goods) in a kiln;

(b) Vapour glazing earthenware or clay with salts.

Clay includes a blend of clay with ash, sand or other materials.

Refractory material means material (such as fireclay, silica, magnesite, chrome magnesite, sillimanite, sintered alumina, beryllia and boron nitride) which is able to withstand high temperatures and to function as a furnace lining or in other similar high temperature applications.

[Schedule 1: Part 1: Pollution Prevention and Control (England and Wales) Regulations 2000]

Part A activities

Part B activities

Pollution Prevention and Control Act 1999

Pollution Prevention and Control (England and Wales) Regulations 2000

Scheduled activities

Change in operation

In relation to an installation or mobile plant, a change in the nature of functioning or an extension of the installation or mobile plant which may have consequences for the environment.

[Pollution Prevention and Control (England and Wales) Regulations 2000]

Installation

Mobile plant

Substantial change in operation

Chemical fertiliser production

These scheduled activities are:

Part A(1)

(a) Producing (including any blending which is related to their production) phosphorus, nitrogen or potassium based fertilisers (simple or compound fertilisers);

(b) Converting chemical fertilisers into granules.

Part A(2)

Nil

Part B

Nil

[Schedule 1: Part 1: Pollution Prevention and Control (England and Wales) Regulations 2000]

Inorganic chemical production

Organic chemicals: manufacture and use

Part A activities

Part B activities

Pharmaceutical production

Scheduled activities

Storage of chemicals in bulk

Chemical Oxygen Demand (COD)

This is a test used in assessing the level of pollution of a sample of water. It is a quantitative measure of the amount of oxygen required to oxidise all organic components in a unit volume of water.

The amount of oxygen required for the chemical oxidation of pollutants in water.

Biochemical Oxygen Demand (BOD)

Chemicals (Hazard Information and Packaging for Supply) (CHIP) Regulations 1994 – 2002

These Regulations cover many important aspects with regard to the classification, labelling, packaging and supply of chemicals and have been subject to regular amendment. The Regulations differentiate between *substances* and *preparations* and specify those *substances dangerous for supply.*

Preparations are mixtures or solutions of two or more substances.

Substances are chemical elements and their compounds in the natural state or obtained by any production process, including any additive necessary to preserve the stability of the product and any impurity deriving from the process used, but excluding any solvent which may be separated without affecting the stability of the substance or changing its composition.

Substances dangerous for supply means:

(a) a substance listed in Part 1 of the Approved Supply List;

(b) any other substance which is in one or more of the categories of danger specified in column 1 of Schedule 1.

Category of danger applies to those substances classified on the basis of:

(a) *Physico-chemical properties*

"Explosive", "Oxidising", "Extremely Flammable", "Highly Flammable" and "Flammable".

(b) *Health effects*

"Very Toxic", "Toxic", "Harmful", "Corrosive", "Irritant", "Sensitising", "Carcinogenic", "Mutagenic", "Toxic for Reproduction" and "Dangerous for the Environment".

With respect to substances and preparations dangerous for supply, the Regulations cover:

(a) classification;

(b) safety data sheets;

(c) advertisements;

(d) packaging requirements;

(e) labelling;

(f) particular labelling requirements for certain preparations;

(g) methods of marking or labelling packages;

(h) child-resistant fastenings and tactile warning devices;

(i) retention of classification data;

(j) notification of the constituents of certain preparations dangerous for supply to the Poisons Advisory Centre; and

(k) exemption certificates.

Approved Supply List

Hazardous substances: classification

Safety data

Chimney heights

Local authorities are empowered to control the height of chimneys for the purposes of regulating air pollution. This philosophy is based on the principle of 'dilute and disperse'.

Where anyone is seeking to:

(a) erect a new chimney to serve a furnace;

(b) enlarge an existing chimney to serve a furnace; or

(c) replace a chimney with an increased combustion space,

they must apply to the local authority for approval of the chimney height. The local authority will determine the application by reference to the Third Memorandum on Chimney Heights (Department of the Environment) which provides guidance on this issue. The local authority must take into account many factors and must be satisfied that the proposed height will be sufficient to prevent, so far as is practicable, the chimney emissions becoming prejudicial to health or a nuisance.

The local authority can either approve the chimney height with or without conditions.

Air pollution

Clean Air Act 1993

Emission

Local Air Pollution Control (LAPC)

Nuisance

Chlorine

Chlorine is a highly irritant gas and may be evolved from a number of processes and in the transport of liquid chlorine in tank cars and cylinders. As it is heavier than air, it tends to accumulate in low places and is not readily diluted or dispersed unless it is subjected to strong currents. Chlorine has a direct effect on the lungs causing bronchitis and difficulty in breathing due to the formation of fluid in the lungs (pulmonary oedema).

Chlorofluorocarbons (CFCs)

Hazardous substances: classification

Chlorofluorocarbons (CFCs)

These are any of several organic compounds composed of carbon, fluorine, chlorine and hydrogen. These halogenated hydrocarbons, notably trichlorofluoromethane and dichlorodifluoromethane have been used extensively as aerosol spray propellants, refrigerants, solvents and foam blowing agents.

CFCs represent a serious threat to the environment in that, when released into the atmosphere, they accumulate in the stratosphere, where they have a damaging effect on the ozone layer. Stratospheric ozone shields living organisms from the harmful effects of the sun's ultra violet radiation. It has been demonstrated that even a relatively small decrease in the stratospheric ozone concentration can result in increased incidence of skin cancer and in genetic damage to many organisms.

In the stratosphere, the CFC molecules break down by the action of solar ultra violet radiation and release their constituent chlorine atoms. These then react with the ozone molecules, resulting in their removal.

Chlorine

Environmental Protection (Controls on Ozone-Depleting Substances) Regulations 2002

Organic solvents

Ozone-depleting substances

Ozone depletion

Ozone layer

Ultra violet light

Civil liability

Civil law, namely the law relating to the duties owed by one person to another, is derived from, and incorporated in, common law. Civil liability is based on civil law. It generally arises from an act or omission which the law regards as allowing a party, a person, a company, an organisation or undertaking, the right to take an action against another party.

Such action may take the form of a claim for damages based on the extent of the injury, damage or loss.

Civil law is a branch of the law concerned with the relationships between individual persons, and between persons and organisations, and the effect of a wrongful act or omission resulting in injury, damage or loss to one of the parties concerned. This may result in one individual, a claimant, taking a civil action against a second party, the defendant.

The main area of civil law which impinges on environmental protection is the law of tort, a collective name for certain rights of action. A civil action generally takes the form of a claim made by a claimant against a defendant based on the torts of negligence or breach of statutory duty. Certain aspects of civil law are based on statute, such as the Occupiers' Liability Acts of 1957 and 1984.

The civil courts are the County Court and the High Court, with appeal to the Court of Appeal (Civil Division). A civil case must be proved on 'the balance of probabilities', which is a lesser standard than 'beyond reasonable doubt' required in a criminal case.

Breach of statutory duty

Duty of care

Negligence

Waste: duty of care

Waste offences

Waste unlawfully deposited

Classification of Dangerous Goods

There are nine classifications of dangerous goods, thus:

1. *Explosives*

These are sub-divided into six groups, Classes 1.1 to 1.3 being the most dangerous. Different substances are also assigned a 'compatibility group' which help a carrier determine which substances may be carried together.

2. *Gases*

This classification covers all compressed gases including those classified as 'flammable' and 'toxic', thus:

- Flammable gases
- Non-toxic, non-flammable compressed gases
- Toxic gases

3. *Flammable liquids*

These are liquids which give off a vapour and which burn in air if ignited.

4. *Other flammables*

These are sub-divided into:

- Flammable solids which ignite and burn when heated
- Spontaneously combustible (pyrophoric) which ignite when they come into contact with air
- Dangerous when wet, which ignite or give off flammable gas when wet

5. *Oxidisers*

These are sub-divided into:

- Oxidising agents which produce oxygen helping to sustain any fire that may start
- Organic peroxides – unstable compounds which give off oxygen and may heat up; can explode

6. *Toxics*

These are sub-divided into:

- Poisonous/toxic substances which may be inhaled, swallowed or absorbed through eyes
- Infectious substances which may represent a biological hazard

7. Radioactives

These are not sub-divided but there are three levels of danger. The most dangerous, 'Radioactive', should be accompanied by a sign with three red bars upon it.

8. Corrosives

These substances may cause serious burns.

9. Miscellaneous

This classification covers any other substance regarded as dangerous by the UN which does not readily fit into the classes above.

Warning diamonds

Each class or sub-class is assigned a warning diamond depicting the nature of the associated hazard. Warning diamonds are colour coded depending upon the nature of the hazard and incorporate a pictorial representation of the hazard within the diamond and its class.

Airborne particulates

Biological agents

Chemicals (Hazard Information and Packaging for Supply) (CHIP) Regulations 1994 – 2002

Hazardous substances: classification

Radioactive substances and wastes

Clean Air Act 1993

The Clean Air Act (CAA) 1993 controls emissions of smoke, dust and grit by means of criminal offences. The main offences under the CAA are:

(a) emission of dark smoke from a chimney or from industrial premises other than from a chimney;

(b) emission of dust and grit from non-domestic furnaces;

(c) emission of smoke from a chimney in a Smoke Control Area; and

(d) various offences relating to the installation of furnaces.

Prosecutions under most provisions of the Act are dealt with summarily in the Magistrates' Court.

It is important to note the relationship between controls under the CAA and those under Part I of the EPA (Integrated Pollution Control and Local Authority Air Pollution Control) as amended. The provisions of Parts I – III of the CAA do not apply to any process regulated under Part I of the EPA.

Chimney heights

Dark smoke offences

Emission

Grit, dust and fumes

Ringelmann Chart

Clean Neighbourhoods and Environment Act 2005

This statute covers a range of matters relating to:

Crime and disorder

Crime and disorder reduction partnerships must take into account anti-social behaviour and other behaviour adversely affecting the local environment, and make provision for the gating of minor highways that attract anti-social behaviour through the making of gating orders.

Vehicles

This Part of the Act deals with nuisance parking, including exposing vehicles for sale on a road, repairing vehicles on a road and amends the law relating to abandoned and illegally parked vehicles with the power of the local authority to issue Fixed Penalty Notices for such offences.

Litter and refuse

The statutory offence of dropping litter was extended to all open places.

Graffiti and other defacement

This Part amended the law relating to graffiti, fly-posting and the illegal display of advertisements.

Waste

This Part makes provision for the registration of carriers of particular kinds of waste and covers the illegal deposit of waste (fly-tipping).

Dogs

Local authorities and community councils can create offences relating to the control of dogs.

Noise

Local authorities were given new powers to deal with noise from intruder alarms.

Architecture and the Built Environment

This Part established a statutory body to take the place of a non-departmental public body, the Commission for Architecture and the Built Environment.

Built environment

Litter

Litter Control Notice

Litter Fixed Penalty Notice

Noise nuisance

Statutory nuisances

Stray dogs

Waste offences

Climate change

Climate change refers to the average weather experienced over a long period of time. It includes temperature, wind and rainfall patterns. Climate change is considered by world governments as the most serious environmental threat to the planet and is associated with the production of greenhouse gases, such as carbon dioxide and methane, from the burning of fossil fuels, such as gas, oil and coal. Current climate models predict that global temperatures could increase from between 1.4°C to 5.8°C over the next century depending on the amounts of greenhouse gases emitted and the sensitivity of the climate system.

The implications of climate change are wetter winters and drier summers, higher temperatures, higher sea levels leading to flooding of coastal areas and less snow. This may be accompanied by droughts, flooding, the spread of disease and shortages of food.

The United Kingdom is committed to the Kyoto Protocol, an international agreement which aims to limit greenhouse gas emissions and slow the warming of the Earth's atmosphere. The UK is committed to reducing its greenhouse gas emissions by 12.5%, based on 1990 levels, by 2008 – 2012.

Climate Change Agreements

Climate Change Levy

Fossil fuels

Greenhouse effect

Greenhouse gases

Kyoto Protocol (US)

Climate Change Agreements

These are international non-binding agreements on tackling climate change whereby:

(a) developing countries must face targets for cutting greenhouse gas emissions as well as the rich countries;

(b) a limit should be decided for maximum acceptable carbon dioxide levels in the atmosphere; and

(c) a global market should be formed to cap and trade carbon emissions.

Climate change

Climate Change Levy

Greenhouse gases

Climate Change Levy

This is a tax on the use of energy in industry, commerce and the public sector, with offsetting cuts in employers' National Insurance contributions and additional support for energy efficiency schemes and renewable sources of energy. It is designed to stimulate business improvements in energy efficiency.

Legislation to implement the levy was incorporated in the Finance Act 2000.

Climate change

Climate Change Agreements

Greenhouse gases

Closed landfills

Waste Regulation Authorities have a duty to inspect their area from time to time, except where a current site licence applies. The purpose of such inspections is to detect whether any land is in such a condition that it may cause pollution to the environment or harm to human health due to noxious gases or noxious liquids caused by deposits of controlled waste in land.

For this purpose, the authority may enter and inspect any land:

(a) on which controlled waste has been deposited at any time under a Waste Management Licence or a Disposal Licence;

(b) where the authority has reason to believe that controlled waste has been deposited in the land at any time; or

(c) in which there are, or the authority has reason to believe there may be, concentrations or accumulations of noxious gases or noxious liquids.

Where an inspection indicates that any land is in such a condition due to noxious gases or liquids, the authority has a duty to carry out whatever works or other measures appear to be reasonable to avoid pollution of the environment or harm to health. The authority may recover all or part of the cost from the current owner of the land, unless there was a licence which has been surrendered. The authority must have regard to any hardship the recovery of the cost may cause to the owner of the land.

[Environmental Protection Act 1990]

Landfill sites

Landfill (England and Wales) Regulations 2002 – 2005

Landfill: disposal of waste

Landfill tax

Coastal waters

Waters which are within the area which extends landward from the baseline of the territorial sea as far as the limit of the highest tide or, in the case of the waters of any relevant river or watercourse, as far as the fresh water limit of the river or watercourse, together with the waters of any enclosed dock which adjoins waters within that area.

[Water Resources Act 1991]

Controlled waters

Fresh water limit

Ground waters

Inland fresh waters

Relevant lake or pond

Relevant river or watercourse

Watercourse

Water Resources Act 1991

Coating activities, printing and textile treatment

These scheduled activities are:

Part A(1)

(a) Applying or removing a coating material containing any tributyltin compound or triphenyltin compound, if carried out at a shipyard or boatyard where vessels of a length of 25 metres or more can be built, maintained or repaired;

(b) Pre-treating (by operations such as washing, bleaching or mercerisation) or dyeing fibres or textiles in plant with a treatment capacity of more than 10 tonnes per day;

(c) Treating textiles if the activity may result in the release into water of any substance listed in paragraph 13 of Part 2 of this Schedule in a quantity which, in any period of 12 months, is greater than the background quantity by more than the amount specified in that paragraph in relation to that substance.

Part A(2)

(a) Unless falling within Part A(1) of this Section, surface treating substances, objects or products using organic solvents, in particular for dressing, printing, coating, degreasing, waterproofing, sizing, painting, cleaning or impregnating, in plant with a consumption capacity of more than 150 kg per hour or more than 200 tonnes per year.

Part B

(a) Unless falling within Part A(1) or A(2) of this Section or paragraph (c) of Part A(2) of Section 2.1 (ferrous metals), any process (other than for the repainting or re-spraying of or of parts of aircraft or road or railway vehicles) for applying to a substrate, or drying or curing after such application, printing ink or paint or any other coating material as, in the course of a manufacturing activity, where the process may result in the release into the air of particulate matter or of any volatile organic compound and is likely to involve the use in any period of 12 months of:

   (i) 20 tonnes or more of printing ink, paint or other coating material which is applied in solid form;

   (ii) 20 tonnes or more of any metal coating which is sprayed on in molten form;

   (iii) 25 tonnes or more of organic solvents in respect of any cold set web offset printing activity or any sheet fed offset litho printing activity; or

   (iv) 5 tonnes or more of organic solvents in respect of any activity not mentioned in sub-paragraph (iii);

(b) Unless falling within Part A(2) of this Section, repainting or re-spraying road vehicles or parts of them if the activity may result in the release into the air of particulate matter or of any volatile organic compound and the carrying on of the activity is likely to involve the use of 1 tonne or more of organic solvents in any period of 12 months;

(c) Repainting or re-spraying aircraft or railway vehicles or parts of them if the activity may result in the release into the air of particulate matter or of any volatile organic compound and the carrying out of the activity is likely to involve the use in any period of 12 months or more of:

   (i) 20 tonnes or more of any paint or other coating material which is applied in solid form;

(ii) 20 tonnes or more of any metal coatings which are sprayed on in molten form; or

(iii) 5 tonnes or more of organic solvents.

Coating material means paint, printing ink, varnish, lacquer, dye, any metal oxide coating, any elastomer coating, any metal or plastic coating and any other coating material.

The amount of organic solvents used in an activity shall be calculated as:

(a) the total input of organic solvents into the process including both solvents contained in coating materials and solvents used for cleaning or other purposes; less

(b) any organic solvents that are removed from the process for re-use or for recovery for re-use.

[Schedule 1: Part 1: Pollution Prevention and Control (England and Wales) Regulations 2000]

Ferrous metals

Organic solvents

Part A activities

Part B activities

Particulate matter

Pollution Prevention and Control Act 1999

Pollution Prevention and Control (England and Wales) Regulations 2000

Scheduled activities

Co-incineration

This means the use of wastes as a regular or additional fuel in a co-incineration plant or the thermal treatment of waste for the purpose of disposal in a co-incineration plant.

[Waste Incineration (England and Wales) Regulations 2002]

Co-incineration plant

Incineration

Incineration and co-incineration of waste

Incineration plant

Scheduled activities

Co-incineration plant

Any stationary or mobile plant whose main purpose is the generation of energy or production of material products and:

(a) which uses waste as a regular or additional fuel; or

(b) in which waste is thermally treated for the purpose of disposal.

Note

If co-incineration takes place in such a way that the main purpose of the plant is not the generation of energy or production of material products but rather the thermal treatment of waste, the plant shall be regarded as an incineration plant.

This definition covers the site and the entire plant including all co-incineration lines, waste reception, storage, on-site pre-treatment facilities, waste-, fuel- and air supply systems, boiler, facilities for the treatment of exhaust gases, on-site facilities for treatment or storage of residues and waste water, stack devices and systems for controlling incineration operations, recording and monitoring incineration conditions, but does not cover co-incineration in an excluded plant.

[Waste Incineration (England and Wales) Regulations 2002]

Co-incineration

Incineration

Incineration and co-incineration of waste

Incineration plant

Scheduled activities

Combined Heat and Power

Environment Act 1995

Combustion activities

These scheduled activities are:

Part A(1)

(a) Burning any fuel in an appliance with a net rated thermal input of 50 megawatts or more;

(b) Burning any of the following fuels in an appliance with a rated thermal input of 3 megawatts or more but less than 50 megawatts unless the activity is carried out as part of a Part A(2) or B activity:

(i) waste oil;

(ii) recovered oil;

(iii) fuel manufactured from, or comprising, any other waste.

Part A(2)

Nil

Part B

Unless falling within paragraph (a) of Part A(1) of this Section:

(a) Burning of any fuel, other than a fuel mentioned in paragraph (b) of Part A(1) of this Section, in a boiler or furnace or a gas turbine or compression ignition engine with, in the case of these appliances, a rated thermal input of 20 megawatts or more but less than 50 megawa

(b) Burning any of the following fuels in an appliance with a rated thermal input of less than 3 megawatts:

(i) waste oil;

(ii) recovered oil;

(iii) a solid fuel which has been manufactured from waste by an activity involving the application of heat;

(c) Burning fuel manufactured from or including waste, other than a fuel mentioned in paragraph (b), in any appliance:

(i) with a rated thermal input of less than 3 megawatts but at least 0.4 megawatts; or

(ii) which is used together with other appliances which each have a rated thermal input of less than 3 megawatts, where the aggregate rated thermal input of all the appliances is at least 0.4 megawatts.

Fuel does not include gas produced by biological degradation of water.

Waste oil means any mineral based lubricating or industrial oil which has become unfit for the use for which it was intended and, in particular, used combustion oil, gearbox oil, mineral lubricating oil, oil for turbines and hydraulic oil.

Recovered oil means waste oil which has been processed before being burned.

[Schedule 1: Part 1: Pollution Prevention and Control (England and Wales) Regulations 2006]

Gasification, liquefaction and refining activities

Part A activities

Part B activities

Pollution Prevention and Control Act 1999

Pollution Prevention and Control (England and Wales) Regulations 2000

Scheduled activities

Waste oil

Comfort ventilation

Comfort is essentially a subjective feeling or assessment of the conditions in which a person works, sleeps, travels, etc and the sensation of comfort is commonly associated with age, state of health and vitality. Comfort is associated with the ambient air temperature, relative humidity and the rate of air movement in a building. Comfort ventilation, therefore, may be related to the rate of air movement, the number of air changes per hour and the external ambient temperature. When external temperatures are low, the rate of air movement must be reduced to maintain comfort. In hot summer months, the opposite must take place.

Ventilation systems, whether natural or artificial, are commonly designed assuming a maximum air temperature of 32°C and a minimum air temperature of 0°C and should operate within these extremes. Much will depend upon the nature of the work undertaken.

A commonly used standard for recommended air changes per hour is shown in the Table below.

	Summer	Winter
Offices	6	4
Corridors	4	2
Amenity areas	6	4
Storage areas	2	2
Production areas with heat producing plant	20	20
Production area – assembly, finishing	6	6
Workshops	6	4

Figure 4: RECOMMENDED VENTILATION RATES

Comfort ventilation criteria

In considering comfort ventilation, the following criteria should be considered:

(a) incoming air should be drawn from a clean source or subject to a filtration process;

(b) an atmosphere which is cool rather that hot, dry rather than damp, and with a variable rate of air movement according to season, must be produced;

(c) relative humidity should vary between 40% and 70%;

(d) every occupied part of a workplace should be separately ventilated;

(e) input units should be located so as to give a flow of air from operating positions towards sources of heat and finally to extract units;

(f) total extract volume should be around 80% of the input volume to allow for a positive plenum or pressure within the building;

(g) fresh air intakes at roof level should stand at least 0.66 m above the roof surface to avoid collecting heated, and sometimes contaminated, air from extracts.

Legal requirements

Regulation 6 of the Workplace (Health, Safety and Welfare) Regulations 1992 places an absolute duty on employers to ensure that effective and suitable provision is made to ensure that every enclosed workplace, for example, a factory, office, shop or workshop, is ventilated by a sufficient quantity of fresh or purified air.

Further detail on this requirement is incorporated in the ACOP to the Regulations.

Local exhaust ventilation (LEV) systems

Ventilation of buildings

Work environment

Commercial waste

This includes waste from premises used wholly or mainly for the purposes of a trade or business; or for the purposes of sport, recreation or entertainment, except household, industrial, mining, quarrying and agricultural waste, or any other waste specified in the Controlled Waste Regulations 1992.

Controlled waste

Controlled Waste Regulations 1992

Environmental Protection Act 1990

Waste

Waste Collection Authorities (WCAs)

Waste Disposal Authorities (WDAs) and Companies

Waste Disposal Plans by Waste Regulation Authorities

Waste: environmental consequences

Waste hierarchy

Waste Local Plans

Waste Management Licences

Waste management option

Waste Minimisation Act 1998

Waste offences

Waste on land

Waste planning and recycling

Waste Recycling Plans

Waste Regulation Authorities (WRAs)

Waste Regulatory Authorities

Waste transfer

Waste unlawfully deposited

Common law

Common law is the body of case law of universal or common application formed by the judgements of the courts. Each judgement contains the judge's enunciation of the facts, a statement of the law applying to the case and his *ratio decendi* or legal reasoning for the finding at which he has arrived. These various judgements are recorded in the series of Law Reports and have thus developed into the current body of decided case law and continue to develop.

Common law is, then, accumulated case law, recorded for the most part in the Law Reports, underpinned by the doctrine of precedent, under which a court is bound to follow earlier decisions of courts of its own level and of the decisions of superior courts.

One of the principal functions of the common law is to protect interests in land.

Breach of statutory duty

Negligence

Rylands v Fletcher

Tort

Competent person

At common law, "competence" implies that the person has the appropriate skill, knowledge and experience to undertake certain tasks correctly, safely and efficiently. (The term "competent person" appears frequently in health and safety legislation.)

A person could be said to be technically competent if he holds a relevant qualification in this field, such as a certificate awarded by the Waste Management Industry Training and Advisory Board.

Waste offences

Complaint to a Magistrates' Court

A person who is aggrieved by the existence of a statutory nuisance need not necessarily pursue the matter through the local authority. Under Section 82 of the EPA, a Magistrates' Court may act on a complaint made by any person on the ground that he is aggrieved by the existence of a statutory nuisance.

If the court is satisfied that the alleged nuisance exists, or that although abated it is likely to recur on the same premises, the court shall make an order for either or both of the following purposes –

(a) requiring the defendant to abate the nuisance (Abatement Order), within a time specified in the Order, and to execute any works necessary for that purpose;

(b) prohibiting a recurrence of the nuisance (Prohibition Order) and requiring the defendant, within a time specified in the Order, to execute any works necessary to prevent the recurrence,

and may also impose on the defendant a fine not exceeding level 5 on the standard scale.

If the court is satisfied that the alleged nuisance exists and is such as, in the opinion of the court, to render premises unfit for human habitation, an Order (as above) may prohibit the use of the premises for human habitation until the premises are, to the satisfaction of the court, rendered fit for that purpose.

Abatement Order

Environmental Protection Act 1990

Prohibition Order

Statutory nuisances

Composting

A process in which bacteria in soil is mixed with refuse and degradable waste eventually breaking down this mixture into organic fertiliser, a relatively stable humus material.

Aerobic digestion

Conceptual Model

The Conceptual Model for a site relates to the potential pollution linkages. It should identify:

(a) each of the receptors;

(b) the pathways by which they could be exposed;

(c) the substances associated with former uses or likely to be present; and

(d) a preliminary assessment of the likelihood of a pollutant linkage for each combination of source, pathway and receptor.

Contaminated Land (England) Regulations 2000

Pollutant linkage

Receptor

Consents: controlled waters

A person wishing to discharge into controlled waters must make application to the National Rivers Authority (NRA) providing all the information which may reasonably be required by the Authority. Such an application must be advertised. The NRA is under a duty to consider any written representations or objections made with respect to the application.

Discharge consent

Discharge to controlled waters

Effluent

National Rivers Authority

Conservation

Protection and preservation with respect to soil, herbage, species or the environment.

Conservation Area

Conservation Area

The Town and Country Planning Act 1990 reinforced much of the former legislation relating to Conservation Areas, such as the Civic Amenities Act 1967.

A Conservation Area is defined in Section 69 of the Town and Country Planning Act 1990 as 'an area of special architectural or historic interest, the character or appearance of which it is desirable to preserve or enhance'.

Every local planning authority (LPA), the Secretary of State for National Heritage and, in London, the Historical Monuments and Buildings Commission, i.e. English Heritage, has the power to designate a Conservation Area. Designation is by a resolution of the LPA, who do not need to consult owners or occupiers. However, the Secretary of State must consult LPAs, who may hold a public meeting. Notice of designation must be given by the Secretary of State and English Heritage in the London Gazette and, in the case of LPAs, local residents are informed via a local newspaper insertion. A designation may be modified or cancelled. No ministerial consent is required.

Designation has the following impact upon development:

(a) Control of demolition

Section 74 stipulates that LPA consent is required to demolish any building except:

- (i) church buildings;
- (ii) listed buildings;
- (iii) ancient monuments; and
- (iv) buildings subject to ministerial direction,

in which cases, other authorities must be consulted and consent given e.g. English Heritage.

(b) Trees

Sections 211- 214 of the TCPA 1990 deal with the subject of Tree Preservation Orders (TPOs). Every tree in a Conservation Area is deemed to be covered by a TPO, whether or not such an order formally exists. Notice must be given to the planning authority by the property owner of the intention to either remove, top, lop, etc. and the planning authority has 6 weeks in which to consider making a TPO. If no TPO is made, the tree may be removed up to two years after the original notification.

(c) Advertisements

The planning authority has the power to declare an area of special control with regard to advertisements, which must be confirmed by the Secretary of State.

Improvements in Conservation Areas

Section 71 of the Planning (Listed Buildings and Conservation Areas) Act 1990 requires a LPA to publish proposals for preservation and enhancement of Conservation Areas and to hold a public meeting into its proposals at which it considers the views of members of the public.

Section 77 allows for grants and loans to be made by the Secretary of State and English Heritage for preservation and enhancement, subject to wide-ranging criteria. Normally arrangements under Section 77 entail an agreement between English Heritage and an individual.

Area preservation is covered in Section 79 by means of a Town Scheme. In this case English Heritage and a local authority each agree to set aside a specific sum of money for a specified number of years to make grants for the repair of buildings included in either a Town Scheme List or shown on a Town Scheme Map.

Section 80 of the Act allows for Repair Grant Agreements to be made which are linked with certain conditions. This entails the planning authority making an offer to an owner of a grant for repairs to a listed building. If the offer is not responded to within 21 days, there may be two consequences:

(a) a fine of up to £400 in a Magistrates' Court; and/or

(b) the service of an Enforcement Notice under the Act.

There is no right of appeal in this case.

Enforcement Arrangements

Under Section 187 a Breach of Condition Notice can be served by the planning authority for failure to comply with a condition imposed in connection with a planning permission. The planning authority must give 28 days notice to the applicant to enable compliance to take place. Failure to comply can result in a fine as above and/or the service of a Planning Contravention Notice. There is no right of appeal.

Typical offences under the Act include:

1. Failure to comply with the time limits imposed under a Planning Control Notice or Breach of Condition Notice. (Enforcement action must be taken with 4 years of the breach of control.)
2. Carrying out works without planning permission e.g. building, engineering, mining or other operations in, on, over or under land from the date on which the operations were substantially completed (undefined).

Breach of Condition Notice

Civil liability

Conservation

Injunction

Conservation sites

These are protected sites recognised for their distinctive plants, animals, habitats, geology or landforms.

Areas of Outstanding Natural Beauty

Conservation

Habitat

Special Areas of Conservation

Special Protection Areas

Contained use

With respect to genetically modified organisms, the process where control measures are used to limit contact between these organisms and humans and the environment so as to provide a high level of safety. In practice, this involves work in laboratories, animal houses, plant growth facilities (including growth rooms in buildings and suitable glasshouses) and large-scale production facilities on industrial sites.

The vast majority of work with genetically modified organisms in contained use is inherently safe. This is because most of the work involves the insertion of genes into micro-organisms that have been deliberately "crippled" with disabling mutations so that they will not grow outside of the controlled environment of a laboratory test tube. Safety is thus built into the experimental design. Only a small number of activities involve genetically modified micro-organisms that are not disabled and still capable of growth outside of the laboratory.

Environmental Protection Act 1990

Genetically modified organism (GMO)

Genetically Modified Organisms (Contained Use) Regulations 2000

Genetic engineering

Genetic modification

Contaminant

A substance which is in, on or under land which has the potential to cause harm or to cause pollution of controlled waters.

Contaminated land

Controlled waters

Harm

Pollutant

Pollution: definition

Pollution incidents

Pollution of controlled waters

Pollution of the environment

Contaminated land

Any land which appears to the local authority in whose area it is situated to be in such a condition, by reason of substances in, on or under the land, that:

(a) significant harm is being caused or there is a significant possibility of such harm being caused; or

(b) pollution of controlled waters is being, or is likely to be, caused.

[Environmental Protection Act 1990]

Contaminated Land (England) Regulations 2000

Environment Act 1995

Environmental Protection Act 1990

Harm

Pollution of controlled waters

Remediation

Remediation Notice

Contaminated Land (England) Regulations 2000

These Regulations set out detailed provisions with respect to special sites, Remediation Notices, compensation for rights of entry, etc, appeals and public registers of contaminated land.

The Regulations require contaminated land of the following descriptions to be prescribed for the purposes of Section 78(c)(8) as land required to be designated as a special site:

(a) land where there is the potential for pollution of controlled waters;

(b) land which is contaminated land by reason of waste acid tars in, on or under the land;

(c) land on which any of the following activities have been carried on at any time:

 (i) the purification (including refining) of crude petroleum or of oil extracted from petroleum, shale or any other bituminous substance except coal; or

 (ii) the manufacture or processing of explosives;

(d) land on which a prescribed process designated for central control has been or is carried on under an authorisation where the process does not comprise solely things being done which are required by way of remediation;

(e) land within a nuclear site;

(f) land owned or occupied by or on behalf of:

 (i) the Secretary of State for Defence;

 (ii) the Defence Council;

 (iii) an international headquarters or defence organisation; or

 (iv) the service authority of a visiting force, being land used for naval, military or air force purposes;

(g) land on which the manufacture, production or disposal of:

 (i) chemical weapons;

 (ii) any biological agent or toxin which falls within Section 1(1)(a) of the Biological Weapons Act 1974 (restriction on development of biological weapons and toxins); or

 (iii) any weapon, equipment or means of delivery which falls within Section 1(1)(b) of that Act (restriction on development of biological weapons), has been carried out at any time;

(h) land comprising premises which are or were designated by the Secretary of State by an order made under Section 1(1) of the Atomic Weapons Establishment Act 1991 (arrangements for development etc. of nuclear devices);

(i) land to which Section 30 of the Armed Forces Act 1996 applies; and

(j) land which:

    (i) is adjoining or adjacent to land of a description specified in sub-paragraphs (b) to (i) above; and

    (ii) is contaminated land by virtue of substances which appear to have escaped from land of such a description.

Contaminated Land Regime

Controlled waters

Harm

Imminent danger of serious harm

Nuclear waste

Radioactive substances and wastes

Remediation

Remediation Notice

Special sites

Waste acid tars

Contaminated Land Regime

The Contaminated Land Regime is set out in Part IIA of the EPA. This provides a risk-based approach to the identification and clean up (remediation) of land where contamination poses an unacceptable risk to human health and the environment.

Contaminated land

Contaminated Land (England) Regulations 2000

Environmental Protection Act 1990

Remediation

Remediation Notice

"Control"

With respect to genetically modified organisms, organisms of any description are under the control of a person where he keeps them contained by any system of physical, chemical or biological barriers (or combination of such barriers) used for either or both of the following purposes, namely:

(a) for ensuring that the organisms do not enter the environment or produce descendants which are not so contained; or

(b) for ensuring that any of the organisms which do enter the environment, or any descendants of the organisms which are not so contained, are harmless.

"Damage to the environment"

Environmental Protection Act 1990

Genetically modified organism (GMO)

Genetically Modified Organisms (Contained Use) Regulations 2000

"Released" and "release"

Controlled waste

Controlled wastes are those wastes that are controlled by the EPA, namely household, industrial and commercial waste or any such waste.

Not all types of waste are 'controlled'. For example, waste from agricultural premises, waste from mines and quarries and explosive or most radioactive waste are not defined as controlled wastes. Litter is, however, classified as controlled waste.

Commercial waste

Controlled Waste Regulations 1992

Household waste

Industrial waste

Litter

Waste

Controlled Waste Regulations 1992

These Regulations classified the forms of waste in terms of the provisions relating to collection. Most household waste is collected free of charge whereas charges are made for the collection of industrial and commercial waste.

(a) *Household waste* includes waste from domestic properties, caravans, residential homes, educational establishments, hospitals and nursing homes;

(b) *Industrial waste* (trade waste) means waste from any of the following premises – factories, public transport premises, premises used to supply gas, water and electricity, sewerage, postal or telecom services; waste from construction or demolition operations is also included in this definition as is waste from contaminated land;

(c) *Commercial waste* includes waste from premises used wholly or mainly for the purposes of a trade or business, or for the purposes of sport, recreation or entertainment, except household, industrial, mining, quarrying and agricultural waste, or any other waste specified in the Waste Management Licence Regulations 1992.

Commercial waste

Controlled waste

Household waste

Industrial waste

Litter

Waste

Waste Management Licences

Waste Management Licensing Regulations 1994 – 2006

Waste offences

Controlled waters

The Water Resources Act 1991 deals with the control of pollution in 'controlled waters' only.

Section 104 of the EPA defines 'controlled waters' as including:

(a) *inland fresh waters* – including lakes, ponds, rivers or water courses above the fresh water limit;

(b) *ground waters* – that is waters contained in the underground strata; and

(c) *coastal waters* – including all estuarine waters up to the fresh water limits of rivers and water courses. The Contaminated Land (England) Regulations 2000 apply the contaminated land requirements with respect to the potential for pollution of controlled waters from such land where:

(a) controlled waters which are, or are intended to be, used for the supply of drinking water for human consumption are being affected by the land and, as a result, require a treatment process or a change in such a process to be applied to those waters before use, so as to be regarded as wholesome within the meaning of Part III of the Water Industry Act 1991;

(b) controlled waters are being affected by land and, as a result, those waters do not meet or are not likely to meet the criterion for classification applying to the relevant description of waters specified in Regulations made under Section 82 of the Water Resources Act 1991; or

(c) controlled waters are being affected by the land and:

   (i) any of the substances by reason of which the pollution of the waters is being or is likely to be caused falls within any of the families or groups of substances listed in paragraph 1 of Schedule 1 to these Regulations; and

   (ii) the waters, or any part of the waters, are contained within underground strata which comprise wholly or partly any of the formation of rocks listed in paragraph 2 of Schedule 1 to these Regulations.

Coastal waters

Contaminated land

Contaminated Land (England) Regulations 2000

Drinking water

Remediation

Remediation Notice

Water classification

Water quality objectives and standards

Water Resources Act 1991

Control of Asbestos at Work Regulations 2006

Under these Regulations, employers have extensive duties to manage asbestos in workplaces. They must identify the types of asbestos present, assess the risk arising from work exposing employees to asbestos, produce written plans of work in respect of work with asbestos, notify the enforcing authority prior to commencing work with asbestos, provide information, instruction and training for employees who may be exposed, take measures to prevent or reduce, so far as is reasonably practicable, the exposure of employees to asbestos, ensure any control measures are used by employees, maintain the appropriate control measures, provide and clean protective clothing for employees.

There must be procedures for dealing with accidents, incidents and emergencies, premises and plant must be kept clean and designated areas established where work involves exposure to asbestos. Designated areas must be subject to regular air monitoring, ensuring compliance with established Air Quality Standards. Health records must be maintained and exposed employees must receive regular medical surveillance. Separate washing and changing facilities must also be provided for exposed workers.

Asbestos

Asbestos: activities involving

Pollution Prevention and Control (England and Wales) Regulations 2000

Scheduled activities

Control of Major Accident Hazards (COMAH) Regulations 1999

The Regulations are concerned with the prevention of major accidents, i.e. uncontrolled, unexpected or unplanned events, involving one or more defined dangerous substances.

A *major accident* is broadly defined as one having the potential to cause serious danger to people or the environment. In this context, *serious danger* means risk of death, physical injury or ill health whether acute (immediate) or chronic (delayed) to persons on the site or outside it, including the general public.

COMAH applies to all sites where dangerous substances listed in Schedule 1 to the Regulations:

(a) are present at or above a threshold quantity;

(b) where any dangerous substance at the threshold quantity is generated either intentionally or unintentionally, for instance, as a result of an accident or malfunction in a process;

(c) nuclear and licensed explosives sites, where dangerous substances are stored or used at or above the threshold quantities.

Operators are required to notify the Health and Safety Executive (HSE) in terms of the operator, the site and the processes carried out and provide an inventory of all dangerous substances held on site.

Operators must take all necessary measures to prevent major accidents and undertake risk analysis with a view to understanding and predicting how a major accident, such as a major chemical spillage, explosion or major fire, could arise on site and the possible consequences of same. They must further prepare a Major Accident Prevention Policy and a document indicating the safety management system on site. This document must incorporate the organisational structure, responsibilities of on-site personnel, procedures and resources for implementing the Policy.

The HSE require documented evidence that appropriate precautions are being taken to avoid major accidents, including plans, systems and procedures.

Environmental occurrences

Hazardous substances: classification

Health and Safety Executive (HSE)

Pollution incidents

Control of Noise at Work Regulations 2005

The Regulations cover not only the noisy industries and sites, but virtually all workplaces with few exceptions. They apply to motor cycle couriers and call centre workers who are exposed to noise (including speech) through headphones.

The Regulations specify *action values* and *exposure limit values* for daily personal noise exposure (or weekly personal noise exposure) and peak sound level.

Daily personal noise exposure ($L_{\cdot EPd}$) is a measure of the total noise received by an employee over the working day. They depend upon both noise levels experienced at work and the time spent in the noise, i.e. noise dose. For an eight-hour working day, the average noise level over the eight hours is numerically equal to the daily personal noise exposure.

Weekly personal noise exposure ($L._{EP.w}$) is a measure of the total noise received by an employee during a 40-hour working week, i.e. five eight-hour days instead of an eight- hour day.

Peak sound pressure level ($L._{Cpeak}$) is the instantaneous C-weighted peak sound pressure level occurring at any time during the working day.

The threshold for providing hearing protection and training on noise and hearing is 80 dB(A)$L_{EP.d}$.

The thresholds for introducing noise control are 85 d(B)A $L_{EP.d}$ and 137 dBL_{peak}.

An *exposure limit value* for daily noise exposure is introduced and weekly averaging of noise exposure is permitted when noise exposures vary from day to day. Considerable emphasis is placed on consultation between employers and employees and their representatives and there is a specific requirement for health surveillance and hearing testing where a risk is identified.

The Regulations apply in aircraft in flight over British soil.

Employers must ensure noise is eliminated at source or, where not reasonably practicable, to as low a level as is reasonably practicable

If one of the Lower Exposure Action Values (LEAVs) is likely to be exceeded, a risk assessment must be carried out to determine whether any employees are likely to be exposed to noise at or above the LEAV, an Upper Exposure Action Value (UEAV) or an Exposure Limit Value (ELV).

Specific factors to be incorporated in risk assessment:

- level, type and duration of exposure
- effects of exposure to employees particularly at risk, etc

LEAVs and UEAVs

At or above the LEAV, employer to make hearing protection available, provide information, instruction and training on specified issues, such as the nature of the risks, the organisational and technical measures taken to reduce exposure, etc.

At or above the UEAV, employer to reduce exposure to noise to as low a level as is reasonably practicable by establishing and implementing a programme of organisational and technical measures, excluding the provision of hearing protection.

ELVs

An ELV must never be exceeded. If an ELV is exceeded, the employer must identify the reason and take steps to prevent a recurrence.

Noise Act 1996

Noise and Statutory Nuisances Act 1993

Noise nuisance

Control of Pollution Act 1974

This statute was the first attempt at achieving a comprehensive pollution control strategy in the UK. In particular, it required local authorities to make plans with respect to waste generated in their areas and introduced a system of licensing to control the location of waste deposit sites. Waste Disposal Authorities were required to draw up a plan for the disposal of all household, commercial and industrial waste likely to arise in their areas. The plans had to contain information on the types and quantities of waste, the methods of disposal, the sites and equipment being provided and the overall cost. Waste Disposal Authorities were also required to consult with the water authorities, other levels of local government and other relevant bodies.

The Act introduced the requirement for a comprehensive licensing system for the disposal of waste on land.

Environmental Protection Act 1990

Waste Disposal Authorities (WDAs) and Companies

Control of Substances Hazardous to Health (COSHH) Regulations 2006

The COSHH Regulations apply to every form of workplace and every type of work activity involving the use of substances which may be hazardous to health to people at work. The Regulations are supported by a number of HSC Approved Codes of Practice, including:

- "Control of substances hazardous to health"
- "Control of carcinogenic substances" and
- "Control of biological agents"

Substance hazardous to health means a substance (including any preparation):

(a) which is listed for supply in Part 1 of the Approved Supply List as dangerous for supply within the meaning of the Chemicals (Hazard Information and Packaging for Supply) Regulations and for which an indication of danger specified for the substance is *very toxic, toxic, harmful, corrosive* or *irritant*;

(b) for which the HSC has approved a maximum exposure limit or an occupational exposure standard (now known as "workplace exposure limit");

(c) which is a biological agent;

(d) which is dust of any kind, except dust which is a substance within paragraph (a) or (b) above, when present at a concentration in air equal to or greater than:

  (i) 10 mg/m^3, as a time-weighted average over an eight-hour period, of inhalable dust; or

  (ii) 4 mg/m^3, as a time-weighted average over an eight-hour period, of respirable dust;

(e) which, not being a substance falling within sub-paragraphs (a) to (d), because of its chemical or toxicological properties and the way it is used or is present at the workplace creates a risk to health.

Under the Regulations, employers must:

(a) assess the risks to health created by work involving substances hazardous to health;

(b) prevent or control exposure to such substances;

(c) ensure the use of control measures;

(d) maintain, examine and test control measures; (such as local exhaust ventilation systems);

(e) monitor exposure in the workplace where the risk assessment identifies the need for same;

(f) provide health surveillance for employees if the risk assessment identifies the need for same;

(g) provide information, instruction and training for persons who may be exposed to substances hazardous to health; and

(h) make arrangements to deal with accidents, incidents and emergencies.

Principles of good practice

Schedule 2A to the COSHH (Amendment) Regulations 2004 outlines the following principles of good practice for the control of exposure to substances hazardous to health:

(a) design and operate processes and activities to minimise emission, release and spread of substances hazardous to health;

(b) take into account all relevant routes of exposure – inhalation, skin absorption and ingestion – when developing control measures;

(c) control exposure by measures that are proportionate to the health risk;

(d) choose the most effective and reliable control options which minimise the escape and spread of substances hazardous to health;

(e) where adequate control of exposure cannot be achieved by other means, provide, in combination with other control measures, suitable personal protective equipment;

(f) check and review regularly all elements of control measures for their continuing effectiveness;

(g) inform and train all employees on the hazards and risks from the substances with which they work and the use of control measures developed to minimise the risks;

(h) ensure that the introduction of control measures does not increase the overall risk to health and safety.

Airborne particulates

Biological agents

Carcinogens

Chemicals (Hazard Information and Packaging for Supply) (CHIP) Regulations 1994 – 2002

Hazardous substances: classification

Local exhaust ventilation (LEV) systems

Workplace exposure limits (WELs)

Control of Vibration at Work Regulations 2005

Employers must undertake vibration risk assessments. The Regulations specify in detail information that must be incorporated in a risk assessment, where there is risk of injury arising from hand-arm vibration or whole-body vibration.

The Regulations specify:

- *Exposure limit values* – a level of daily exposure for any worker which must not be exceeded.
- *Exposure action values* – the level of daily exposure for any worker which, if exceeded, requires specific action to be taken to reduce risk.
- Exposure action values and exposure limit values:
  - *for hand-arm vibration*

    The daily exposure limit value normalised to an eight-hour reference period is 5 m/s^2

    The daily exposure action value normalised to an eight-hour reference period is 2.5 m/s^2
  - *for whole-body vibration*

    The daily exposure limit value normalised to an eight-hour reference period is 1.15 m/s^2

    The daily exposure action value normalised to an eight-hour reference period is 0.5 m/s^2

Employers have a duty to eliminate or control exposure on the basic of "Principles of Prevention" set out in Schedule 1 to the Management of Health and Safety at Work Regulations 1999.

Where it is not reasonably practicable to eliminate the risk of vibration injury at source and the risk assessment indicates an exposure action value is likely to be exceeded, the employer must establish a *programme of organisational and technical measures* appropriate to the activity and consistent with the risk assessment.

Reasonably practicable

Cooling towers and evaporative condensers

A range of items of plant, such as cooling towers and air conditioning systems, which produce aerosols have, in the past, been associated with cases of legionnaires' disease

The Notification of Cooling Towers and Evaporative Condensers Regulations 1992 lay down a regime for the notification by a person in control of premises to ensure that no *notifiable device* is situated on those premises unless the information set out in the Schedule to the Regulations has been notified on the form approved by the Health and Safety Executive to the local authority.

Cooling tower means a device whose main purpose is to cool water by direct contact between that water and a stream of air.

Evaporative condenser means a device whose main purpose is to cool a fluid by passing that fluid through a heat exchanger which is itself cooled by contact with water passing through a stream of air.

Notifiable device means a cooling tower or evaporative condenser except:

(a) where it contains no water that is exposed to air;

(b) where its water supply is not connected; and

(c) where its electrical supply is not connected.

Airborne particulates

Health and Safety Executive (HSE)

Legionnaires' disease

Copper

Heavy metal pollution

Corporate liability

Section 157 of the EPA states:

> Where an offence committed by a body corporate is proved to have been committed with the consent or connivance of, or to have been attributable to any neglect on the part of, any director, manager, secretary or other similar officer of the body corporate or a person who was purporting to act in any such capacity, he as well as the body corporate shall be guilty of that offence and shall be liable to be proceeded against and punished accordingly.

Similar provisions apply in the case of a body corporate which is managed by its members thus:

> Where the affairs of a body corporate are managed by its members, the above requirement shall apply in relation to the acts or defaults of a member

in connection with his functions of management as if he were a director of the body corporate.

The key words in this Section are *consent, connivance* and *neglect*. Where an officer of an enforcement agency can show that an individual consented, connived or neglected to take action with respect to the commission of an offence under the EPA, that individual can also be prosecuted personally in addition to the body corporate.

Environmental Protection Act 1990

Offences

Penalties

Cost-benefit analysis

An assessment of the costs and benefits associated with a process, action, enterprise or system.

Countryside and Rights of Way Act 2000

This statute extended the public's ability to enjoy the countryside whilst also providing safeguards for landowners and occupiers. It created a statutory right of access to open country and registered common land, modernised the rights of way system, gave greater protection to Sites of Special and Scientific Interest, provided better management arrangements for Areas of Outstanding Natural Beauty and strengthened wildlife enforcement legislation.

Areas of Outstanding Natural Beauty

Riparian rights

Sites of Special and Scientific Interest

Cradle to Cradle

A design protocol that advocates the elimination of waste by recycling a material or product into a new or similar product at the end of its intended life, rather than disposing of it.

Cradle to Grave

Recycling and disposal of waste

Cradle to Grave

A manufacturing model, dating to the onset of the Industrial Revolution, which describes the process of disposing of a material or product via landfill, incineration, etc at the end of its presumed useful life.

Cradle to Cradle

Incineration

Landfill sites

Recycling and disposal of waste

Criteria for assessment

The water company undertakes all consultations necessary, plus a technical and economic appraisal of a scheme to provide sewers to the area, and reports back to the applicant on their findings.

The duty to provide a public sewer arises if some or all of the various technical criteria are met, and provision of a sewer is the most cost effective solution.

The *technical criteria* are:

(a) there is a risk to water sources;

(b) there is evidence of a risk to public health from the existing system (but not neglect);

(c) polluting matter is reaching, or can reach, a watercourse;

(d) sewage pollution is damaging the local amenity value;

(e) statutes or other requirements are being breached resulting in environmental problems; and

(f) other practical and technical criteria.

An economic assessment will be undertaken as part of the proposals.

Time

Following application to the water company by an owner or his representative, the water company must then deal with the application reasonably quickly, say, within 6 months.

Appeals

Where an applicant is dissatisfied with the decision of the water company, he may appeal against this decision by making a formal application to the Environment Agency for the decision to be reviewed.

Sewage effluent

Water

Water classification

Water pollution

D

Damages

The normal remedy in a successful civil action is an award of damages to the claimant. The objective is to put the claimant in the position that he would have been in had the harm, loss or damage not arisen.

In the case of damage to the environment, this is hard to calculate. Environmental damage, such as an oil spill or the release of a hazardous liquid into a watercourse, may have long-lasting consequences. Moreover, the cost of cleaning up the damage may involve work lasting several years. In some cases, the damage may never be fully rectified.

Common law

Duty of care

Environmental Protection (Duty of Care) Regulations 1991

Injunction

Negligence

Nuisance

Nuisance at common law

Tort

"Damage to the environment"

Section 107 of the EPA defines a number of terms in connection with genetically modified organisms.

Damage to the environment is caused by the presence in the environment of genetically modified organisms which have (or of a single such organism) escaped or been released form a person's control and are (or is) capable of causing harm to the living organisms supported by the environment.

Environmental Protection Act 1990

Genetically modified organisms (GMO)

Genetically Modified Organisms (Contained Use) Regulations 2000

Dangerous substance sites

The Dangerous Substances (Notification and Marking of Sites) Regulations 1990 require that the person in control of a site must ensure that:

(a) there is not present on the site, at any one time, a total of 25 tonnes or more of dangerous substances unless written notification with specified particulars has been given to the fire and rescue authority, together with the Health and Safety Executive and the local authority;

(b) where there is 25 tonnes or more of dangerous substances on site, that specified safety signs are displayed so as to give adequate warning to fire-fighters of the presence of dangerous substances; and

(c) that safety signs are kept clean and free from obstructions at all times and are in accordance with any directions given by an inspector from the Health and Safety Executive.

Hazardous substances: classification

Health and Safety Executive (HSE)

"Dark smoke"

Dark smoke is smoke which is determined to be as dark or darker than shade 2 on the Ringelmann Chart.

Dark smoke defences

Dark smoke offences

Ringelmann Chart

Smoke

Dark smoke defences

Where a breach of the dark smoke provisions occurs, a number of defences are available in the following circumstances:

(a) when lighting the furnace from cold; or

(b) when there has been some unforeseeable and unavoidable failure of the furnace or apparatus connected with the furnace; or

(c) when unsuitable fuel has been used when suitable fuel is unobtainable and that the least unsuitable fuel was used.

These defences are all subject to the important caveat that 'all practicable steps' were taken to prevent or minimise the emissions of dark smoke. In considering whether 'all practicable steps ' have been taken, consideration must be given to factors such as local conditions and circumstances and the current state of technical knowledge.

[Clean Air Act 1993]

"Dark smoke"

Dark smoke offences

Dark smoke offences

Section 1 of the Clean Air Act prohibits the emission of dark smoke:

(a) from the chimney of any building; or

(b) from a chimney which serves the furnace of any fixed boiler or industrial plant.

This includes emissions from the chimneys of domestic premises as well as industrial and commercial premises.

Where an offence is committed under (a) above, liability rests with the occupier of the building from which the dark smoke is emitted. In the case of an emission from (b) above, the person having possession of the boiler or plant may be liable.

Section 2 of the Clean Air Act prohibits the emission of dark smoke from industrial trade premises. However, the emission need not be through a chimney. An offence may be committed either by the occupier of the premises or any other person causing or permitting the emission.

Under Section 3, a court must be satisfied in any legal proceedings for a breach of Section 1 that the smoke is as dark as defined. There is no requirement for an actual comparison of the smoke with the Ringelmann Chart. It is sufficient that the court is certain that the method was properly applied and that the smoke was thereby determined to be dark.

There is no requirement for the defendant to have caused or knowingly permitted the discharge of dark smoke. The offence is a strict liability offence.

Breach of Section 1 is a criminal offence and a person may be liable on summary conviction to a fine of up to £3,000 (level 3), in the case of emissions from private dwelling houses, and £5,000 (level 5) in other cases.

The occupier of the premises must be notified of the offence 'as soon as may be' by the local environmental health officer. This would normally be a verbal notification, which must be followed up in writing within four days of same.

Clean Air Act 1993

"Dark smoke"

Dark smoke defences

Ringelmann Chart

Decisions

A Decision is an individual Act made by the European Commission which is binding in its entirety upon those to whom it is addressed. Decisions can be addressed to Member States, organisations and individuals. Because a Decision is binding, it has the force of law and does not require any implementation. Decisions are not frequently used by the European Commission in environmental law.

Directives

Recommendations and opinions

Regulations

Defences: criminal proceedings

Duties under environmental protection law are largely of an absolute or strict nature. However, statutes do provide a number of defences, in particular the defence that 'best practicable means' were used to prevent the commission of the offence. The principal statutory defences include:

(a) best practicable means;

(b) that all reasonable precautions were taken and all due diligence exercised;

(c) that the defendant acted on instructions from his employer and that neither knew, or had reason to suppose, that such actions were in contravention of the law;

(d) acts done in an emergency;

(e) the offences were committed due to the act or default of another person; and

(f) reasonable excuse.

Noise emitted from premises

In proceedings for an offence for a statutory nuisance falling within paragraph (g) of Section 79(1) (noise emitted from premises), where the offence consists in contravening requirements imposed by virtue of subsection 1(a), it is a defence to prove :

(a) that the alleged offence was covered by a Notice served under Section 60 or a Consent given under Sections 61 or 65 of the Control of Pollution Act 1974 (construction sites, etc.); or

(b) where the alleged offence was committed at a time when the premises were subject to a Notice under Section 66 of the Act (Noise Reduction Notice), that the level of noise emitted from the premises at that time was not such as to constitute a contravention of the Notice under that Section; or

(c) where the alleged offence was committed at a time when the premises were not subject to a Notice under Section 66 of that Act, and when a level fixed under Section 67 of that Act (new buildings liable to an Abatement Order) applied to the premises, that the level of noise emitted from the premises did not exceed that level.

[Environmental Protection Act 1990]

All reasonable precautions and all due diligence

"Best practicable means"

Environmental crimes

Noise Abatement Notices

Noise Abatement Zone

Noise Act 1996

Offences

Reasonable excuse

Deforestation

The removal of trees or forests of trees associated with the activities of logging companies, the building of highways, construction of buildings on virgin land and the conversion of forest areas to agricultural use.

Ecosystems

Virgin forest

DEFRA

DEFRA, The Department of Environment, Food and Rural Affairs, is charged with regulating the environment. DEFRA's aim is sustainable development.

Within this principal aim of sustainable development, DEFRA has five strategic priorities:

(a) climate change and energy;

(b) sustainable consumption and production;

(c) protecting the countryside and natural resource protection;

(d) sustainable rural communities; and

(e) a sustainable farming and food sector including animal health and welfare.

A significant part of DEFRA's work is concerned with preparedness for emergencies and contingencies which fall within the remit of environment, food and rural affairs.

DEFRA and its executive agencies are responsible for enforcing a wide range of legal obligations, many of which carry criminal sanctions for non-compliance.

Sustainability

Sustainable development

Sustainable use

Deposit of waste from motor vehicles

Where controlled waste is carried in and deposited from a motor vehicle, the person who controls, or is in a position to control, its use is treated as knowingly causing the waste to be deposited, whether or not he gave any instructions for this to be done.

Controlled waste

Controlled Waste Regulations 1992

Environmental Protection Act 1990

Waste disposal: hazardous substances

Waste offences

Waste unlawfully deposited

Deposit of waste: offence

Any person who unlawfully deposits, or knowingly causes or permits the deposit of waste which causes damage, is liable for that damage unless it:

(a) was wholly due to the fault of the person who suffered it; or

(b) was suffered by the person who voluntarily accepted the risk.

Waste

Waste: duty of care

Waste offences

Waste unlawfully deposited

Designated mineral or mineral product

This means:

(a) clay, sand and any other naturally occurring mineral other than coal or lignite;

(b) metallurgical slag;

(c) boiler or furnace ash produced from the burning of coal, coke or any other coal product;

(d) gypsum which is a by-product of any activity.

[Pollution Prevention and Control (England and Wales) Regulations 2000]

Scheduled activities

Diffuse pollution

Diffuse pollution is that form of water pollution which cannot be attributed to a precise point of entry to water or pollution incident. It is the cumulative effect of ongoing activity over a very large area. A number of activities contribute to diffuse pollution, including agriculture, forestry, construction, mining and urban life. In many cases, pollutants deposited on land, roads and open spaces are washed into watercourses and lakes by rain. On this basis, the local climate, geology and other natural phenomena can influence the size and extent of diffuse pollution.

In agriculture, diffuse pollutants include silt from soil erosion, nutrients from the application of fertilisers or the spreading of manure, and pesticides from the application and handling of chemical substances.

Agricultural nitrate pollution

Manures and slurries

Pesticide

Soil erosion

Watercourse

Water pollution

Dioxins

These are chlorinated organic chemicals which are formed unintentionally and released through activities such as the combustion of fuels and incineration of waste. Dioxins travel in air and are eventually deposited on land and in water where they can enter the food chain. Over 90% of the human intake of dioxins is through food, mainly of animal origin, where they tend to accumulate in the liver and body fat. Dioxins can trigger biological effects such as hormonal disturbances and alterations in cell functions.

For workers exposed accidentally to the highest doses of dioxins, studies indicate that the risk of contracting cancer increases by around 40%. Other non-cancerous effects include liver and heart diseases, diabetes, dermatitis (chloracne), slowed nervous responses, conjunctivitis and fatigue.

Chlorine

Combustion activities

Hazardous substances: classification

Incineration

Directions to regulators

The Secretary of State may give directions to regulators of a general or specific character with respect to the carrying out of any of their functions under Regulations, such as the Pollution Prevention and Control (England and Wales) Regulations 2000.

Regulator

Directives

Under the Treaty of Rome, the Council of the European Committees can issue Directives. Directives usually provide for "harmonisation" of the laws of the Member States, including those covering occupational health and safety.

The process commences whereby representatives of the Member States meet to agree the content of draft Directives. Once agreed, drafts are presented to the European Parliament for ratification. Directives impose a duty on each Member State to:

(a) make Regulations to conform to the Directive; and

(b) enforce such Regulations.

Directives are legally binding on all governments who must introduce national legislation or use certain administrative procedures. *Framework Directives* set out overall objectives, which are subsequently dealt with individually by *Daughter Directives*.

Opinions and Directions

Regulations

Single European Act 1986

Directive waste

This is waste referred to in the EC Directive 91/156 on Waste (which amended the original Directive 74/442) and which includes substances that can be recycled. Directive waste is defined by reference to a list of categories of waste. It is any substance or object in the categories laid down in Schedule 4 to the Waste Management Licence Regulations 1994 which the producer or the person in possession of it discards, or intends to discard or is required to discard.

These categories are as follows:

- production or consumption residues;
- off-specification products;
- products whose date for appropriate use has expired;
- materials spilled, lost or having undergone other mishap, including any materials, equipment, etc contaminated as a result of the mishap;
- materials contaminated or soiled as a result of planned actions (e.g. residues from cleaning operations, packing materials, containers, etc);
- unusable parts (e.g. reject batteries, exhausted catalysts, etc);

- substances which no longer perform satisfactorily (e.g., contaminated acids, contaminated solvents, exhausted tempering salts, etc);
- residues of industrial processes (e.g. slags, still bottoms, etc);
- residues from pollution abatement processes (e.g. scrubber sludges, baghouse dusts, spent filters, etc);
- machining or finishing residues (e.g. lathe turnings, mill scales, etc);
- residues from raw materials extraction and processing (e.g. mining residues, oil field slops, etc);
- adulterated materials (e.g. oils contaminated with PCBs etc);
- any materials, substances or products whose use has been banned by law;
- products for which the holder has no further use (e.g. agricultural, household, office, commercial and shop discards, etc);
- contaminated materials, substances or products resulting from remedial action with respect to land;
- any material, substances or products which are not contained in the above categories.

Batteries and accumulators

Controlled waste

Industrial waste

Waste

Waste: environmental consequences

Waste Management (England and Wales) Regulations 2006

Waste Management Licences

Waste Management Licensing Regulations 1994 – 2006

Waste offences

Discharge and scope of functions

The following functions are conferred or imposed on a regulator, together with the purposes for which they are exercisable:

Environment Agency

Those functions in their application to a Part (A)1 installation or a Part A(1) mobile plant which shall be exercisable for the purpose of achieving a high level of protection of the environment taken as a whole by, in particular, preventing or, where that is not practicable, reducing emissions into the air, water and land.

Local authorities

Those functions in their application to a Part A(2) installation or Part A(2) mobile plant in whose area the installation is (or will be) situated or the mobile plant is (or will be) operated which shall be exercisable for the purpose of achieving a high level of protection of the environment taken as a whole by, in particular, preventing, or where that is not practicable, reducing emissions into the air, water or land.

Those functions in their application to a Part B installation in whose area the installation is (or will be) situated which shall be exercisable for the purpose of preventing or, where that is not practicable, reducing emissions into the air.

[Pollution Prevention and Control (England and Wales) Regulations 2000]

DEFRA

Emission

Environment Agency

Installation

Mobile plant

Part A activities

Part B activities

Pollution Prevention and Control (England and Wales) Regulations 2000

Practicable: definition

Regulator

Scheduled activities

Discharge consent

A permit to discharge contaminated water from an industrial site. The permit specifies allowed contamination limits and/or permitted discharge volumes.

Authorised discharge consent

Authorised discharges

Controlled waters

Discharge to controlled waters

Permit

Permit conditions

Discharges to controlled waters

Under Section 85 of the Water Resources Act it is an offence to discharge sewage effluent into controlled waters. Sewerage undertakers are required to obtain a consent from the National Rivers Authority to discharge any treated sewage.

Authorised discharge consent

Authorised discharges

Consents: controlled waters

National Rivers Authority

Permit

Permit conditions

Pollution of controlled waters

Water Resources Act 1991

Discharge of trade effluents to sewers

The discharge to public sewers of, particularly, trade effluents is directly controlled by the sewerage undertakers, who exercise powers under the Water Resources Act 1991, together with the National Rivers Authority.

Sewerage undertakers grant consents for the disposal of effluent into the sewers but they must obtain consent from the National Rivers Authority to release the final treated effluent into controlled waters. The Water Industry Act regulates the discharge of trade effluents into sewers and Section 87 of the Water Resources Act deals with the discharge of sewage effluent into controlled waters.

Controlled waters

Discharge consent

National Rivers Authority

Pollution of controlled waters

Sewage effluent

Trade effluent

Water Resources Act 1991

Disposal

Any of the wide range of operations listed in Schedule 4 to the Waste Management Licensing Regulations, such as tipping of waste above or underground and the release of wastes into seas.

Waste Management Licences

Waste Management Licensing Regulations 1994 – 2006

Waste offences

Disposal of waste other than by incineration or landfill

These scheduled activities are:

Part A(1)

(a) The disposal of hazardous waste (other than by incineration or landfill) in a facility with a capacity of more than 10 tonnes per day;

(b) The disposal of waste oils (other than by incineration or landfill) in a facility with a capacity of more than 10 tonnes per day;

(c) Disposal of non-hazardous waste in a facility with a capacity of more than 50 tonnes per day by:

   (i) biological treatment, not being treatment specified in any paragraph other than paragraph D8 of Annex IIA to Council Directive 75/442/EEC, which results in final compounds or mixtures which are discarded by means of any of the operations number D1 to D12 in that Annex (D8); or

   (ii) physico-chemical treatment, not being treatment specified in any paragraph other than paragraph D9 in Annex IIA to Council Directive 74/442/EEC, which results in final compounds or mixtures which are discarded by means of any of the operations numbered D1 to D12 in that Annex (for example, evaporation, drying, calcination, etc) (D9).

Part A(2)

Nil

Part B

Nil

[Schedule 1: Part 1: Pollution Prevention and Control (England and Wales) Regulations 2000]

Part A activities

Part B activities

Pollution Prevention and Control Act 1999

Pollution Prevention and Control (England and Wales) Regulations 2000

Scheduled activities

Drinking water

Under the Water Act 1989, water companies are placed under a statutory duty when supplying water to any premises for domestic purposes to supply "only water which is wholesome at the time of supply". The wholesomeness of water supplied for domestic purposes, such as drinking, cooking and washing, is defined in the Water Supply (Water Quality) Regulations 1989.

Water

Water abstraction

Water Act 2003

Water classification

Water pollution

Water quality objectives and standards

Drinking Water Inspectorate

It is the responsibility of the Drinking Water Inspectorate to ensure that the drinking water supplied in England and Wales is wholesome and that water companies are complying with the requirements of the Water Supply (Water Quality) Regulations 1989.

Drinking water

Water pollution

Duty of care

The common duty of care exists between all persons and was established in *Donoghue v Stevenson (1932)* The main principle behind the duty of care is the "neighbour principle", namely that 'you must take reasonable care to avoid acts or omissions which you can reasonably foresee would be likely to injure your neighbour'.

Neighbour is defined as 'persons who are so closely and directly affected by my act that I ought reasonably to have them in contemplation as being so affected when I am directing my mind to the acts or omissions which are being called into question'.

The requirements for establishing a duty of care are:

(a) foreseeability of damage;

(b) a proximate relationship between the parties; and

(c) that it is just and reasonable to impose such a duty.

At common law, employers must take reasonable care to protect employees from risk of foreseeable injury, death or disease arising from work. Consequently, where an employer is aware of a risk to the health and safety of his employees, or ought 'in the light of the current state of the art', to have known of such a risk, he may well be liable in the event of injury, illness or death to his employee arising from the risk if it can be established that he failed to take reasonable care in the particular situation.

In its Eleventh Report, *Managing Waste: The Duty of Care* (1985), the Royal Commission for Environmental Pollution recommended that a duty of care be placed on everyone involved in the waste chain thus:

> *The producer (of waste) incurs a duty of care which is owed to society, and we would like to see this duty reflected in public attitudes and enshrined in legislation and codes of practice.*

Duty of care under the EPA

Section 33 of the EPA prohibits the unauthorised or harmful deposit, treatment or disposal, etc of waste and Section 34 sets out the duty of care of persons under the Act. This duty is supplemented by Regulations, the Environmental Protection (Duty of Care) Regulations 1991.

Any person who fails to comply with the duty of care commits a criminal offence. Moreover, it is not necessary for there to have been any form of environmental damage or for there to be an actual breach of Section 33. All that is required is for there to have been a breach of the duty of care.

Civil liability

Controlled waste

Environmental Protection Act 1990

Environmental Protection (Duty of Care) Regulations 1991

Negligence

Nuisance at common law

Statutory nuisances

Tort

Waste

Waste offences

Waste unlawfully deposited

Duty of care in respect of waste

Section 34 of the EPA provides that the duty of care applies to any person who imports, produces, carries, keeps, treats or disposes of controlled waste or, as a broker, has control of such waste. Such persons are classified as "waste holders".

There are four main elements of the duty:

(a) the duty to prevent any other person committing an offence under Section 33 of the EPA (Prohibition on unauthorised or harmful deposits, treatment or disposal, etc of waste);

(b) the duty to prevent the escape of waste from his control or the control of others (Section 34: Duty of care etc in respect of waste)

(c) the duty to ensure waste handed over to another person is in a suitable container and which is suitably labelled (Section 34); and

(d) the duty to transfer to an authorised person or to a person for authorised transport purposes (Section 34).

Authorised transport purposes

Controlled waste

Duty of care

Environmental Protection Act 1990

Environmental Protection (Duty of Care) Regulations 1991

Waste

Waste broker

Waste offences

Waste transfer

Waste unlawfully deposited

Dyestuffs, printing ink and coating materials

These scheduled activities are:

Part A(1)

Nil

Part A(2)

Nil

Part B

(a) Unless falling within Part A(1) or A(2) of any Section in this Schedule:

  (i) manufacturing or formulating printing ink or any other coating material containing, or involving the use of, an organic solvent, where the carrying out of the activity is likely to involve the use of 100 tonnes or more of organic solvents in any period of 12 months;

  (ii) manufacturing any powder for use as a coating material where there is the capacity to produce 200 tonnes or more of such powder in any period of 12 months.

[Schedule 1: Part 1: Pollution Prevention and Control (England and Wales) Regulations 2000]

Coating activities, printing and textile treatment

Part A activities

Part B activities

Pollution Prevention and Control Act 1999

Pollution Prevention and Control (England and Wales) Regulations 2000

Scheduled activities

E

Eco-efficiency

The delivery of competitively priced goods and services that satisfy human needs and bring quality of life, while progressively reducing environmental impacts and resource intensity throughout the life cycle, to a level at least in line with the Earth's estimated carrying capacity.

Eco-label

Environmental impact

Eco-label

An eco-label is a mark that can be placed on a product to indicate that it meets (or exceeds) certain criteria for environmental performance. These criteria are generally based on an analysis of where, in its whole lifecycle, the product causes the greatest environmental impacts.

Environmental impact

Ecology

The study of living creatures and organisms in their natural surroundings or environment.

Ecosystems

Ecosystems

A given habitat and its community which interact and form an ecological unit which is largely self-contained.

The interacting system of a biological community and its non-living environmental surroundings.

Many smaller ecosystems can be found within larger ones. These systems include both living and non-living substances interacting to produce an exchange of materials between the living and non-living units.

Ecology

Habitat

Effluent

Any liquid, including particles of matter and other substances in suspension in the liquid.

[Water Resources Act 1991]

Controlled waters

Sewage effluent

Trade effluent

Water Resources Act 1991

EMAS (European) Eco-management and Audit Scheme

A European Commission voluntary scheme which accredits industrial sites that undertake an environmental audit of their operations. An organisation wishing to register under EMAS must have a clearly-defined strategy for environmental management equivalent to ISO 14001, complete with quantified objectives, and produce a site environmental report that is verified by an approved third party body.

Environmental audit

Environmental management system (EMS)

ISO 14001: Environmental Management Systems

Emission

The release of any gas, particle or vapour into the environment from a commercial, industrial or residential source including flues, chimneys and vehicles.

Means:

(i) in relation to Part A installations, the direct or indirect release of substances, vibrations, heat or noise from individual or diffuse sources in an installation into the air, water or land;

(ii) in relation to Part B installations, the direct release of substances or heat from individual or diffuse sources in an installation into the air;

(iii) in relation to Part A mobile plant, the direct or indirect release of substances, vibrations, heat or noise from the mobile plant into the air, water or land;

(iv) in relation to Part B mobile plant, the direct release of substances or heat from the mobile plant into the air.

[Pollution Prevention and Control (England and Wales) Regulations 2000]

Airborne particulates

Emission limit value

Installation

Mobile plant

Part A activities

Part B activities

Scheduled activities

Emission limit value

The mass, expressed in terms of specific parameters, concentration or level of emission, which may not be exceeded during one or more periods of time.

[Pollution Prevention and Control (England and Wales) Regulations 2000]

Emission

Emissions Trading Scheme

Emissions trading is a mechanism for achieving emissions reductions in a whole economy (national, regional or global) for the lowest cost. Organisations taking part in an Emissions Trading Scheme are allocated a certain quantity of emissions for a fixed period, normally one year. Where an organisation does not use its full allocation, it can sell any spare in an open market. Where it needs to exceed its allocation, it can buy permits in the same market. Those who can reduce emissions for the lowest cost have an incentive to do so as they profit from the difference between their costs and the market price of permits.

Because the total allocation of emission permits is centrally controlled, overall reductions can be achieved by reducing the amount of permits issued each year. As permits for unused allocations become scarcer, the price rises and more emissions-reducing investments become viable.

Emission

Permit

Endangered species

A population of a particular species which because it is either:

(a) few in number; or

(b) threatened by a changing environment or predation parameters, is at risk of becoming extinct.

Ecosystems

Habitat

Wildlife

Wildlife and Countryside Act 1981

Endocrine disruptors

Endocrine systems incorporate glands, which secrete hormones, together with receptor cells which detect and react to the hormones. (A hormone is described as "a chemical messenger".)

Disruption of the endocrine system can occur where:

(a) some chemicals mimic a natural hormone, resulting on over-response to a stimulus;

(b) blocking the effects of a hormone from certain receptors by blocking the receptor site on a cell;

(c) directly stimulating or inhibiting the endocrine system, resulting in the over-production or under-production of hormones.

Typical endocrine disrupting chemicals are dioxins, polychlorinated biphenyls (PCBs), phenols and certain pesticides, such as DDT.

Dioxins

Pesticide

Polychlorinated biphenyls (PCBs) and other dangerous sustances

End-of-life vehicles (ELVs)

These are scrapped motor vehicles that fall into the category of 'waste' as defined by the EU Waste Directive.

They are subject to the End-of-Life Vehicles Regulations 2003 which aim to:

(a) tighten existing controls and support pollution prevention;

(b) standardise disposal requirements throughout the European Union;

(c) influence the design of vehicles so that they, and their components, are easier to recycle;

(d) reduce the quantity of waste remaining after recovery and recycling have been undertaken; and

(e) reduce the use of certain hazardous materials in vehicle manufacture and, therefore, in vehicles being disposed of.

Hazardous substances: classification

Pollution: definition

Recovery of waste

Recycling and disposal of waste

Waste

Waste: environmental consequences

Energy intensive sector

A sector which carries out activities which are listed under Part A(1) or A(2) headings in Part 1 to Schedule 1 of the Pollution Prevention and Control (England and Wales) Regulations 2000 (as amended).

There are ten major energy intensive sectors – aluminium, cement, ceramics, chemicals, food and drink, foundries, glass, non-ferrous metals, paper and steel and over thirty smaller sectors. DEFRA has the responsibility for climate change agreements with these sectors.

Climate Change Agreements

DEFRA

Part A activities

Part B activities

Pollution Prevention and Control (England and Wales) Regulations 2000

Scheduled activities

Energy recovery

This is the recovery of useful energy in the form of heat and/or power from burning waste. The term is generally applied to incineration, but can also include the combustion of landfill gas and gas produced during anaerobic digestion.

Anaerobic digestion

Environmental Act 1996

Incineration

Enforcement activities

Regulators and their inspectors have significant powers including the power to:

(a) enter any premises to ascertain whether an offence is being or has been committed;

(b) carry out inspections, take measurements and undertake tests;

(c) remove samples of water, effluent, land or articles;

(d) carry out experimental borings; and

(e) install and operate monitoring equipment.

They are further authorised to serve a range of Notices on those breaching environmental protection legislation and to enforce requirements in the courts.

Abatement Notice

Abatement Order

All reasonable precautions and all due diligence

Breach of Conditions Notice

Causing pollution (offence)

Dark smoke offences

Defences: criminal proceedings

Enforcement by the High Court

Enforcement Notice

Health and Safety Executive (HSE)

Litter Abatement Notice

Litter Control Notice

Litter Fixed Penalty Notice

Noise Abatement Notices

Noise Abatement Zone

Penalties

Planning Contravention Notice

Powers of inspectors

Prohibition Notice

Prohibition Order

Regulator

Remediation Notice

Service of Notices

Street Litter Control Notice

Suspension Notice

Variation Notice

Warning Notice

Waste offences

Water Resources Act 1991

Works Notice

Enforcement by the High Court

Where the enforcement authority (or regulator) is of the opinion that proceedings for an offence under the EPA or Pollution Prevention and Control (England and Wales) Regulations, would afford an ineffectual remedy against a person who has failed to comply with the requirements of an Enforcement Notice or Suspension Notice, the authority or regulator may take proceedings in the High Court for the purpose of securing compliance with the Notice.

Enforcement Notice

Environmental Protection Act 1990

Offences

Pollution Prevention and Control (England and Wales) Regulations 2000

Regulator

Suspension Notice

Enforcement Notice

Where the regulator is of the opinion that an operator has contravened, is contravening or is likely to contravene any condition of his permit, the regulator may serve on him an Enforcement Notice.

An Enforcement Notice shall:

(a) state that the authority is of that opinion;

(b) specify the matters constituting the contravention or the matters making it likely that the contravention will arise, as the case may be;

(c) specify the steps that must be taken to remedy the contravention or to remedy the matters that make it likely that the contravention will arise, as the case may be; and

(d) specify the period within which those steps must be taken.

[Pollution Prevention and Control (England and Wales) Regulations 2000]

Permit

Regulator

Environment

The *environment* consists of all, or any, of the following media, namely the air, water and land; and the medium of air includes the air within buildings and the air within other natural or man-made structures above or below ground.

[Environmental Protection Act 1990]

The surroundings of a plant or animal, both living and non-living; the natural surroundings of human beings.

Built environment

Environmentally friendly

Environmental media

Habitat

Wildlife

Environment Act 1995

This Act brought in a number of new arrangements for dealing with environmental pollution, in particular the creation of the Environment Agency for England and Wales.

The Act brought together HM Inspectorate of Pollution, the National Rivers Authority and local Waste Regulation Authorities. Similar arrangements were made for Scotland with the creation of the Scottish Environment Protection Agency. Local air pollution control, formerly the responsibility of district and islands councils, comes under this Agency.

The Act contains detailed provisions for dealing with a range of environmental problems and issues, namely:

Air quality

(a) The setting of legislation to establish a national strategy and framework of ambient Air Quality Standards and targets for nine main pollutants.

(b) New powers for local authorities to review air quality in their districts and create *Air Quality Management Areas* where levels fall short of targets.

The Act provides the statutory framework for the new system.

Contaminated land

The Polluter Pays Principle was reinforced, but there was also recognition that land-owners should be responsible for some aspects of the land, if the original polluters cannot be found. No new classes of liability were created.

The measures are based on the *suitable for use* approach, the removal of real environmental hazards without the imposition of unnecessary costs. This approach requires remedial action only where there is *significant harm* or pollution of controlled waters and where there are appropriate and cost effective means available to take such action, taking into account the actual or intended use of the site.

Contaminated land is defined as any land which appears to be in such a condition that significant harm or pollution of controlled waters is being caused or is likely to be caused. *Harm* relates to the health of living organisms, or interference with the ecological systems of which they form part.

Pollution from abandoned mines

Statutory protection was removed from the owners and operators of all mines abandoned after the end of 1999. This allowed the national agencies to deal with discharges through *consents*, as with other pollution discharges. Failure to comply with these consents will lead to prosecution. Mine operators are required to give the agencies six months' notice of their intention to abandon a mine, thus allowing steps to be taken to prevent future mine water pollution.

National Parks Authorities (NPAs) in England and Wales

Local authority members are drawn from parish, rather than county, councils and are appointed by the Secretary of State. NPAs are required to foster the economic and social well-being of their local communities as well as protecting the natural beauty of the areas in their stewardship. Government and other public bodies must consider National Park purposes in carrying out their functions.

Waste strategy

National waste strategies were drawn up by the new agencies for England and Wales and for Scotland and national waste surveys carried out. *Sustainable development* was the cornerstone of the strategy, that is, making the best possible use of unavoidable waste and minimising the risk of pollution or harm to human health arising from waste disposal or recovery.

Producer responsibility

Regulations were introduced to impose *producer responsibility* to increase the reuse, recovery or recycling of any product or material. The powers are applicable to any waste stream.

Minerals planning permissions

There was an initial review and updating of old mineral permissions phased over six years. Future reviews of mineral permissions will be held every fifteen years.

Water conservation

Water companies are required to promote the efficient use of water by their customers. The Director General of Water Services will monitor this work and publish conservation performance league tables.

Water quality

The Environment Agency has powers to require action to prevent water pollution and require polluters to clean up after pollution incidents.

Combined Heat and Power (CHP)

The Act amends the Electricity Act 1989 to enable CHP to compete effectively for support under the fossil fuel levy with other forms of non-fossil electricity generating schemes.

Nuisance provisions

The framework for the control of statutory nuisance contained in Part III of the Environmental Protection Act 1990 was extended to Scotland.

Air Quality Management Area

Packaging

Producer Responsibility Obligations (Packaging Waste) Regulations 2005

Recovery

Recovery and recycling obligations

Recovery of waste

Recycling and disposal of waste

Statutory nuisances

Sustainable development

Water quality

Environment Agency

The Environment Act introduced a number of arrangements for dealing with environmental pollution, in particular the creation of the Environment Agency for England and Wales. The Environment Act brought together HM Inspectorate of Pollution, the National Rivers Authority and local Waste Regulation Authorities. Similar arrangements were made for Scotland with the creation of the Scottish Environment Protection Agency. Local air pollution control, formerly the responsibility of district and islands councils, comes under this Agency.

The Environment Agency is the leading body for protecting the environment in England and Wales. The Agency was established by the Environment Act 1995. As a non-departmental public body, it is sponsored largely by the Department of Environment, Food and Rural Affairs (DEFRA) and the National Assembly for Wales. It provides a number of national services, such as the National Laboratory Service and the National Library and Information Service. The Agency operates on a regional basis. Regional Offices support the local Area Offices.

The Agency provides high quality environmental protection and improvement, working with businesses and organisations to prevent damage to the environment by providing education and guidance. Where necessary, the Agency enforces Regulations, in some cases resulting in prosecution of offenders.

The Agency contributes to the worldwide environmental goal of sustainable development, which has been defined as *development that meets the needs of the present without compromising the ability of future generations to meet their own needs.*

Regulatory functions

The Environment Agency is the most important environmental regulator in England and Wales and undertakes the following functions:

Authorisations

The issue of permits, licences, consents and registrations, such as major industrial authorisations to, for example, abstract water from rivers.

Provision of advice

The provision of advice, prior to the issue of licences, on the best ways of reducing the effects of certain activities on the environment.

Inspection and monitoring

Regular inspection and monitoring of licence holders' activities with a view to ensuring environmental standards are being maintained. The Agency also assesses safety reports for sites covered by the Control of Major Accident Hazards (COMAH) Regulations and has a supervisory duty on flood defence.

Enforcement

The Agency prosecutes offenders for breaches of environmental legislation.

Information and education

In addition to running a number of print and on-line publications, the Agency promotes and influences sustainable development education in professional organisations, universities and other training institutions. The Agency also establishes standards for sustainable development qualifications, producing learning materials and courses and supporting sustainable development education in the workplace.

Working with others

Much of the Agency's work is delivered in partnerships with, for instance, local businesses and interest groups. It works closely with local authorities on a large range of activities, such as flood defence and tackling fly tipping. As well as advising businesses on pollution issues, the Agency provides a consultancy service to local authorities in the preparation of their development plans, advising and providing environmental information.

Consents: controlled waters

Control of Major Accident Hazards (COMAH) Regulations 1999

DEFRA

Enforcement activities

Powers of inspectors

Regulator

Sustainable development

Water abstraction

Environment and Safety Information Act 1988

This Act is concerned with ensuring the public learn more about possible risks to their health and safety by requiring enforcement authorities to provide and maintain public registers in which are entered the following details:

(a) Improvement Notices;

(b) Prohibition Notices;

(c) Notices (not Improvement Notices) served by Fire Authorities under Section 10 of the Fire Precautions Act 1971 (repealed by Regulatory Reform (Fire Safety) Order 2005);

(d) Notices served by local authorities under Section 10 of the Safety of Sports Grounds Act 1975;

(e) Notices served by responsible authorities under Section 10 of the Food and Environment Protection Act 1985.

The registers must be kept open to the public with free access. Copies of entries must be supplied on request with payment of a fee.

Environmental accounting

Any quantitative approach to linking financial and environmental performance.

Environmental management system (EMS)

ISO 14001: Environmental Management Systems

Environmental Assessment and Planning

Under the Town and Country Planning (Assessment of Environmental Effects) Regulations 1988-94, developers are required to produce Environmental Impact Statements (Environmental Statements) for various types of development.

Environmental Impact Statements

Environmental audit

An independent assessment of the current status of a party's compliance with applicable environmental requirements or of a party's environmental compliance policies, practices and controls.

Environmental law

Environmental management system (EMS)

Environmental measures

Environmental crimes

Breaches of environmental law are criminal offences and can be categorised thus:

(a) causing pollution;

(b) permitting pollution;

(c) breach of the conditions of a licence;

(d) breach of a statutory duty; and

(e) failure to comply with a Notice.

Breach of licence conditions

Breach of statutory duty

Breach of statutory duty of care

Causing pollution (offence)

Defences: criminal proceedings

Enforcement activities

Environmental Protection Act 1990

Environmental Protection (Duty of Care) Regulations 1991

Offences

Permitting pollution: offence

Pollution: definition

Polluter Pays Principle

Environmental (ecological) footprint

The amount of land and water area a human population would theoretically need in order to provide sufficient resources for it to be self-supporting and to deal with its waste products.

The impact of an organisation in environmental terms, such as resource use, waste generation, physical environment changes, etc.

The concept of footprinting is widely used as a measure or indicator of environmental sustainability.

Sustainable development

Sustainable use

Sustainability

Waste to energy

Environmental impact

Any change to the environment, good or bad, that wholly or partially results from industrial or manufacturing activities, products or services.

Environmental Impact Assessments

Environmental Impact Statements

Environmental Impact Assessments

An Environmental Impact Assessment (EIA) is a formal study process used to predict the environmental consequences of a proposed development project. Such an assessment concentrates on problems, conflicts or constraints that could affect the viability of the project. It examines how the project will affect people, the land around the project and other nearby developments.

After predicting potential problems, the EIA identifies measures to minimise the problems and outlines ways to improve the project's suitability for its proposed environment.

The aim of an EIA is to ensure that potential problems are addressed at an early stage in the project's planning and design. To achieve this goal, the assessment's findings are communicated to all the various groups who will make decisions about the proposed project. This report, called *An Environmental Impact Statement,* is submitted to the appropriate regulatory authorities as part of the planning application.

Developments for which a mandatory Environmental Impact Statement are required are listed in Schedule 1 to the Regulations, whereas those developments for which an Environmental Statement may be required are listed in Schedule 2.

Schedule 1

1. A crude oil refinery or an installation for the gasification or liquefaction of 500 tonnes or more of coal or bituminous shale per day.
2. A thermal power station or other combustion installation with a heat output of 300 megawatts or more, or a nuclear power station or other nuclear reactor (excluding a research installation the maximum power of which does not exceed 1 kilowatt continuous thermal load).
3. An installation designed solely for the permanent storage or final disposal of radioactive waste.

4. An integrated works for the initial melting of cast iron and steel.
5. An installation for the extraction of asbestos or for the processing or transformation of asbestos or products containing asbestos (subject to various limits).
6. An integrated chemical installation for the manufacture of olefins from petroleum products, or sulphuric acid, nitric acid, hydrofluoric acid, chlorine or fluorine.
7. A special road, a line for long-distance railway traffic or an aerodrome with a basic runway of 2100 metres or more.
8. A trading port, an inland waterway for the passage of vessels of over 1350 tonnes, or a port for inland waterway traffic capable of handling such vessels.
9. A waste disposal installation for the incineration or chemical treatment of special waste.
10. The carrying out of operations to fill land with special waste, or the change of use of land (where a material change) to use for the deposit of such waste.

Schedule 2

Development for any of the following purposes (selected examples):

1. Agriculture, including pig rearing.
2. Extractive industry, including sand, gravel, open cast and underground coal.
3. Energy industry, including overhead electricity cables, surface storage of fossil fuels, and a wind generator.
4. Processing of metal, including coating of metals, assembly of motor vehicles, shipyards.
5. Glass making.
6. Chemical industry, including the manufacture of pesticides and pharmaceuticals.
7. Food industry, including brewing, sugar factory, slaughterhouses.
8. Textile, leather, wood and paper industries, including a tannery.
9. Rubber industry.
10. Infrastructure projects, including industrial estate development, yacht mooring, underground railway, motorway service area and coast protection works.

11. Other projects including a holiday village, hotel complex, waste water treatment plant.
12. Modification of development listed in Schedule 1.
13. Development listed in Schedule 1 which is for developing and testing new methods or products and will not be permitted for longer than one year.

Environmental impact

Environmental Impact Statements

Environmental Impact Statements

An Environmental Impact Statement is required for Schedule 2 developments where there is -

> "likelihood of significant environmental effects and not the amount of opposition or controversy to which a project gives rise except to the extent that the substance of opponents' arguments indicates that there may be significant environmental issues".

Standard tests for Environmental Impact Statements

DoE Circular (15) 1988 indicates that Environmental Impact Statements can be requested by the local planning authority if one or more of the following tests led to that conclusion:

(a) for major projects which are of more than local importance;

(b) for projects on a small scale which are proposed for particularly sensitive or vulnerable locations;

(c) for projects with unusually complex and potentially adverse environmental effects, where expert and detailed analysis of those effects would be desirable and would be relevant to the issue of principal, as to whether or not the development should be permitted.

Contents of an Environmental Impact Statement

The 'specified information' to be incorporated in an Environmental Impact Statement is set out in Schedule 3 to the Regulations, e.g.

1. Description of the development proposal.
2. The date necessary to identify and assess the main effects on the environment.

3. A description of the possible impact on human beings, flora, fauna, etc.
4. A summary of items 1 to 3 above in non-technical language.
5. Other information may be included as detailed in the Schedule.

See also *Evaluation of environmental information for planning projects: a good practice guide DoE (1994) HMSO*

Submission of Environmental Impact Statements

If an application is made to a local planning authority (LPA) without an Environmental Impact Statement, the LPA can require one to be submitted. If, after three weeks, the developer does not accept the requirement or apply to the Secretary of State for a Direction, the application is deemed to be refused. There is no right of appeal against this type of refusal.

The LPA is required to advertise applications which are accompanied by Environmental Statements, or which subsequently receive a Statement as a result of an opinion or Direction.

Where applications have Environmental Statements, the period for issuing a decision is extended from 8 weeks to 16 weeks, or such longer period as may be agreed.

Summary

The general rule is that any planning application for development of the types listed in the Schedule, whether by a private individual or by a public authority, must include an Environmental Impact Statement.

No planning permission may be granted by the LPA or the Secretary of State unless they have taken the environmental information into consideration.

A developer may ask a LPA for an *opinion* on whether an Environmental Statement is required for a proposed development. If the developer is not satisfied, he may ask the Secretary of State for a *Direction* on the matter. The LPA must give its opinion within 3 weeks of the request, although this period may be extended in writing. The Secretary of State must give a Direction in three weeks or such longer periods as may be required.

Environmental impact

Environmental Impact Assessments

Environmental Information Regulations 1992

These Regulations came into operation on 31st December 1992 enacting the provisions of EC Directive 90/313/EEC on the *freedom of access to information on the environment*. In December 1992, the Department of Environment issued guidance on the implementation of the Regulations.

The Regulations set a minimum standard for the availability of environmental information irrespective of the legislation under which it was gathered. A range of provisions sets out the circumstances in which information must, may or may not be made available.

Application for information

Any person or organisation can apply for access to environmental information under these Regulations. No justification is needed for such a request.

Provision of information

The Regulations provide that every *relevant person* is under a duty to make environmental information available. This imposes a clear duty on all local authorities, Ministers and government departments, and their local and regional offices.

As far as other bodies are concerned, the same duty is imposed on organisations under the control of one of the organisations mentioned above which has public responsibility for the environment. The guidance states that:

'*Control* is taken to mean a relationship constituted by statute, rights, contracts or other means which either separately or jointly confer the possibility of directly or indirectly exercising a decisive influence on a body.'

This would include bodies such as the National Rivers Authority, English Nature, etc.

Information to be made available

Information which relates to the environment must be made available. The Regulations feature an extensive definition of same, which is clarified by the guidance as follows:

Information relating to the environment includes information on the state of water, air, flora, fauna, soil, natural sites and other land. This should be taken to include physical, chemical and biological conditions at any moment in time (i.e. past, present and future).

Flora and fauna should be taken to include species both living and dead.

Land should be taken to include all land surfaces, buildings, land covered by water and underground strata.

Soil should be taken to include all the in situ upper layer of the mantle rock in which plants grow.

A natural site should be taken to include areas identified by reason of their flora, fauna, geological or physio-graphical features (e.g. Sites of Special and Scientific Interest) or general environmental quality (e.g. Areas of Outstanding Natural Beauty).

The guidance suggests that since the environment impacts on human health, either directly or indirectly, such information affecting the state of human health comes within the definition.

Information held by a body, whether or not it was obtained as a result of environmental responsibilities, is included, as is information which pre-dates the Regulations. The information can exist in virtually any form.

Disclosure of information

Information must be made available as soon as possible and in any event within 2 months of the request. Any refusal to make information available must be in writing and specifying the reasons for the refusal. As information may not already be in published form, the information may, in those cases, be provided orally, in correspondence or by allowing the relevant documents to be inspected. A charge can be made for the provision of information, but it must not exceed the cost of supplying the information.

In view of the possible information collected from other sources, the guidance suggests that, in such cases, a disclaimer should be attached, as well as details of the source of the information.

In recognition of the difficulties faced by people in knowing whether information is available and, if so, what information and where it can be found, the guidance suggests that these details should be publicised, with the name and address of a contact point, or 'information co-ordinator'.

Refusal of disclosure

The presumption built into the Regulations is that environmental information must be disclosed unless there is a very good reason for not doing so. There are, however, a number of circumstances where disclosure is restricted:

(a) information held for purposes of judicial or legislative functions is excluded from the Regulations and need not be disclosed;

(b) a request for information which is manifestly unreasonable or formulated in too general a manner can be refused;

(c) access to information falling into the following categories may be treated as confidential and, therefore, refused:

(i) information relating to matters affecting international relationships, national defence or public security;

(ii) information concerning any legal or other proceedings (whether existing or proposed);

(iii) information relating to the confidential deliberations of the body or internal communications of the body;

(iv) where the information is part of a record which is not yet finished; and

(v) where the information is covered by commercial or industrial confidentiality.

Access to information must be refused if:

(a) it is capable of being treated as confidential under one of the categories above and disclosure would be unlawful or in breach of an agreement;

(b) it is personal information in records relating to an individual who has not consented to its disclosure;

(c) it was supplied to the body voluntarily and the supplier could not have been compelled to supply it, and the supplier had not consented to its disclosure; and

(d) where disclosure of the information would increase the likelihood of damage to the environment.

Where a refusal to make information available is given, the provision only justifies the excluded information to be withheld. Any information which is capable of being separated from it must be made available.

Information already available

The basic aim of the Regulations is to improve the accessibility of information to a minimum standard. This means that where information can be required under other statutory provisions, it must also be provided as soon as possible and, in any event, no more than two months after the request was made.

Where the response contains a refusal to make information available, the refusal must be in writing giving reasons. No charge, excepting a reasonable charge, can be made for the information relating to the environment. If any legislation contains more generous access to information provisions, such provisions would apply.

Unreasonable withholding of information

Where a person is aggrieved in connection with reasons given for refusal of information, the guidance suggests the following remedies:

(a) to ask the body to review its reasons for refusing to provide the information or to go to the head of the body concerned;

(b) in the case of a local authority, to apply to the local government ombudsman on grounds of maladministration giving rise to injustice;

(c) to ask the local MP to pursue the matter; and

(d) to seek the assistance of the courts, presumably by means of a judicial review of the decision.

Areas of Outstanding Natural Beauty

Control

Environment

National Rivers Authority

Regulator

Sites of Special and Scientific Interest

Environmentalism

Environmentalism is a broad social, philosophical and political movement that advocates a range of actions and policies aimed at:

(a) protecting what nature remains in the natural environment; and

(b) restoring or expanding the role of nature in this environment.

It is concerned with the preservation, restoration or improvement of the natural environment, such as the conservation of natural resources, prevention of pollution and certain land use actions.

Biodiversity

Climate change

Ecosystems

Endangered species

Environmental management system (EMS)

Global warming

Greenhouse gases

Natural environment

Sustainability

Environmental law

Environmental law is a branch of law that has had increasing prominence since the Clean Air Act 1956. It is made up of law from a number of sources:

(a) statutes, such as the EPA, and Regulations made under same;

(b) consumer protection law;

(c) occupational health and safety law;

(d) public health law;

(e) land law:

(f) town and country planning law; and

(g) the torts of nuisance, negligence and trespass, together with the rule in *Rylands v Fletcher*.

Environmental law has three main functions or objectives:

(a) prevention of pollution by controlling emissions to all three environmental media;

(b) the setting of Environmental Quality Standards; and

(c) clean up/remediation following pollution incidents and environmental damage.

Three basic tenets of environmental law are:

(a) the polluter should pay for the administration of the pollution control system;

(b) the polluter should pay for the consequences of pollution; and

(c) the Preventive Principle, i.e. prevention sooner than cure.

Emission

Enforcement activities

Environmental crimes

Environmental law sources

Environmental management system (EMS)

Environmental media

Environmental Protection Act 1990

Polluter Pays Principle

Pollution incidents

Precautionary principle

Preventive Principle

Remediation

Rylands v Fletcher

Scheduled activities

Environmental law sources

Environmental law comprises many sources:

(a) environmental legislation, such as the Environmental Protection Act and Regulations made under the Act;

(b) international treaties, conventions and protocols;

(c) the torts of nuisance, negligence and trespass;

(d) case law;

(e) town and country planning legislation;

(f) land law;

(g) consumer protection legislation;

(h) public health legislation;

(i) health and safety legislation.

These sources of law are supported by:

(a) government departmental notes, such as Planning Policy Guidance Notes;

(b) government circulars;

(c) Environment Agency Guidance Notes;

(d) Codes of Practice.

It should be appreciated that international agreements, such as the Treaty of Rome, play an important part in the framing of environmental law and policy.

Environment Act 1995

Environment Agency

Environmental Protection Act 1990

Negligence

Nuisance

Nuisance at common law

Pollution Prevention and Control (England and Wales) Regulations 2000

Statutory nuisances

Tort

Trespass

Environmental licences

Consents: controlled waters

Permit

Environmental management system (EMS)

Any set of controls that enables an organisation to control the environmental impacts arising from its activities. Certification of such a system to ISO 14001 is common.

An environmental management system provides a framework for managing environmental management responsibilities so they become more efficient and are more integrated into overall business operations.

They are based on standards which specify a process of achieving continuously improved environmental performance and compliance with regulatory requirements.

ISO 14001: Environmental Management Systems

Environmental measures

The Fifth Environmental Action Programme provided the broad policy framework from which the European Commission can initiate legislative proposals. The Programme recognised that environmental protection cannot be secured entirely by legal and regulatory measures. The Commission stated that future environmental policy would be based on four types of measure:

(a) regulatory instruments;

(b) market-based measures;

(c) support measures, such as education, information and research; and

(d) financial support mechanisms.

Environmental law

Environmental Information Regulations 1992

Environmental law sources

Environmental media

There are three environmental media, namely air, water and land.

"Damage to the environment"

Environment

Harm

"Released" and "release"

Release into the air: substances

Release into water

Release to land

Offences

Environmental monitoring in the workplace

Environmental monitoring implies the continuous or intermittent sampling of air in the working environment with a view to detecting the presence of contaminants. Contaminants may take many forms, such as gases, fogs, fumes, dusts and mists.

Environmental monitoring can be undertaken through the taking of air samples on a long-term or short-term basis.

Short-term sampling techniques

Generally known as "snap" sampling or "grab" sampling, this implies taking an immediate sample of air from the workplace and, in most cases, passing it through a particular chemical reagent which responds to the contaminant being monitored.

Long-term sampling techniques

Instruments which are used for long-term sampling are, broadly, of two types – personal samplers and static sampling systems.

(a) Personal samplers

These devices are attached to the person and may take a number of forms e.g. gas monitoring badges, filtration devices and impingers.

(b) Static sampling systems

These are sampling systems stationed in the working area. They sample continuously over a period of time e.g. a working shift of 8 hours, or over longer periods if necessary. They operate using mains or battery-operated pumps. Long-term stain tube detectors are available for this purpose.

Personal sampling devices

Sampling of the exposures of specific individuals is undertaken through the use of:

Gas monitoring badges

These incorporate a solid sorbent or impregnated carrier in a badge worn by the operator. Contact is by diffusion. The level of exposure is indicated by a change in colour or through analytical determination.

Filtration devices

These entail the use of a low flow or constant flow sample pump attached to a sampling head. The filter in the sampling head is located close to the operator's breathing zone.

Determination of the results is by gravimetric analysis, solvent extraction, gas chromatography or atomic absorption.

Impingers

Air is bubbled through the impinger (a glass bubble tube) which contains an appropriate absorbing medium. Impingers work in conjunction with a constant flow sample pump attached to the operator. Analysis is by gas chromatography or spectrophotometry.

Sorbent tubes

These incorporate a tube filled with two layers of solid adsorbent capable of completely removing chemicals from the air. The tube has breakable end tips and is inserted into a tube holder located in the breathing zone of the operator. They operate in conjunction with a constant flow sample pump.

Static sampling equipment

This form of equipment is located in the working area and samples continuously in most cases. Various devices are available.

Constant flow pump devices

These incorporate a pump which takes in a measured quantity of air on a continuing basis. For sampling dusts, selective filters are used, whereas, in the case of volatile substances, various absorbing media are used.

Long-term stain detector tubes

These are linked to a constant flow pump and tube holder, sampling over an eight-hour period in most cases.

Direct monitoring devices

These include multi-gas detection and monitoring devices, which are capable of monitoring the concentrations of a number of gases at any one time. They incorporate a digital display and give an instant read out. In some cases, they can be linked to an alarm where a predetermined concentration of a substance in air is exceeded.

Airborne particulates

Control of Substances Hazardous to Health (COSHH) Regulations 2006

Work environment

Environmental occurrences

Also known as 'major pollution incidents', these are occurrences which have significant potential for causing pollution of one or more of the three environmental media. Typical environmental occurrences include major oil and chemical spillages, radiation leakages, major fires in industrial and waste landfill sites and oil pollution from ships.

Control of Major Accident Hazards Regulations (COMAH) 1999

Environmental crimes

Environmental media

Environmental pollution

Environmental pollution

Pollution of the environment has been a matter for public concern since the Industrial Revolution. As such, the term implies some form of contamination of the surrounding air, water and land which is prejudicial to the health of both workers and the general public.

Numerous legal measures have been taken over the last century with a view to curbing these forms of pollution, including the Public Health Acts 1936 and 1961, Clean Air Acts 1956 and 1993, Control of Pollution Act 1984, the Environmental Protection Act 1990, the Noise and Statutory Nuisances Act 1993, the Environment Act 1995 (EA) and the Pollution Prevention and Control Act 1999, together with numerous Regulations made under the above statutes.

Environmental pollution means pollution of the air, water or land which may give rise to any harm; and for the purposes of this definition (but without prejudice to its generality):

(a) *pollution* includes pollution by noise, heat or vibration or any other kind of release of energy; and

(b) *air* includes air within buildings and air within other natural or man-made structures above or below ground.

[Environmental Protection Act 1990]

Many industries have, over the last century or more, been guilty of polluting the environment, such as the fuel and power industry (gasification and carbonisation plants), the mineral industry (cement, asbestos and ceramic manufacture), the chemical industry (petrochemical, pharmaceutical and pesticide manufacture), the metal industry (iron and steel manufacture) and other industries, such as paper manufacturing.

Environmental crimes

Environmental Protection Act 1990

Pollution Prevention and Control Act 1999

Pollution Prevention and Control (England and Wales) Regulations 2000

Scheduled activities

Environmental Protection Act 1990

This Act is the principal statute and is split into eight specific parts.

1. Integrated pollution control and air pollution control by local authorities (revoked)
2. Waste on land
3. Statutory Nuisances and Clean Air
4. Litter etc.
5. Amendment to the Radioactive Substances Act 1960
6. Genetically modified organisms
7. Nature conservancy
8. Miscellaneous provisions

Part 8 contains a number of miscellaneous provisions. The most significant are:

(a) power to restrict the importation, use, supply or storage of substances or articles for the purpose of avoiding pollution, or harm to man, animals or plants;

(b) power to restrict the importation or exportation of waste for the purpose of preventing pollution or harm to human health or for conserving facilities or resources for dealing with waste;

(c) power to make provision for the obtaining of information about substances with potential to cause pollution or harm to human health;

(d) provision of public registers of potentially contaminated land;

(e) amendments of the legislation of control of hazardous substances;

(f) increase in the maximum penalties in respect of water pollution offences;

(g) amendments on legislation as to marine deposits and the creation of public registers as to such deposits and marine incineration;

(h) amendments of the provisions as to oil pollution offences from ships;

(i) provisions for the control of stray dogs; and

(j) provision as to the banning of straw, stubble and other crop residues.

Part I of the Act was replaced by the Pollution Prevention and Control (England and Wales) Regulations 2000.

Abatement

Abatement Notice

Action in default

Best Available Techniques (BAT)

Best Available Techniques Not Entailing Excessive Cost (BATNEEC)

"Best practicable means"

Causing pollution (offence)

Conservation Area

Defences: criminal proceedings

Enforcement by the High Court

Enforcement Notice

Environmental media

Environmental Protection (Duty of Care) Regulations 1991

Genetically modified organisms (GMO)

Litter Control Area

Local Air Pollution Control (LAPC)

Nature Conservancy Council

Powers of inspectors

Prior approval of industrial installations

Prohibition Notice

Prohibition Order

Public Registers of Information (various)

Scheduled activities

Service of Notices

Shopping and luggage trolleys

Statutory nuisances

Street Litter Control Notice

Waste Collection Authorities (WCAs)

Waste Disposal Authorities (WDAs) and Companies

Waste Disposal Plans by Waste Regulation Authorities

Waste holders' duties

Waste Local Plans

Waste Management Licences

Waste offences

Waste Regulation Authorities (WRAs)

Waste Regulatory Authorities

Environmental Protection (Controls on Ozone-Depleting Substances) Regulations 2002

These Regulations apply controls over the production, importation, exportation, placing on the market, emission, recovery, recycling and destruction of substances that have an adverse impact on the ozone layer in the upper atmosphere.

The principal ozone-depleting substances are indicated below. However, the Regulations apply to substances less commonly used and reference should be made to the complete list. The controls apply to ozone-depleting substances irrespective of whether such substances occur on their own or in a mixture. The level of control applying to individual substances varies considerably.

The more common ozone-depleting substances are:

Refrigerants

(a) Chlorofluorocarbons (CFCs): 11, 12, 13, 113, 114, 500, 502, 503;

(b) Hydrochlorofluorocarbons (HCFCs): 22, 123, 124;

(c) HCFC blends: various including R401a, R402a, R403a, R406a, R408a, R411b.

Common trade names: *Arcton, Forane, Freon, Isceon, Solkane, Suva*

Solvents

(a) 1,1,1 trichloroethane;

(b) HCFCs: 141b;

(c) Bromochloromethane (CBM).

Common trade names: *Arklone, Freon, Flugene, Forane, Kaltron, Fluorisol, Gensolv, Genklene*

Foam blowing agents

HCFCs: 22, 141b, 142b.

Fire fighting fluids

Halons: 1211, 1301.

The Regulations more commonly apply to anyone using or handling:

(a) refrigeration, air conditioning or dry cleaning equipment;

(b) insulating foam;

(c) industrial solvents; and

(d) halon fire-extinguishing systems.

The Regulations established a timetable for the virtual prohibition and elimination of CFCs, HCFCs, virgin HCFCs for maintenance and servicing, and Halons (virgin, recovered, reclaimed and recycled) thus:

1. The supply and use of CFCs was banned with effect from October 2000, subject to a number of exemptions.
2. The use of HCFCs was banned, including their use in aerosols, solvents, refrigerants and foam.
3. A prohibition on the use of virgin HCFCs for maintenance and servicing of refrigeration and air conditioning systems comes into effect in 2010, with a prohibition on all HCFCs with effect from 2015.
4. There is a prohibition on the use of Halons, (virgin, recovered, reclaimed and recycled).
5. All fire protection systems containing Halons were required to be decommissioned by the end of 2003.

Chlorofluorcarbons (CFCs)

Hazardous substances: classification

Organic solvents

Ozone

Ozone depletion

Ozone layer

Environmental Protection (Duty of Care) Regulations 1991

The EPA brought in a statutory duty of care in relation to waste with effect from 1st April 1992. This duty of care is set out in Section 34 of the Act and is supplemented by the Environmental Protection (Duty of Care) Regulations 1991 and a Code of Practice.

Fundamentally, any person who fails to comply with the duty under Section 34 of the EPA or with the Regulations commits a criminal offence. It is not necessary for any environmental damage to have been caused. All that is required is that there has been a breach of the duty of care. On summary conviction, a breach of this duty of care can lead to a fine of £5,000 or, on indictment, an unlimited fine.

Section 34(1) provides that the duty of care applies to any person who imports, produces, carries, keeps, treats or disposes of controlled waste or, as a broker, has control of such waste (i.e. a 'waste holder'.) A broker is a person who may exercise control over waste, but may not necessarily hold it.

Any person bound by the duty must take all such measures applicable to him in that capacity as are reasonable in the circumstances:

(a) to prevent any other person committing the offences in Section 33, e.g. unlawful deposit of waste on land;

(b) to prevent the escape of the waste from his control or that of any other person;

(c) to ensure that if the waste is transferred, it is transferred only to an authorised person or to a person for authorised transport purposes;

(d) when waste is transferred, to make sure that it is accompanied by a written description of the waste which will enable other persons to avoid a contravention of Section 33 of the Act and to comply with a duty under Section 34(1)(b) to prevent the escape of waste.

These Regulations (made under Section 34(5) of the EPA) established a system of Transfer Notes and record keeping of waste transfers to help waste holders comply with their elements of the duty of care.

The aim of this system is to enable the Waste Regulation Authority (WRA) to keep track of the movement of all wastes within their area and a written description is needed to be provided when waste is transferred. The Regulations place responsibilities on the transferor and transferee of waste to keep records of all waste transfers. On completion of the transfer of the controlled waste (household, commercial or industrial waste), both the giver and receiver must complete and sign a Transfer Note.

The Transfer Note must incorporate the following details:

(a) identification of the waste;

(b) quantity;

(c) whether it is loose or in a container at the time of transfer;

(d) place and time of transfer;

(e) name and address of both transferor and transferee;

(f) whether the transferor is the producer or importer; and

(g) if the transferee is authorised for transport purposes.

All parties involved in the transfer must keep a copy of the Transfer Note and the written description for at least two years. The WRA may serve a Notice demanding copies of Transfer Notes which must be supplied within seven days.

The Code of Practice, *Waste Management, The Duty of Care,* recommends a series of steps which would normally be sufficient to satisfy the requirements of this duty of care. This Code of Practice is admissible in evidence and, if any provision of the Code appears to the court to be relevant to any question arising in the proceedings, it shall be taken into account in determining that question.

Penalties

Any person who fails to comply with the duty of care or the documentation requirements laid down in the Regulations commits a criminal offence and is liable on summary conviction to a fine not exceeding £5,000. On indictment, the Crown Court can impose an unlimited fine. Directors and senior managers may also be personally liable for a breach of Section 34 of the EPA.

Breach of these Regulations does not give rise to civil liability, although damages may be available through common law actions such as nuisance.

Duty of care

Environmental Protection Act 1990

Transfer Note

Waste broker

Waste disposal Plans by Waste Regulation Authorities

Waste hierarchy

Waste holders' duties

Waste offences

Waste Regulation Authorities (WRAs)

Waste transfer

Waste unlawfully deposited

Environmental Quality Standard

A value, generally defined by Regulations, which specifies the maximum permissible concentration of a potentially hazardous chemical in an environmental sample, generally of air or water. It is sometimes referred to as an "ambient standard".

The set of requirements which must be fulfilled at a given time by a given environment or particular part thereof, as set out in community legislation.

[Pollution Prevention and Control (England and Wales) Regulations 2000]

Environmental Statement

A project submitted to a planning authority must be accompanied by an Environmental Statement. Such a Statement must provide an objective account of the significant environmental effects which may arise as a result of the project. The Environmental Statement is a document, or series of documents, submitted by a developer in support of the planning application. Whilst there is no standard format for such a Statement, Schedule 3 of the Town and Country Planning (Assessment of Environmental Effects) Regulations 1994 (as amended) lays down the minimum requirements for the coverage of an Environmental Statement. A Statement must contain information on the following:

(a) a description of the proposed development comprising information about the site and the design and scale of the development;

(b) the data necessary to identify and assess the main effects which the development is likely to have on the environment;

(c) a description and assessment of the likely significant effects, direct or indirect, which the development is likely to have upon its environment explained by reference to its possible impact upon the following:

    (i) human beings;

    (ii) flora and fauna;

    (iii) soil;

    (iv) water;

    (v) air;

    (vi) climate;

    (vii) landscape;

    (viii) interaction between any of the above;

    (ix) material assets; and

    (x) cultural heritage;

(d) where significant adverse effects are identified, a description of the measures envisaged to avoid, reduce or remedy those effects; and

(e) a non-technical summary of the information provided above.

Environmental Assessment and Planning

Environmental Impact Assessments

Environmental Impact Statements

Publicity requirements

Environmentally friendly

This term refers to goods, services and activities or practices considered to inflict little or least harm on the environment. As such, it entails activities such as:

(a) recycling and composting, as opposed to incineration of waste; and

(b) intense control over the use of chemicals, such as pesticides, and its replacement by biological pest control methods.

Composting

"Damage to the environment"

Harm

Incineration

Pesticide

Recycling and disposal of waste

European Commission

The European Commission comprises a President and Commissioners who are appointed by the governments of the Member States. Commissioners must be independent and act in the interests of the Community. They are generally appointed for a five year period. Each Commissioner has a specific portfolio for which he is responsible.

The Commission has executive capacity and plays a significant role in the setting and enforcement of European law. The Commission has the power to bring Member States before the European Court of Justice.

European Court of Justice

European Court of Justice

This is the supreme law court whose decisions on the interpretation of EC law are sacrosanct. EC law is enforced through a network of courts and tribunals in all member states. Cases can only be brought before this court by organisations or individuals representing organisations.

European Directive

A European Union legal instruction, binding on all Member States, but which must be implemented through national legislation within a prescribed time scale.

Directives

European Environment Agency

This Agency was set up in 1994 following the adoption by the Council of Ministers in May 1990 of Council Regulation 1210/90. It is based in Copenhagen.

The functions of the European Environment Agency (EEA) are:

(a) to provide Member States with objective, reliable and comparable information about the environment; and

(b) to ensure that the public is properly informed about the state of the environment.

The Management Board of the EEA is made up of one representative from each Member State, two representatives from the European Commission and a further two designated by the European Parliament.

The EEA is assisted by the European Environment Information and Observation Network. The principal criticism of the EEA is that it has no role to play in the enforcement of environmental law across Member States.

Environment Agency

Eutrophication

This is the enrichment of water by nutrients, such as nitrate or phosphate, causing an accelerated growth of algae and higher forms of plant life. This leads to an undesirable disturbance to the balance of organisms present in the water and to the quality of the water concerned.

Water pollution

Water Protection Zones

Water quality objectives and standards

Exempt activity

Animal and vegetable matter and food industries

Exempt facility

A waste recovery operation (also occasionally certain disposal at the waste producer and some storage activities) registered with, but not licensed by, the Environment Agency. Exempt facilities are subject to general rules, e.g. on the types and quantities of wastes received.

Waste

Waste activity

Waste offences

Existing waste incineration installation

This is a waste incineration installation which:

(a) in the case of an installation which is a co-incineration plant, is put into operation before 28th December 2004 subject to a relevant approval; or

(b) in any other case:

(i) is put into operation before 28th December 2003 subject to a relevant approval granted before 28th December 2002; or

(ii) is put into operation before 28th December 2004 subject to a relevant approval granted on the basis of a duly made application submitted before 28th December 2002;

and where an installation becomes authorised as a waste incineration installation for the first time as a result of a modification or variation pursuant to Section 10, 11 or 37 of the EPA or Regulation 17 of the 2000 Regulations, references in this definition to a relevant approval shall be construed as references to that modification or variation and not to the original relevant approval, and references to the grant of an approval shall be construed as references to the service of a Notice effecting the modification or variation.

[Waste Incineration (England and Wales) Regulations 2002]

Co-incineration

Co-incineration plant

Environmental Protection Act 1990

Incineration

Incineration plant

Part A activities

Part B activities

Pollution Prevention and Control (England and Wales) Regulations 2000

Relevant approval

Scheduled activities

Explosives production

These scheduled activities are:

Part A(1)

Producing explosives

Part A(2)

Nil

Part B

Nil

[Schedule 1: Part 1: Pollution Prevention and Control (England and Wales) Regulations 2000]

Part A activities

Part B activities

Pollution Prevention and Control Act 1999

Pollution Prevention and Control (England and Wales) Regulations 2000

Scheduled activities

F

Failure to comply with an Abatement Notice

Local authorities have three options available in the event of failure to comply with a Notice. As far as noise nuisance is concerned, the environmental health officer has powers to take steps to abate the nuisance. This may mean the officer can remove stereo/audio equipment. If the noise is from a car alarm the officer has power to open the car, if necessary by force, and immobilise the offending alarm.

Expenses incurred by a local authority in abating a nuisance can be recovered with interest. The local authority can also place a charge on the premises.

Abatement

Neighbour noise

Noise Abatement Notices

Noise Abatement Zone

Noise Act 1996

Noise nuisance

Ferrous metals

These scheduled activities are:

Part A(1)

(a) Roasting or sintering metal ore, including sulphide ore, or any mixture of iron ore with or without other materials;

(b) Producing, melting or refining iron or steel or any ferrous alloy, including continuous casting, except where the only furnaces used are:

  (i) electric arc furnaces with a designed holding capacity of less than 7 tonnes; or

  (ii) cupola, crucible, reverbatory, rotary, induction or resistance furnaces;

(c) Processing ferrous metals and their alloys by using hot-rolling mills with a production capacity of more than 20 tonnes of crude steel per hour;

(d) Loading, unloading or otherwise handling or storing more than 500,000 tonnes in total in any period of 12 months of iron ore, except in the course of mining operations, or burnt pyrites.

Part A(2)

(a) Producing pig iron or steel, including continuous casting, in a plant with a production capacity of more than 2.5 tonnes per hour unless falling within paragraph (b) of Part A(1) of this Section;

(b) Operating hammers in a forge, the energy of which is more than 50 kilojoules per hammer, where the calorific power used is more than 20 megawatts;

(c) Applying protective fused metal coatings with an input of more than 2 tonnes of crude steel per hour;

(d) Casting ferrous metal at a foundry with a production capacity of more than 20 tonnes per day.

Part B

(a) Producing pig iron or steel, including continuous casting, in a plant with a production capacity of 205 tonnes or less per hour, unless falling within paragraph (b) of Part A(1) of this Section;

(b) Producing, melting or refining iron or steel or any ferrous alloy (other than producing pig iron or steel, including continuous casting) using:

   (i) one or more electric arc furnaces, none of which has a designed holding capacity of 7 tonnes or more; or

   (ii) a cupola, crucible, reverbatory, rotary, induction or resistance furnace,unless falling within paragraph (a) or (d) of Part A(2) of this Section;

(c) Desulphurising iron, steel or any ferrous alloy;

(d) Heating iron, steel or any ferrous alloy (whether in a furnace or other appliance) to remove grease, oil or any other non-metallic contaminant (including such operations as the removal by heat of plastic or rubber covering from scrap cable) unless:

   (i) it is carried out in one or more furnaces or other appliances, the primary combustion chambers of which have, in aggregate, a rated thermal input of less than 0.2 megawatts;

   (ii) it does not involve the removal by heat of plastic or rubber covering from scrap cable or of any asbestos contaminant; and

   (iii) it is not related to any other activity falling within this Part of this Section;

(e) Casting iron, steel or any ferrous alloy from deliveries of 50 tonnes or more of molten metal, unless falling within Part A(1) or Part A(2) of this Section.

Ferrous alloy means an alloy of which iron is the largest constituent or equal to the largest constituent, by weight, whether or not that alloy also has a non-ferrous metal content greater than any percentage specified in Section 2.2 (Non-ferrous metals).

[Schedule 1: Part 1: Pollution Prevention and Control (England and Wales) Regulations 2000]

Part A activities

Part B activities

Pollution Prevention and Control Act 1999

Pollution Prevention and Control (England and Wales) Regulations 2000

Scheduled activities

"Fit and proper person"

The regulator is required to determine whether a person is or is not a fit and proper person to carry out a specified waste management activity. Whether a person is or is not a fit and proper person shall be determined by reference to the fulfilment of the conditions of the permit which apply or will apply to the carrying out of that activity.

A person shall be treated as not being a fit and proper person if it appears to the regulator that:

(a) he or another relevant person has been convicted of a relevant offence;

(b) the management of the specified waste management activity which is or is to be carried out is not or will not be in the hands of a technically competent person; or

(c) the person who holds or is to hold the permit has not made and either has no intention of making or is in no position to make financial provision adequate to discharge the obligations arising from the permit in relation to the specified waste management activity.

The "fit and proper person" test does not simply apply to the applicant but also relates to "another relevant person" in relation to the holder or proposed holder of a permit, which includes:

(a) any person who has been convicted of a relevant offence committed by him in the course of his employment by the holder or proposed holder of the permit or in the course of carrying on any business by a partnership one of the members of which was the holder or proposed holder of the permit;

(b) a body corporate which has been convicted of a relevant offence committed when the holder or proposed holder of the permit was a director, manager, secretary or similar officer of that body corporate; or

(c) where the holder or proposed holder of the permit is a body corporate, a person who is a director, manager, secretary or similar officer of that body corporate and who:

    (i) has been convicted of a relevant offence;

    (ii) was a director, manager, secretary or other similar officer of another body corporate at a time when a relevant offence for which that other body corporate has been convicted was committed.

[Pollution Prevention and Control (England and Wales) Regulations 2006]

Competent person

Corporate liability

Permit

Regulator

Relevant offences

Scheduled activities

Waste Management Licences

Waste offences

Fluorides

These are organic and inorganic compounds containing the element fluorine. Examples of fluoride compounds are hydrofluoric acid, sodium fluoride and calcium fluoride. Fluorides occur naturally in low concentrations in drinking water and dome foods, such as tea. Fresh water supplies generally contain between 0.01 and 0.3 ppm of fluorides.

Fluorides, such as sodium fluoride and calcium fluoride, have a beneficial effect when added to drinking water, toothpaste and other oral hygiene products as fluoride strengthens the tooth enamel.

However, fluorides have many toxic effects on the body and, when exposed to high concentrations over a period of time, it can cause death due to the condition, fluorosis. Skin or eye contact with many fluorides in high concentrations can also be dangerous.

Hazardous substances: classification

Fluorocarbon

A non-flammable heat-stable hydrocarbon liquid or gas, commonly used as a propellant in spray cans. Fluorocarbons are classed as ozone-depleting substances and many industries are seeking to reduce or eliminate their use in the manufacture and operation of their products.

Environmental Protection (Controls on Ozone-Depleting Substances) Regulations 2002

Ozone-depleting substances

Ozone depletion

Fossil fuels

Biological materials which have been subjected to long-term geological effects, i.e. coal, oil, natural gas, peat.

Fresh water limit

In relation to any river or watercourse, means the place for the time being shown as the fresh water limit of that river or watercourse in the latest map deposited by the Secretary of State with the National Rivers Authority for that purpose.

[Water Resources Act 1991]

Coastal waters

Controlled waters

Ground waters

Inland fresh waters

Relevant river or watercourse

Watercourse

Water Resources Act 1991

Fuel from waste

These scheduled activities are:

Part A(1)

(a) Making solid fuel (other than charcoal) from waste by any process involving the use of heat.

Part A(2)

Nil

Part B

Nil

[Schedule 1: Part 1: Pollution Prevention and Control (England and Wales) Regulations 2000]

Incineration

Part A activities

Part B activities

Pollution Prevention and Control Act 1999

Pollution Prevention and Control (England and Wales) Regulations 2000

Recovery of waste

Recycling and disposal of waste

Scheduled activities

G

Gaia Theory

The Gaia Theory states that selected aspects of the atmosphere, sediments and hydrosphere are controlled by growth, metabolic activities and other interactions in the biosphere.

It is a theory of the atmosphere and surface sediments of the planet Earth taken as a whole. In its most general form the theory states that the temperature and composition of the Earth's atmosphere are actively regulated by the sum of life on the planet, that is, the 'biota', namely animals, plants, micro-organisms, and the non-living parts, such as rocks, oceans and the atmosphere. In the Gaian Theory of the atmosphere, life continually synthesises and removes the gases necessary for its own survival.

Gasification, liquefaction and refining activities

These scheduled activities are:

Part A(1)

(a) Refining gas where this is likely to involve the use of 1,000 tonnes or more of a gas in any period of 12 months;

(b) Reforming natural gas;

(c) Operating coke ovens;

(d) Coal or lignite gasification;

(e) Producing gas from oil or other carbonaceous material or from mixtures thereof, other than from sewage, unless the production is carried out as part of an activity which is a combustion activity (whether or not that combustion activity is described in Section 1.1);

(f) Purifying or refining any product of any of the activities falling within paragraphs (a) to (e) or converting it into a different product;

(g) Refining mineral oils;

(h) The loading, unloading or other handling of, the storage of, or the physical, chemical or thermal treatment of:

- (i) crude oil;
- (ii) stabilised crude petroleum;
- (iii) crude shale oil;

(iv) where related to another activity described in this paragraph, any associated gas or condensate;

(v) emulsified hydrocarbons intended for use as a fuel;

(i) The further refining, conversion or use (otherwise than as a fuel or solvent) of the product of any activity falling within paragraphs (g) or (h) in the manufacture of a chemical;

(j) Activities involving pyrolysis, carbonisation, distillation, liquefaction, gasification, partial oxidation or other heat treatment of coal (other than the drying of coal), lignite, oil, other carbonaceous material or mixtures thereof otherwise than with a view to making charcoal.

Carbonaceous material includes such materials as charcoal, coke, peat, rubber and wood.

Part A(2)

(a) Refining gas where this activity does not fall within paragraph (a) of Part A(1).

Part B

(a) Odorising natural gas or liquefied petroleum gas, except where that activity is related to a Part A activity;

(b) Blending odorant for use with natural gas or liquefied petroleum gas;

(c) The storage of petrol in stationary storage tanks at a terminal, or the loading or unloading at a terminal of petrol into or from road tankers, rail tankers or inland waterway vessels;

(d) The loading or unloading of petrol into stationary storage tanks at a service station, if the total quantity of petrol unloaded into such tanks at the service station in any period of 12 months is likely to be 100 m^3 or more.

[Schedule 1: Part 1: Pollution Prevention and Control (England and Wales) Regulations 2000]

Combustion activities

Fossil fuels

Part A activities

Part B activities

Pollution Prevention and Control Act 1999

Pollution Prevention and Control (England and Wales) Regulations 2000

Scheduled activities

General binding rules

The Secretary of State may make rules ("general binding rules") containing requirements applying to certain types of installation or mobile plant.

[Pollution Prevention and Control (England and Wales) Regulations 2000]

General binding rules condition

Installation

Mobile plant

Permit

General binding rules condition

Where the Secretary of State makes general binding rules, a regulator may, at the request of the operator, include in a permit authorising the operation of an installation or mobile plant covered by the rules a condition ("a general binding rules condition") providing that aspects of the operation of the installation or mobile plant covered by the requirements in the rules shall be subject to those requirements instead of to conditions included in the permit.

[Pollution Prevention and Control (England and Wales) Regulations 2000]

General binding rules

Installation

Mobile plant

Permit

Genetically modified organism (GMO)

An organism is genetically modified if any of the genes or other genetic material in the organism:

(a) have been modified by means of an artificial technique prescribed in Regulations by the Secretary of State; or

(b) are inherited or otherwise derived, through any number of replications, from genes or other genetic material (from any source) which were so modified.

Part 6 of the EPA has effect for the purpose of preventing or minimising any damage to the environment which may arise from the escape or release from human control of genetically modified organisms (GMOs).

The following definitions are important –

Organism means any acellular, unicellular or multicellular entity (in any form), other than humans or human embryos; and unless the context otherwise requires, the term also includes any article or substance consisting of biological matter.

Biological matter means anything (other than an entity mentioned above) which consists of or includes:

(a) tissue or cells (including gametes or propagules) or subcellular entities, of any kind, capable of replication or of transferring genetic material; or

(b) genes or other genetic material, in any form, which are so capable,

and it is immaterial, in determining if something is or is not an organism or biological matter, whether it is the product of natural or artificial processes of reproduction and, in the case of biological matter, whether it has ever been part of a whole organism.

Techniques

The *techniques* which may be prescribed for the above purposes include -

(a) any technique for the modification of any genes or other genetic material by the recombination, insertion or deletion of, or of any component parts of, that material from its previously occurring state; and

(b) any other technique for modifying genes or other genetic material which in the opinion of the Secretary of State would produce organisms which should for the purposes of this Part be treated as having been genetically modified,

but do not include techniques which involve no more than, or no more than the assistance of, naturally occurring processes of reproduction (including selective breeding techniques or in vitro fertilisation).

Risk Assessment

Section 108 of the Act requires that no person shall import or acquire, release or market any GMOs unless, before that act -

(a) he carries out an assessment of the risks of damage to the environment being caused as a result of that act; and

(b) in prescribed cases and circumstances, has given notice of intention and prescribed information to the Secretary of State.

General duties relating to the importation, acquisition, keeping, release or marketing of GMOs are detailed in Section 109.

Enforcement

Section 110 empowers the Secretary of State to serve a Prohibition Notice on any person he has reason to believe -

(a) is proposing to import or acquit, release or market GMOs; or

(b) is keeping any such organisms,

if he is of the opinion that doing any such act to those organisms or continuing to keep them would involve a risk of causing damage to the environment.

A system of *consents*, however, is operated through the Secretary of State whereby a person importing or acquiring, releasing or marketing GMOs may be subject to certain limitations and conditions. (Sections 111 and 112)

Similar provisions relating to enforcement, offences and the powers of a court to make orders apply as with other Parts of the EPA.

Environmental Protection Act 1990

Genetically Modified Organisms (Contained Use) Regulations 2000

These Regulations provide for:

(a) human health and safety and environmental protection from genetically modified micro-organisms in contained use; and

(b) the human health and safety from genetically modified plants and animals (genetically modified organisms).

The Regulations require risk assessment of:

(a) activities involving genetically modified micro-organisms; and

(b) activities involving organisms other than micro-organisms.

All activities must be assessed for risk to humans and those involving genetically modified micro-organisms assessed for risk to the environment.

A classification system was introduced based on the risk of the activity independent of the purpose of the activity. The classification is based on the four levels of containment for microbial laboratories.

Other requirements include:

(a) notification of all premises to the Health and Safety Executive before they are used for genetic modification activities for the first time;

(b) notification of individual activities of Class 2 (low risk) to Class 4 (high risk) to the competent authority, which is administered by the HSE.

Consents are issued for all Class 3 (medium risk) and Class 4 (high risk) activities. Class 1 (no or negligible risk) activities are non-notifiable, although they are open to scrutiny by HSE's specialist inspectors who enforce the Regulations.

Activities involving genetically modified animals and plants which are more hazardous to humans than the parental non-modified organism also require notification;

(c) fees to be payable for the notification of premises for first time use, Class 2, 3 and 4 activities notifications, and notified activities involving genetically modified animals and plants; and

(d) the maintenance of a public register of premises undertaking genetic modification and certain activities.

Contained use

Genetically modified organism (GMO)

Genetic engineering

Genetic modification

Genetic engineering

The science of modifying the genetic constitution of plants and animals directly.

Genetically modified organism (GMO)

Genetic modification

Genetic modification

Genetic modification occurs where the genetic material in an organism (either DNA or RNA) is altered by use of a method that does not occur in nature and the modification can be replicated and/or transferred to other cells or organisms. Typically, genetic modification involves the removal of DNA, its manipulation outside the cell and reinsertion into the same or another organism. The aim of genetic modification is often to introduce a new or altered characteristic to the target organism.

The organism which has been modified is referred to as a *genetically modified organism (GMO)*. GMOs may be plants, animals or, most commonly, micro-organisms (including bacteria, viruses, parasites and fungi).

Biological agents

Contained use

Genetic engineering

Genetically modified organism (GMO)

Genetically Modified Organisms (Contained Use) Regulations 2000

Geothermal energy

This form of energy is obtained by tapping the heat of the Earth itself, usually from distances deep into the Earth's crust. This energy derives from the radioactive decay in the core of the Earth, which heats the Earth from the inside out.

This energy can be used as:

(a) geothermal electricity;

(b) geothermal heating, through deep earth pipes; and

(c) geothermal heating, through the use of a heat pump.

Biofuels

Renewable energy

Solar energy

Water power

Wind power

Glass and glass fibre manufacturing

These scheduled activities are:

Part A(1)

(a) Manufacturing glass fibre;

(b) Manufacturing glass frit or enamel frit and its use in any activity where that activity is related to its manufacture and the aggregate quantity of such substances manufactured in any period of 12 months is likely to be 100 tonnes or more.

Part A(2)

(a) Manufacturing glass, unless falling within Part A(1) of this Section, where the melting capacity of the plant is more than 20 tonnes per day.

Part B

Unless falling within Part A(1) or A(2) of this Section:

(a) Manufacturing glass at any location where the person concerned has the capacity to make 5,000 tonnes or more of glass in any period of 12 months, and any activity involving the use of glass which is carried out at any such location in conjunction with its manufacture;

(b) Manufacturing glass where the use of lead or any lead compound is involved;

(c) Manufacturing any glass product where lead or any lead compound has been used in the manufacture of the glass except:

- (i) the making of products from lead glass blanks;
- (ii) the melting, or mixing with another substance, of glass manufactured elsewhere to produce articles such as ornaments and road paint;

(d) Polishing or etching glass or glass products in the course of any manufacturing activity if:

- (i) hydrofluoric acid is used; or
- (ii) hydrogen fluoride may be released into the air;

(e) Manufacturing glass frit or enamel frit and its use in any activity where that activity is related to its manufacture.

[Schedule 1: Part 1: Pollution Prevention and Control (England and Wales) Regulations 2000]

Part A activities

Part B activities

Pollution Prevention and Control Act 1999

Pollution Prevention and Control (England and Wales) Regulations 2000

Scheduled activities

A term referring to the increased interdependence in the economic, social, cultural, technological, ecological and political processes between world states.

A process of increasing communication and integration between national industrial organisations, states and households.

Globalisation relies on three areas of development, namely international trade, the role of human migration and the rapid movement of capital and integration of financial markets.

Globally Harmonised System (GHS)

Globally Harmonised System (GHS)

The Globally Harmonised System of Classification and Labelling of Chemicals (GHS) (the 'Purple Book') provides a framework for integrating various national and regional hazard communication systems which control the supply of hazardous chemicals in very much the same way that the 'Orange Book' offers a global framework for the transport of dangerous goods.

The aim of GHS is to provide a single globally harmonised system to address the classification of chemicals, labels and safety data.

Chemicals (Hazard Information and Packaging for Supply) (CHIP) Regulations 1994 – 2006

Hazardous substances: classification

Global warming

Certain gases, such as carbon dioxide, methane, nitrous oxides and chlorofluorocarbons (CFCs) absorb reflected infra-red radiation and trap it within the Earth's atmosphere. This heat, which would normally be dissipated to space, brings about an increase in the temperature of the Earth arising from this greenhouse effect. Although greenhouse gases are present in the atmosphere naturally, the application of modern agricultural and industrial processes, particularly those burning fossil fuels, means that their concentration is increasing more rapidly than ever before.

Global warming is the observed increase in the average temperature of the Earth's atmosphere and oceans over recent decades and its projected continuation. Models used by the Intergovernmental Panel on Climate Change (IPCC) predict that global temperatures are likely to increase by 1.1°C to 6.4°C between 1990 and 2100. The uncertainty in this range results from two factors, namely different future greenhouse gas emission scenarios and uncertainties regarding climate sensitivity. The prevailing scientific opinion on climate change is that most of the observed increase in globally-averaged temperatures since the mid-twentieth century is very likely due to the observed increase in anthropogenic greenhouse gas concentrations. This leads to warming of the surface and lower atmosphere by increasing the greenhouse effect.

An increase in the Earth's temperature would have a significant effect on sea levels and climate.

Carbon dioxide

Climate change

Chlorofluorocarbons (CFCs)

Fossil fuels

Greenhouse effect

Greenhouse gases

Nitrogen oxides

Green energy

The use of environmentally-friendly power and energy that comes from renewable and non-polluting energy sources. Primary green energy sources include solar, wind, geothermal, hydropower and biomass (wood and animal waste).

Solar energy

Wind power

Greenhouse effect

A greenhouse operates on a simple principle. Light passes through a clear roof but the heat created is trapped within, increasing the temperature inside the greenhouse. In the case of global warming, the Earth operates on the same basis as a greenhouse. The current scientific view is that the continuing production of high levels of carbon dioxide from industrial processes will eventually create a blanket around the Earth that allows the penetration of light but retards or reduces heat escaping to outer space.

Where global warming raises temperatures by several degrees, some predictions are that changes in the Earth's climate could have severe impacts on normal life and agriculture. The control of greenhouse gases is, therefore, vital.

Climate change

Global warming

Greenhouse Gas Emissions Trading Scheme

Greenhouse gases

Greenhouse Gas Emissions Trading Scheme

The EU Emissions Trading Scheme is a policy developed across Europe to tackle greenhouse gas emissions and to combat the ever-increasing threat of climate change. The main objective of the Scheme is to promote reductions of greenhouse gas emissions in a cost-effective and economically efficient manner.

The first phase of the Scheme ran from 2005 to 2007 and the second phase from 2008 to 2012 to coincide with the Kyoto Protocol Commitment Period. Further five-year phases will follow.

Climate change

Emissions Trading Scheme

Global warming

Greenhouse gases

Greenhouse Gas Emissions Trading Scheme Regulations 2005

Kyoto Protocol (US)

Greenhouse Gas Emissions Trading Scheme Regulations 2005

Operators of installations covered by the Scheme must hold a greenhouse gas permit issued by the Environment Agency. A permit can incorporate conditions that must be met, including monitoring and reporting requirements. The installations covered by the Scheme are set out in Schedule 1 dealing with 'Activities and Specified Emissions'.

One of the conditions of a permit is that the operator must, by 30th April each year, surrender allowances equal to the total emissions from that installation during the preceding year. Operators are able to select whether to make emission reductions themselves or purchase surplus allowances from other operators.

Each Member State must produce a National Allocation Plan indicating:

(a) the total allowances to be allocated for any given phase of the Scheme; and

(b) how those allowances will be allocated to all installations participating in the Emissions Trading Scheme in that country.

Allowances will be allocated free of charge to incumbent installations in accordance with the methodology set out in the UK National Allocation Plan.

Operators are allocated an account on the UK Emissions Trading Registry that enables them to manage their allowances, including transferring and surrendering allowances.

The Regulations set out the fees and charges for operators. These include:

(a) fees relating to permits, e.g. application, variation and surrender fees;

(b) fees relating to new entrant applications; and

(c) annual subsistence charges.

A fee also applies to non-permit holders, i.e. individuals, companies and other organisations who are not classed as operators of installations covered by the Scheme, who open accounts with the Registry.

Operators of installations that do not surrender sufficient allowances to cover their annual emissions are liable to a penalty. In the first phase of the Scheme, the penalty is 40 Euros for each tonne of carbon dioxide equivalent emitted by that installation for which the operator has not surrendered allowances. In the second phase, the penalty is 100 Euros per tonne. Payment of a penalty does not release the operator from the obligation to surrender the required amount of allowances the following year.

The Regulations also provide that it is an offence to fail to comply with certain other obligations, such as undertaking an activity covered by the Scheme without having a greenhouse gas emissions permit. A person guilty of an offence under the Regulations is liable to a fine and/or imprisonment.

Appeals may be made against certain Decisions or Notices that are made or served under the Regulations. Those Decisions or Notices that are the subject of appeal are:

(a) Decisions relating to permits, e.g. refusal of a permit;

(b) Decisions on new entrant applications; and

(c) Enforcement Notices and Civil Penalty Notices.

As with the Pollution Prevention and Control regime, the Secretary of State, Scottish Ministers, National Assembly for Wales or the Department of the Environment in Northern Ireland may delegate responsibility for determining an appeal or any element of that appeal to a person appointed for that purpose.

Appeals

Enforcement Notice

Greenhouse gases

Permit

Pollution Prevention and Control (PPC)

Greenhouse gases

These are gases that contribute to the greenhouse effect by which infra-red radiation is absorbed by molecules in the atmosphere. Most of these gases are found naturally in the environment but their levels have been raised artificially by emissions from vehicles, electricity generation and industrial processes.

The principal greenhouse gases are carbon dioxide, methane, nitrous oxide, hydrofluorocarbons, sulphur hexafluoride and perfluorocarbons. Greenhouse gases are released by activities such as the burning of fossil fuels, land clearing and agriculture.

The major natural greenhouse gases are water vapour, which causes between 36 – 70% of the greenhouse effect on Earth, carbon dioxide, which causes 9 – 26%, methane, 4 – 9% and ozone, 3 – 7%. Greenhouse gases, in particular carbon dioxide, play an important part in keeping the Earth at a habitable temperature. Increasing concentrations of these gases and the release of more powerful organic gases are behind concerns about climate change.

Carbon dioxide

Climate change

Fossil fuels

Global warming

Greenhouse effect

"Green" products

These are those products that have been manufactured or produced in an environmentally friendly way or which are less damaging to the environment. They include recycled products, such as paper products, CFC-free aerosols and various chemical products, such as chlorine-free bleaches.

Chlorine

Chlorofluorocarbons (CFCs)

Grit, dust and fumes

Section 5 of the Clean Air Act 1993 establishes similar offences to the dark smoke offences in relation to the emission of grit, dust and fumes.

Where, on any day, the grit or dust emitted from a chimney serving a specified furnace is over the prescribed emission limits, as prescribed in the Clean Air (Emission of Grit and Dust from Furnaces) Regulations 1971, the occupier will be guilty of an offence unless he can successfully raise the defence that the best practicable means had been used to minimise or prevent the emission

[Clean Air Act 1993]

"Best practicable means"

Clean Air Act 1993

"Dark smoke"

Dark smoke offences

Ringelmann Chart

Ground waters

Any waters which are contained in underground strata. *Underground strata* means strata subjacent to the surface of any land.

[Water Resources Act 1991]

Coastal waters

Controlled waters

Fresh water limit

Inland fresh waters

Relevant lake or pond

Relevant river or watercourse

Watercourse

Water Resources Act 1991

Groundwater pollution

This form of pollution is regulated by the Groundwater Regulations 1998. The Regulations are designed to ensure that substances which could pollute groundwater are properly controlled and that authorisation is required for any listed substance to be disposed of on the land.

The Regulations also place a duty on environment agencies to serve Notices controlling activity on land to avoid the pollution of groundwater.

Regulator

Groundwater Regulations 1998

These Regulations control the disposal of certain listed substances to groundwater.

List I substances are the most damaging and toxic. They must be prevented from directly or indirectly entering groundwater. They include:

(a) many pesticides and herbicides;

(b) many solvents;

(c) mineral oils and hydrocarbons;

(d) cadmium and mercury.

Activities resulting in direct discharges may be authorised following prior investigation.

List II substances are less harmful but must be controlled to prevent pollution of groundwater. They include:

(a) many metals, such as zinc, lead and copper;

(b) many biocides;

(c) phosphorus;

(d) fluorides;

(e) ammonia and nitrates;

(f) anything that will make groundwater unfit to drink.

Where an operator intends to dispose of a listed substance in a way that might cause a discharge into groundwater, he must apply for an authorisation to discharge same. This may take the form of a Groundwater Authorisation, a Discharge Consent, an Integrated Pollution Control Authorisation or Pollution Prevention and Control Permit, and the type of authorisation will depend upon the circumstances of the disposal.

Where a person carries on, or proposes to carry on, an activity on or in the ground, he must take all necessary measures to prevent an accidental discharge of listed substances to groundwater. Activities that can lead to pollution of groundwater as a result of indirect discharges of listed substances include:

(a) storage or use of sheep dip or other agricultural pesticides;

(b) storage or use of industrial chemicals;

(c) storage of hydrocarbons such as oil;

(d) operation of a dirty water drainage system;

(e) operation of an oil pipeline or underground oil-filled cable.

A regulator has the power to serve a Prohibition Notice on a person undertaking such activities.

Biocides

Fluorides

Ground waters

Heavy metal pollution

Pesticide

Prohibition Notice

Solvent emissions

Water Resources Act 1991

Groundwater remediation

Remediation

Grouped packaging

Packaging

Guidance to regulators

The Secretary of State may issue guidance to regulators with respect to the carrying out of any of their functions under Regulations, such as the Pollution Prevention and Control (England and Wales) Regulations 2000.

Regulator

H

Habitat

The area of an environment where an organism lives, feeds and breeds.

Harm

Wildlife

Harm

Harm means harm to the health of living organisms or other interference with the ecological systems of which they form part and, in the case of man, includes offence caused to any of his senses or harm to his property; and harmless has a corresponding meaning.

[Environmental Protection Act 1990]

With respect to the definition of *environmental pollution*, *harm* means:

- (a) harm to the health of human beings or other living organisms;
- (b) harm to the quality of the environment, including:
  - (i) harm to the quality of the environment taken as a whole;
  - (ii) harm to the quality of the air, water or land; and
  - (iii) other impairment of, or interference with, amenities or other legitimate uses of the environment.

[Pollution Prevention and Control Act 1999]

Environmental pollution

Environmental Protection Act 1990

Habitat

Pollution Prevention and Control Act 1999

Hazard

Something with the potential to cause harm.

The property of a substance, or a situation with the potential to cause harm.

Hazardous substances: classification

Hazardous substances are classified according to Schedule 1 of the Chemicals (Hazard Information and Packaging for Supply) (CHIP) Regulations 2002.

Schedule 1 – Part I – Classification of Hazardous Substances **Part I – Categories of Danger**		
Column 1	**Column 2**	**Column 3**
Category of letter	Property	Symbol-danger

Figure 5: CLASSIFICATION OF HAZARDOUS SUBSTANCES UNDER THE 'CHIP' REGULATIONS

Physico-chemical properties		
Category of letter	Property	Symbol -danger
Explosive	Solid, liquid, pasty or gelatinous substances and preparations which may react exothermically without atmospheric oxygen thereby quickly evolving gases, and which under defined test conditions detonate, quickly deflagrate or upon heating explode when partially confined.	E
Oxidising	Substances and preparations which give rise to a exothermic reaction in contact with other substances, particularly flammable substances.	O
Extremely flammable	Liquid substances and preparations having an extremely low flash point and a low boiling point and gaseous substances and preparations which are flammable in contact with air at ambient temperature and pressure.	F+

Physico-chemical properties		
Category of letter	Property	Symbol -danger
Highly flammable	The following substances and preparations, namely: (a) substances and preparations which may become hot and finally catch fire in contact with air at ambient temperature without any application of energy; (b) solid substances and preparations which may readily catch fire after brief contact with a source of ignition and which continue to burn or to be consumed after removal of the source of ignition; (c) liquid substances and preparations having a very low flash point; (d) substances and preparations which, in contact with water or damp air, evolve highly flammable gases in dangerous quantities. (See Note 2)	F
Flammable	Liquid substances and preparations having a low flash point.	None

Health effects		
Category of letter	Property	Symbol -danger
Very toxic	Substances and preparations which in very low quantities can cause death or acute or chronic damage to health when inhaled, swallowed or absorbed via the skin.	T+
Toxic	Substances and preparations which in low quantities can cause death or acute or chronic damage to health when inhaled, swallowed or absorbed via the skin.	T
Harmful	Substances and preparations which may cause death or acute or chronic damage to health when inhaled, swallowed or absorbed via the skin.	Xn
Corrosive	Substances and preparations which may, on contact, with living tissues, destroy them.	C

Health effects		
Category of letter	Property	Symbol -danger
Irritant	Non-corrosive substances and preparations which through immediate, prolonged or repeated contact with the skin or mucous membrane, may cause inflammation.	Xi
Sensitising	Substances and preparations which, if they are inhaled or if they penetrate the skin, are capable of eliciting a reaction by hypersensitisation such that on further exposure to the substance or preparation, characteristic adverse effects are produced.	
Sensitising by inhalation		Xn
Sensitising by skin contact		Xi
Carcinogenic	Substances and preparations which, if they are inhaled or ingested or if they penetrate the skin, may induce cancer or increase its incidence.	
Category 1		T
Category 2		T
Category 3		Xn

Health effects		
Category of letter	Property	Symbol -danger
Mutagenic	Substances and preparations which, if they are inhaled or ingested or if they penetrate the skin, may induce heritable genetic defects or increase their incidence.	
Category 1		T
Category 2		T
Category 3		Xn
Toxic for reproduction	Substances and preparations which, if they are inhaled or ingested or if they penetrate the skin, may produce or increase the incidence of non-heritable adverse effects in the progeny and/or an impairment of male or female reproductive functions or capacity.	
Category 1		T
Category 2		T
Category 3		Xn
Dangerous for the environment	Substances which, were they to enter into the environment, would present or might present an immediate or delayed danger for one or more components of the environment.	N

Chemicals (Hazard Information and Packaging for Supply) Regulations 1994 – 2002

Hazardous waste

Hazardous waste is, according to EU legislation, the most harmful form of waste to human health and the environment. Hazardous wastes have, in the last century or more, been associated with a wide range of industrial processes where little or no attention was given to the long-term effects of pollution of the ground and water sources. They include solvents, acids, alkalis, pesticides, lead batteries, asbestos, electrical equipment containing hazardous components, chemical wastes, fluorescent tubes and various industrial sludges. The waste may have been deposited on land or in landfill sites or discharged to watercourses.

The Hazardous Waste (England and Wales) Regulations 2005 define *hazardous waste* as waste with one or more properties that are hazardous to health or the environment. Such waste is defined on the basis of:

(a) any waste listed as 'hazardous' in the List of Waste Regulations 2005;

(b) any specific batch of waste that the Secretary of State determines as hazardous; and

(c) any specific consignment of waste that the Secretary of State determines is exceptionally to be classified as 'hazardous'.

Typical hazardous wastes are computer monitors, televisions, fluorescent tubes, dental amalgam and un-depolluted end-of-life vehicles.

Both Regulations:

(a) implement an EU definition of 'hazardous waste' in domestic legislation;

(b) require producers of hazardous waste to notify their premises to the Environment Agency;

(c) terminate the requirement to pre-notify wastes to the Environment Agency;

(d) require operators to ensure safe management of hazardous waste;

(e) require operators to provide Cradle to Grave documentation for the movement of hazardous waste; and

(f) require consignees to keep thorough records of hazardous waste and provide the Agency with quarterly disposal and recovery information.

These Regulations ensure hazardous waste is managed correctly under the Environmental Protection (Duty of Care) Regulations and apply to any site which produces more than 200 kg of hazardous waste in any 12 month period.

Operators are recommended to:

(a) minimise hazardous waste production wherever possible and to review waste management arrangements in accordance with the duty of care;

(b) explore the possibilities for using alternative materials and practices that do not result in the production of hazardous waste;

(c) store liquid hazardous waste in watertight containers in a dedicated bunded area with adequate space to allow for inspection and access;

(d) provide information, instruction and training for employees on dealing with spillages of hazardous waste, including the correct use of personal protective equipment and the correct disposal of contaminated clean-up materials.

Operators must further ensure that hazardous waste is transported by a registered or exempt waste carrier and is transferred to a facility authorised to accept that type of waste. Specific requirements apply in the case of waste transfer stations which accept waste and subsequently consign the waste onwards. In this case:

(a) where hazardous waste is to be removed from one site to another, the operator must notify the Environment Agency of the destination site;

(b) in accepting waste as a consignee, an operator must complete the appropriate part of the Consignment Note or multiple collection Consignment Note;

(c) as a consignee, an operator must record details of hazardous wastes received, together with the quantities involved, nature, origin and hazardous properties, and maintain an inventory indicating its location at the site; these records must be kept for three years;

(d) as a consignee, an operator must send returns to the producer or holder of the waste either using the form specified in Schedule 8 to the Regulations or a copy of the Consignment Note;

(e) operators must submit quarterly returns of the Agency indicating details of the consignments they have received.

Attention should also be paid to safety data provided by suppliers under the Chemicals (Hazard Information and Packaging for Supply) (CHIP) Regulations with respect to substances classified as toxic, corrosive, harmful, irritant, dangerous for the environment, etc.

All organisations that produce hazardous waste must register their premises with the Environment Agency before they consign their hazardous waste. Moreover, each type of hazardous waste must be disposed of at a landfill site that is authorised to accept it. The waste must be pre-treated before it can be disposed of. This treatment must take account of the limit values set by the established Waste Acceptance Criteria for the landfill site.

Chemicals (Hazard Information and Packaging for Supply) (CHIP) Regulations 1994 – 2002

Cradle to Grave

End-of-life vehicles (ELVs)

Environmental Protection (Duty of Care) Regulations 1991

Hazardous substances: classification

Landfill: disposal of waste

Landfill (England and Wales) Regulations 2002 – 2005

Safety data

Transfer Note

Waste

Waste disposal: hazardous substances

Waste electrical and electronic equipment

Waste: environmental consequences

Waste hierarchy

Waste offences

Waste oil

Waste on land

Waste unlawfully deposited

Health and Safety Executive (HSE)

The HSE is the national body responsible for enforcing health and safety law, namely the Health and Safety at Work Act 1974 and Regulations made under the Act. Certain enforcement duties are allocated to local authorities.

Health Criteria Values

Authoritative Health Criteria Values for contaminants are established through a review of scientific literature and are provided in the Contaminated Land Regime TOX reports *"Contamination in soil: Collation of toxicological data and intake values for humans"*.

The following values are derived for threshold contaminants:

(a) mean daily intake (MDI) from background sources other than soil;

(b) tolerable daily intake (TDI); and

(c) tolerable daily soil intake (TDSI).

Tolerable daily soil intake is defined as the difference between the tolerable daily intake (TDI) and the mean daily intake (MDI). The only exception to this is when the mean daily intake is greater than or equal to 80% of the tolerable daily intake, in which case the tolerable daily soil intake is set at 20% of the tolerable daily intake.

Contaminated land

Index dose

Soil Guideline Values (SGVs)

Heavy metal pollution

Heavy metals include zinc, copper, lead, cadmium, nickel and mercury. They are used in the manufacture of a wide range of products and have been responsible for much occupational ill-health, such as lead and mercury poisoning, together with polluting global environments, for over 200 years. Heavy metal pollution arises as a result of processes, such as heat treatment, incineration, mining, textile manufacture, dyeing processes, smelting and electro-plating. The metal-based waste products from these processes pollute the air, water and soil.

There is increasing evidence to indicate that roads and vehicles are one of the most common sources of heavy metals. Zinc, copper and lead are three of the most common heavy metals released from road travel. Apart from the lead concentrations released from petrol, brakes are understood to release copper whilst the wear on tyres can release zinc. On the road surface, most heavy metals become bound to the surfaces of the road dust or other particulates. During precipitation, the bound metals will either become soluble or be swept off the roadway with the dust. In either case, the metals enter the soil or are washed down storm drains.

Heavy metal pollution of water is caused by the presence of unacceptable levels of the ions of arsenic, cadmium, copper, chromium, mercury, nickel, lead and zinc. Sources of heavy metal pollution include rivers, sewage treatment plants, tidal exchange, urban run off, combined sewer outflows and deposition from the atmosphere in the form of smoke, smog, dusts and fumes from the burning of fossil fuels and industrial processes.

Heavy metals, such as lead, silver and cadmium are particularly toxic to aquatic life in very minute amounts. They accumulate in sediments and, over a period of time, are gradually released into water. Moreover, aquatic algae can take up metal ions in polluted water and store them in their tissues. Once ingested by an animal, or absorbed through the skin or gills, metals can be concentrated as they progress from smaller to larger organisms in the food chain.

Simple techniques to identify the presence of heavy metals include precipitation and flame testing. Techniques to quantitatively determine heavy metals include volumetric and gravimetric analyses, colorimetry, chromatography and spectroscopy, particularly atomic absorption spectroscopy and mass spectroscopy.

Airborne particulates

Combustion activities

Copper

Environmental pollution

Incineration

Petroleum

Release into water: substances

Waste

High activity sealed radioactive sources and orphan sources

The High Activity Sealed Radioactive Substances and Orphan Sources Regulations 2005 (the HASS Regulations), contain relevant provisions aimed at preventing exposure to radiation resulting from the inadequate control of high activity sealed radioactive sources.

The HASS Regulations apply in cases where a person:

(a) is a user of high activity types of sealed radioactive sources, e.g. for radiotherapy, medical therapy and sterilisation; or

(b) handles waste sealed radioactive sources.

High activity sealed radioactive sources, together with other sealed sources of a similar level of potential hazard, represent the greatest risk. On this basis, they are subject to a more detailed and rigorous regime of regulatory control and site security under the Regulations by way of additional requirements and authorisation conditions.

The HASS Regulations further contain provisions for detecting, recovering and dealing appropriately with radioactive sources that are not under regulatory control (orphan sources).

Mobile radioactive source

Open radioactive sources

Radiation

Radioactive substances and wastes

Sealed radioactive sources

Household waste

This includes waste from domestic properties, caravans, residential homes, educational establishments, hospitals and nursing homes.

Controlled waste

Environmental Protection Act 1990

Public registers of information: waste disposal

Waste

Waste Collection Authorities (WCAs)

Waste Disposal Authorities (WDAs) and Companies

Waste Disposal Plans by Waste Regulation Authorities

Waste: environmental consequences

Waste holders' duties

Waste Local Plans

Waste management facility (licensed site)

Waste Management Licences

Waste Minimisation Act 1998

Waste offences

Waste on land

Waste planning and recycling

Waste Recycling Plans

Waste Regulation Authorities (WRAs)

Waste Regulatory Authorities

Waste transfer

Waste unlawfully deposited

Humidity

Humidity is the amount of water vapour present in air.

Relative humidity

Hydrological cycle

The cycle of water evaporated from wet surfaces and plants and precipitated as rain.

Hydrology

This is, fundamentally, the study of water. It is concerned with the quality, movement, storage and distribution of water throughout Earth, in particular the hydrological cycle and water resources.

Imminent danger of damage to the environment

Where in the case of anything found by him on any premises which he has power to enter, an inspector has reason to believe that it is a genetically modified organism or that it consists of or includes genetically modified organisms and that, in the circumstances in which he finds it, it is a cause of *imminent danger of damage to the environment*, he may seize it and cause it to be rendered harmless (whether by destruction, by bringing it under proper control or otherwise).

[Environmental Protection Act 1990]

"Control"

"Damage to the environment"

Environment

Environmental Protection Act 1990

Genetically modified organism (GMO)

Genetically Modified Organisms (Contained Use) Regulations 2000

Harm

Imminent danger of serious harm

Where in the case of any article or substance found by him on any premises which he has power to enter, an inspector has reasonable cause to believe that, in the circumstances in which he finds it, the article or substance is a cause of *imminent danger of serious harm* he may seize it and cause it to be rendered harmless (whether by destruction or otherwise).

[Environmental Protection Act 1990]

Contaminated Land (England) Regulations 2000

Environmental Protection Act 1990

Harm

Incineration

The burning of waste at high temperatures in the presence of sufficient air to achieve complete combustion, either to reduce its volume (as with municipal solid waste) or its toxicity e.g. organic solvents. Municipal solid waste incinerators recover heat and/or power. The main emissions are carbon dioxide, water and ash residues.

Incineration is an effective form of waste disposal and, currently, 7% of all waste in the UK is disposed of in this way. Incineration results in a reduction in volume of waste of up to 90% and of weight by around 60%. The resulting ash is generally biologically inert, but may contain pollutants, such as heavy metals. Prevention of air pollution is critical and such a strategy must be linked to energy recovery.

Controlled Waste Regulations 1992

Incineration and co-incineration of waste

Incineration plant

Part A activities

Part B activities

Pollution Prevention and Control Act 1999

Pollution Prevention and Control (England and Wales) Regulations 2000

Recovery

Scheduled activities

Incineration and co-incineration of waste

These scheduled activities are:

Part A(1)

(a) The incineration of hazardous waste in an incineration plant;

(b) Unless carried out as part of another Part A(1) activity, the incineration of hazardous waste in a co-incineration plant;

(c) The incineration of non-hazardous waste in an incineration plant with a capacity of 1 tonne or more per hour;

(d) Unless carried out as part of any other activity in this Part, the incineration of hazardous waste in plant which is not an incineration plant or co-incineration plant;

(e) Unless carried out as part of any other activity in this Part, the incineration of non-hazardous waste in a plant which is not an incineration plant or a co-incineration plant but which has a capacity of 1 tonne or more per hour.

Part A(2)

(a) The incineration of non-hazardous waste in an incineration plant with a capacity of less than 1 tonne per hour;

(b) Unless carried out as part of any other Part A activity, the incineration of non-hazardous waste in a co-incineration plant.

Part B

(a) The incineration of non-hazardous waste in an incineration plant which is not an incineration plant or a co-incineration plant but which has a capacity of 50 kilogrammes or more per hour but less than 1 tonne per hour;

(b) The cremation of human remains.

Co-incineration

Co-incineration plant

Hazardous waste

Incineration

Incineration plant

Part A activities

Part B activities

Pollution Prevention and Control (England and Wales) Regulations 2000

Scheduled activities

[Pollution Prevention and Control (England and Wales) Regulations 2000 as amended by the Waste Incineration (England and Wales) Regulations 2002]

Incineration plant

Any stationary or mobile technical unit and equipment dedicated to the thermal treatment of wastes with or without recovery of the combustion heat generated. This includes the incineration by oxidation of waste as well as other thermal treatment processes such as pyrolosis, gasification or plasma processes in so far as the substances resulting from the treatment are subsequently incinerated.

[Waste Incineration (England and Wales) Regulations 2002]

Co-incineration

Co-incineration plant

Hazardous waste

Incineration

Incineration and co-incineration of waste

Pollution Prevention and Control (England and Wales) Regulations 2000

Scheduled activities

Index dose

A dose that poses a minimal risk level from a possible exposure to contamination in soil with the additional requirement that exposure needs to be reduced to as low as is reasonably practicable.

Contaminant

Contaminated land

Contaminated Land Regime

Health Criteria Values

Industrial waste

This means waste from any of the following premises: factories; public transport premises; premises used to supply gas, water, electricity, sewerage, postal or telecom services. Waste from construction or demolition operations is also termed industrial waste as is waste from contaminated land. Industrial waste is sometimes referred to as "trade waste".

Commercial waste

Controlled waste

Environmental Protection Act 1990

Household waste

Waste

Waste Collection Authorities (WCAs)

Waste Disposal Authorities (WDAs) and Companies

Waste disposal: hazardous substances

Waste Disposal Plans by Waste Regulation Authorities

Waste: environmental consequences

Waste holders' duties

Waste hierarchy

Waste Local Plans

Waste management facility (licensed site)

Waste Management Licences

Waste management option

Waste management strategies and policies

Waste Minimisation Act 1998

Waste offences

Waste on land

Waste planning and recycling

Waste Recycling Plans

Waste Regulation Authorities (WRAs)

Waste Regulatory Authorities

Waste transfer

Waste unlawfully deposited

Industry-led compliance schemes

Any compliance scheme is required to provide the relevant Agency with a statement showing its policies on the following:

(a) the steps that the scheme intends to take to increase the amount of recyclate used in the packaging and packaging materials, and other products, supplied by its member businesses;

(b) the main methods which the scheme proposes to use to recover and recycle packaging waste and an indication of the role that the consumer can play in helping the scheme use these methods.

[Producer Responsibility (Packaging Waste) Regulations 1997]

Inert waste

Chemically inert, non-combustible, non-biodegradable and non-polluting waste defined in the EU Directive on the Landfill of Waste.

Landfill: disposal of waste

Injunction

In a civil action, a claimant may seek an injunction against another party in addition to, or as an alternative to, an award of damages. An injunction allows the court to require the defendant to take action in respect of the activities causing damage.

Injunctions can be:

(a) *Mandatory*, in which case the court will require the defendant to 'undo' the wrongful act; and

(b) *Prohibitory*, ordering the defendant not to commit a wrongful act, for example, operating a process which is causing a nuisance to inhabitants of the neighbourhood from dust emissions.

A claimant may apply for an interim or interlocutory injunction. This has the effect of preventing the offending activities from continuing pending the setting of a full hearing.

Negligence

Nuisance

Nuisance at common law

Tort

Inland fresh waters

The waters of any relevant lake or pond or of so much of any relevant river or watercourse as is above the fresh water limit.

Coastal waters

Controlled waters

Fresh water limit

Ground waters

Inland fresh waters

Relevant lake or pond

Relevant river or watercourse

Watercourse

Water Resources Act 1991

Inorganic chemical production

These scheduled activities are:

Part A(1)

(a) Producing inorganic chemicals such as:

(i) gases, such as ammonia, hydrogen chloride, hydrogen fluoride, hydrogen cyanide, hydrogen sulphide, oxides of carbon, sulphur compounds, oxides of nitrogen, hydrogen, oxides of sulphur, phosgene;

(ii) acids, such as chromic acid, hydrofluoric acid, hydrochloric acid, hydrobromic acid, hydroiodic acid, phosphoric acid, nitric acid, sulphuric acid, oleum and chlorosulphonic acid;

(iii) bases, such as ammonium hydroxide, potassium hydroxide, sodium hydroxide;

(iv) salts, such as ammonium chloride, potassium chlorate, potassium carbonate, sodium carbonate, perborate, silver nitrate, cupric acetate, ammonium phosphomolybdate;

(v) non-metals, metal oxides, metal carbonyls or other inorganic compounds such as calcium carbide, silicon, silicon carbide, titanium dioxide;

(vi) halogens or interhalogen compound comprising two or more of halogens, or any compound comprising one or more of those halogens and oxygen;

(b) Unless falling within another Section of this Schedule, any manufacturing activity which uses, or which is likely to result in the release into the air or into water of, any halogens, hydrogen halides or any of the compounds mentioned in (a)(vi), other than the treatment of water by chlorine;

(c) Unless falling within another Section of this Schedule, any manufacturing activity involving the use of hydrogen cyanide or hydrogen sulphide;

(d) Unless falling within another Section of this Schedule, any manufacturing activity, other than the application of glaze or vitreous enamel, involving the use of any of the following elements or the recovery of any compound of the following elements:

antimony	beryllium	indium	palladium	selenium	thallium
arsenic	gallium	lead	platinum	tellurium	

where the activity may result in the release into the air of any of those elements or compounds or the release into water of any substance listed in paragraph 13 of Part 2 of this Schedule;

(e) Recovering of any compound of cadmium or mercury;

(f) Unless falling with another Section of this Schedule, any manufacturing activity involving the use of mercury or cadmium or any compound of either element or which may result in the release into air of either of those elements or their compounds;

(g) Unless carried out as part of any other activity falling within this Schedule:

   (i) recovering, concentrating or distilling sulphuric acid or oleum;

   (ii) recovering nitric acid;

   (iii) purifying phosphoric acid;

(h) Any manufacturing activity (other than the manufacture of chemicals or glass or the coating, plating or surface treatment of metal) which:

(i) involves the use of hydrogen fluoride, hydrogen chloride, hydrogen bromide or hydrogen iodide or any of their acids; and

   (ii) may result in the release of any of those compounds into the air;

   (i) Unless carried out as part of any other activity falling within this Schedule, recovering ammonia;

(j) Extracting any magnesium compound from sea water.

Part A(2)

Nil

Part B

Nil

[Schedule 1: Part 1: Pollution Prevention and Control (England and Wales) Regulations 2000]

Chemical fertiliser production

Nitrogen oxides

Organic chemicals: manufacture and use

Part A activities

Part B activities

Pharmaceutical production

Plant health products and biocides

Pollution Prevention and Control (England and Wales) Regulations 2000

Scheduled activities

Storage of chemicals in bulk

Sulphur oxides

Installation

Means:

(i) any stationary technical unit where one or more activities listed in Part 1 of Schedule 1 are carried out; and

(ii) any other location on the same site where any other directly associated activities are carried out which have a technical connection with the activities carried out in the stationary technical unit and which could have an effect on pollution.

[Pollution Prevention and Control (England and Wales) Regulations 2000]

Installations handling hazardous substances

Installations handling hazardous substances

The Notification of Installations Handling Hazardous Substances Regulations 1982 require any person who undertakes any activity in which there is likely to be a notifiable quantity or more of a hazardous substance on any site or in any pipeline to:

(a) notify the Health and Safety Executive in writing of specified particulars at least three months before commencing the activity;

(b) notify the Health and Safety Executive of specified particulars where there are changes in a previously notified activity; and

(c) where the hazardous substance involved has increased to three or more times the amount originally notified, to re-notify as if it were a new activity.

[Dangerous Substances (Notification and Marking of Sites) Regulations 1990]

Hazardous substances: classification

Health and Safety Executive (HSE)

Integrated Pollution Prevention and Control (IPPC)

This is an approach arising from an EC Directive implemented in the UK by the Pollution Prevention and Control (England and Wales) Regulations 2000. It is an approach to controlling, through Regulation and operating permits, all environmentally-damaging emissions from an industrial site in a coherent fashion, rather than applying separate controls to different media (air, water and land) through separate independent authorities.

It is broader in scope than the former Integrated Pollution Control and covers more industrial sectors. In particular, it requires the avoidance of waste production wherever possible and more efficient use of energy. It also covers noise, vibration, resource minimisation, environmental accidents and site protection.

The regime is now known as Pollution Prevention and Control (PPC).

Part A activities

Part B activities

Pollution Prevention and Control (PPC)

Pollution Prevention and Control Act 1999

Pollution Prevention and Control (England and Wales) Regulations 2000

Scheduled activities

Integrated Product Policy

A specific policy, the essence of which is that public policy should use a range of mechanisms to reduce the environmental harm associated with whole product systems across the lifecycle of products. The policy incorporates a number of objectives, including influencing the choice of buyers of products and the offerings of suppliers through the application of market instruments, fiscal incentives and labelling requirements. Other aspects, such as product return legislation, mandatory producer responsibility schemes and consumer education, feature as part of such a policy.

Market instrument

Intensive farming

These scheduled activities are:

Part A(1)

(a) Rearing poultry or pigs intensively in an installation with more than:

(i) 40,000 places for poultry;

(ii) 2,000 places for production pigs (over 30 kg); or

(iii) 750 places for sows.

Part A(2)

Nil

Part B

Nil

[Schedule 1: Part 1: Pollution Prevention and Control (England and Wales) Regulations 2000]

Agricultural nitrate pollution

Agricultural waste

Part A activities

Part B activities

Pollution Prevention and Control Act 1999

Pollution Prevention and Control (England and Wales) Regulations 2000

Scheduled activities

Isocyanates

A range of isocyanates is used in industry, principally in the manufacture of urethane foams and resins, for example, toluene di-isocyanate (TDI) and methylene bisphenyl di-isocyanate (MDI).

TDI is the most volatile of the isocyanates and one of the most toxic. It should only be used under closely controlled conditions in an enclosed system or with well-controlled ventilation. The vapour can be evolved during the manufacture of foams and also during cutting of the finished product with a hot wire.

A dust hazard may arise from the use of 1:5 naphthylene di-isocyanate (NDI) as it is sometimes used in powder form. In the latter case, there is a potential hazard from the spray when NDI in solid form is being sprayed with polyurethane lacquers, a practice commonly used in the furniture and allied industries. The spraying of polyurethane foams is a particularly hazardous operation which requires a high degree of environmental and personal protection.

Most isocyanates can produce varying degrees of dermatitis and exposure can result in skin sensitisation effects in rare cases. The main consideration, however, is that they are a potent primary irritant to the respiratory tract and, in some cases, cause dramatic sensitisation, ie asthmatic attacks once the individual has become sensitised. Eye splashes may cause severe chemical conjunctivitis. Handling and transference, therefore, should be in closed systems. Health supervision should include pre-employment health examinations and routine periodic health examinations with a view to detecting asthmatic conditions in particular.

Airborne particulates

Hazardous substances: classification

ISO 9000

ISO 9000 is a group of standards covering quality management systems maintained by ISO, the International Organisation for Standardisation, administered by various accreditation and certification bodies.

The ISO 9000 group includes the following standards:

ISO 9000: Quality management systems: Fundamentals and vocabulary

This document incorporates a description of quality management standards, together with the basic language of the ISO 9000 series of standards.

ISO 9001: Quality management systems: Requirements

This document is intended for use in any organisation which designs, develops, manufactures, installs and/or services any product or provides any type of service. It identifies a number of requirements which an organisation must meet if it is to achieve customer satisfaction through consistent products and services which meet customer expectations.

ISO 9004: Quality management systems: Guidelines for performance improvements

This document covers the process for continual improvement and provides advice on measures to be taken to enhance a mature system.

ISO 9001

ISO 9001

This document deals with the requirements for quality management systems with particular reference to:

(a) general requirements;

(b) management responsibility;

(c) resource management;

(d) product realisation; and

(e) measurement, analysis and improvement.

The standard specifies six compulsory documents:

(a) Control of Documents;

(b) Control of Records;

(c) Internal Audits;

(d) Control of Non-conforming Product/Service;

(e) Corrective Action; and

(f) Preventive Action.

ISO 9000

ISO 14001: Environmental Management Systems

ISO 14001 is an international standard that specifies a process for controlling and improving an organisation's environmental performance.

ISO 14001 consists of:

(a) General requirements;

(b) Environmental policy;

(c) Planning;

(d) Implementation and operation;

(e) Checking and corrective action; and

(f) Management review.

It implies:

(a) identifying elements of an organisation's operations that impact on the environment and gaining access to requirements of environmental legislation; and

(b) producing objectives for improvement together with a management programme for achieving same, including reviews for continual improvement.

Environmental management system (EMS)

ISO 14021

This is the international standard providing guidance for declarations made by an organisation about the environmental aspects of its products or services.

ISO 14031

This is the international standard providing guidance on environmental performance evaluation. It provides a method for identifying performance indicators that an organisation can use to monitor its progress towards environmental performance objectives. The mechanism shares many of the features of the mechanism for establishing an environmental management system described by ISO 14001.

ISO 14001: Environmental Management Systems

K

Kyoto Protocol (US)

An international agreement, formulated at a meeting in Kyoto, that sets out mechanisms and targets for reducing global emissions of greenhouse gases. This Protocol does not enter into force until it is ratified by 55 countries and this has not yet happened.

L

Land Drainage Act 1994

This Act is largely concerned with flood defence and land drainage. However, it does require local authorities to have regard for the environment when carrying out land drainage and flood defence works.

Landfill sites

Landfill sites are licensed facilities where waste is permanently deposited for disposal on to or in land. This includes sites that receive waste from external sources or are used by waste producers to dispose of their own waste on site.

Landfill operations fundamentally imply the dumping of waste in natural or artificially created depressions in the land or, alternatively, creating such depressions through excavation of land sites. Approximately 90% of household waste is disposed of in this way, which does not generally create an environmental threat.

The advantages and disadvantages of landfill operations are as follows:

Advantages	Disadvantages
Low cost	Needs careful siting
Can deal with a wide range of waste	Needs careful engineering
Can assist restoration of excavated land	Needs careful waste management
Landfill gas (methane) can be migration of landfill gas	Risks include water pollution, reclaimed and gases produced can contribute to the greenhouse effect

Figure 6: LANDFILL OPERATIONS

Landfill: disposal of waste

Landfill tax

Landfill (England and Wales) Regulations 2002 – 2005

These Regulations were implemented in the UK in the European Landfill Directive 1999/31/EC on the landfill of waste.

The Regulations classify landfills as those used for the disposal of :

(a) inert wastes – inert or non-reactive materials, such as concrete, bricks, waste glass, etc;

(b) non-hazardous wastes – such as general household waste and garden waste; and

(c) hazardous wastes – reactive materials, such as chemicals.

The Regulations establish a number of procedures and criteria for the acceptance of waste at landfill sites. Producers of waste, including those creating wastes arising from construction, demolition and excavation work, must be aware of these procedures and criteria in order to identify sites where such waste can be landfilled.

Operators of landfill sites must hold a Pollution Prevention and Control Permit (Landfill Permit) and the site must be classified according to the type of waste it accepts.

Waste, with the exception of:

(a) inert waste that cannot be treated; and

(b) any other waste for which treatment would not reduce its quantity or its danger to human health and the environment,

must be treated before it is landfilled in order to minimise its environmental impact.

Hazardous wastes must not be mixed with non-hazardous wastes due to the risk of reactions which could cause long-term environmental damage. They must be separated and diverted to designated hazardous waste landfills. Other wastes may require treatment before landfilling.

Certain types of wastes are banned from landfilling, namely:

(a) used tyres (whole and shredded), (although this does not apply to bicycle tyres or tyres with an outside diameter greater than 1.4 metres, such as larger earth mover and agricultural tyres);

(b) liquid wastes, including waste water, but excluding sludge;

(c) hospital and other clinical and infectious wastes from medical or veterinary establishments;

(d) waste that may be explosive, corrosive, oxidising or flammable under landfill conditions; and

(e) new or unidentified chemical substances from research and development or teaching activities, and whose effects on Man and the environment are not known.

Part 1 of Schedule 1 of the Landfill (England and Wales) (Amendment) Regulations 2004, as amended in 2005, specifies principles for the acceptance of both hazardous and non-hazardous wastes at relevant landfills. These principles include ensuring that waste will not endanger human health and the environment and satisfy Waste Acceptance Criteria. They further set strict requirements for the acceptance of specific stable and non-reactive hazardous waste into non-hazardous waste landfills.

Hazardous waste

Landfill: disposal of waste

Waste

Waste Acceptance Criteria

Waste activity

Waste: duty of care

Waste holders' duties

Waste Management Licensing Regulations 1994 – 2006

Waste offences

Waste unlawfully deposited

Landfill: disposal of waste

These scheduled activities are:

Part A(1)

(a) The disposal of waste in a landfill receiving more than 10 tonnes of waste in any day or with a total capacity of more than 25,000 tonnes, excluding disposals in landfills taking only inert waste.

Part A(2)

Nil

Part B

Nil

[Schedule 1: Part 1: Pollution Prevention and Control (England and Wales) Regulations 2000]

Landfill sites

Landfill tax

Part A activities

Part B activities

Pollution Prevention and Control Act 1999

Pollution Prevention and Control (England and Wales) Regulations 2000

Scheduled activities

Landfill tax

A tax that applies to active and inert waste, disposed at a licensed landfill. The aim of the tax is to send a tough signal to waste managers to switch to less environmentally damaging alternatives to disposal.

Inert waste

Landfill sites

Land pollution

Land may be polluted by a variety of industrial, commercial and domestic wastes. The contamination can arise as a result of poor standards of controlled tipping or by the indiscriminate, and often unauthorised, dumping, of wastes. The by-products of these wastes can leach into underground water supplies and form pockets of gas, such as methane. Sewage pollution of land is common as a result of defective drains and sewers.

Leaching

Sewage effluent

Waste

Waste offences

Waste on land

Landspreading

This is the process of recovering waste by spreading it on land principally for agricultural benefit or ecological improvement. Sewage sludges and wastes from, for example, the food, brewing and paper pulp industries can be used for this purpose.

Waste

Waste offences

Waste on land

Leaching

The physical removal of nutrients in solution by drainage from the soil.

Land pollution

Lead and lead poisoning

Lead is a microconstituent of many foodstuffs, and is normally found in human tissues and fluids. It may enter the body by inhalation of the fume or dust, by ingestion of contaminated food or through pervasion of the unbroken skin in the form of organic compounds such as tetraethyl lead.

Work in many processes may result in lead poisoning, the most common being lead smelting, melting and burning; vitreous enamelling on glass and metal; the glazing of pottery; the manufacture of lead compounds, such as red and white lead and lead colours; painting; plumbing and soldering activities.

When absorbed, lead rapidly becomes widely distributed and stored in the body. When absorption is slow and continuous over a long period, this storage factor is significant. Lead is a cumulative poison which, in cases of chronic absorption, is deposited in the calcareous portion of the bones as an insoluble and harmless triple phosphate. In certain cases, lead may be released from the bones into the bloodstream, producing symptoms of an acute poisoning.

Lead poisoning occurs through two distinct forms, namely by inorganic lead, and by organic lead, mainly tetraethyl lead and tetramethyl lead. In acute cases, usually arising from exposure to fume, the initial symptoms are a sweetish taste in the mouth – especially when smoking, with anorexia, vomiting and headache, sometimes persistent constipation and intermittent colic. Acute poisoning is often fatal. In severe cases, the effect on the central nervous system is startling with restlessness, compulsive talking, excitement and muscular twitching accompanied by insomnia, delusions, hallucinations and even acute and violent mania.

In more chronic cases, the classical symptoms and signs are headache, pallor, a blue line around the gums, anaemia, palsy (drop wrist), encephalopathy – a form of mental disorder characterised by mental dullness, inability to concentrate, faulty memory, tremors, deafness, convulsions and coma.

The great majority of lead poisoning cases are, in fact, associated with inhalation of fumes containing lead due to heating the metal, for various purposes, above a temperature of 500°C.

Processes involving lead and lead products at work are covered by the Control of Lead at Work Regulations 2002.

Lead pollution

Lead pollution

Lead is one of the oldest known metals going back to Roman times. It is used in batteries, alloys, plastics and, for many years, was a constituent of household and industrial paints. Lead used to be added to petrol to enhance its performance. As a result, vehicles emitted harmful lead compounds in their exhaust gases. This form of pollution has reduced dramatically since the introduction of unleaded petrol.

Lead pollution is also associated with industrial lead processes, such as lead mining, smelting of the ore, the purification of lead, with the burning of fossil fuels as part of these processes. These processes have contributed significantly to the release of lead to the environment over the last 150 years. The production of lead and processes involving the use of lead are now the main sources of emissions.

Heavy metal pollution

Legionnaires' disease

Legionellosis or legionnaires' disease is caused by the inhalation of aerosols containing a specific bacterium, *Legionella pneumophila*. Legionella bacteria are widely distributed in the environment and occur in at least ten different forms. They are commonly encountered in water cooling systems, rivers, streams, ponds, lakes and in soil. Most reported cases occur in the 40 to 70 years age group.

Initial symptoms of the disease include high fever, chills, headache and muscle pains. The incubation period may vary from 2 to 10 days, but commonly 3 to 6 days. After a short period, a dry cough develops and most patients suffer difficulty with breathing. About one third of patients also develop diarrhoea or vomiting and 50% may become confused or delirious. The disease may not always be severe and mild cases may escape detection at the diagnosis stage.

Conditions that affect the proliferation of Legionella bacteria include:

(a) the presence of sludge, scale, rust, algae and organic particulates which are thought to provide nutrients for growth; and

(b) water temperatures in the range 20°C to 45°C which favours growth.

Legionella is frequently found in many recirculating and hot water systems, particularly large complex systems, such as those incorporated in multi-storey office blocks, factories and hospitals. Particular sites for bacterial growth are air conditioning systems, cooling towers, water standing in ductwork and condensate trays, humidifiers, hot and cold water storage tanks, calorifiers, pipework and plant.

Water in these systems should be sampled on a regular basis and the systems subject to regular disinfection.

Cooling towers and evaporative condensers

Licensed site (waste management facility)

A waste disposal or recovery facility licensed under the Environmental Protection Act.

Waste management facility (licensed site)

Life cycle

A system of inputs, outputs, transfers and processes spanning raw material extraction, material processing, manufacture, distribution, use and end-of-life management for any item. A life cycle can be described for any product or service.

End-of-life vehicles (ELVs)

Life Cycle Analysis (Assessment) (LCA)

Life Cycle Analysis (Assessment) (LCA)

A systematic technique for identifying and evaluating the potential environmental benefits and impacts, e.g. use of resources, human health, ecological consequences, associated with a product or function throughout its entire life from extraction of raw materials to its eventual disposal and assimilation into the environment.

LCA helps to place the assessment of the environmental costs and benefits of these various options, and the development of appropriate and practical waste management policies, on a sound and objective basis.

Light pollution

Light pollution from sources such as security lights, fluorescent signs, gardens and local office blocks can be a source of nuisance for many people. This form of obtrusive light can result in stress to individuals as a result of the lack of, or interrupted, sleep.

The Clean Neighbourhoods and Environment Act 2005 amended the EPA to bring artificial light from premises under the statutory nuisance regime. Local authorities have a duty to investigate complaints of light pollution and must take action where they consider light to be a statutory nuisance, such as the service of an Abatement Notice on the person responsible for the light nuisance or, in certain cases, the owner of the premises involved.

In the case of domestic premises, failure to comply with an Abatement Notice without reasonable cause may result in a fine of up to £5000 with a further fine of up to £500 for each day on which the offence continues after conviction. Where the nuisance exists on industrial or commercial premises, the maximum fine is £20,000.

Clean Neighbourhoods and Environment Act 2005

Environmental Protection Act 1990

Statutory nuisances

Listed substances

These are substances listed in paragraph 12 of Schedule 1 to the Pollution Prevention and Control (England and Wales) Regulations. References to, or the release into the air of, a substance listed in this paragraph are to any of the following substances:

- oxides of sulphur and other sulphur compounds
- oxides of nitrogen and other nitrogen compounds
- oxides of carbon
- organic compounds and partial oxidation products
- metals, metalloids and their compounds
- asbestos (suspended particulate matter and fibres), glass fibres and mineral fibres
- halogens and their compounds
- phosphorus and its compounds
- particulate matter

References to, or the release into water, of a substance listed in this paragraph or to its release in a quantity which, in any period of 12 months, is greater than the background quantity by an amount specified in this paragraph are to the following substances and amounts:

Substance	*Amount greater than the background quantity (in grammes) in any period of 12 months*
Mercury and its compounds	200 (expressed as metal)
Cadmium and its compounds	1,000 (expressed as metal)
All isomers of hexachlorocyclohexane	20
All isomers of DDT	5
Pentachlorphenol and its compounds	350 (expressed as PCP)
Hexachlorobenzene	5
Hexachlorobutadiene	20
Aldrin	2
Dieldrin	2
Endrin	1

Substance	*Amount greater than the background quantity (in grammes) in any period of 12 months*
Polychlorinated Biphenyls	1
Dichlorvos	0.2
1,2 – Dichloroethane	2,000
All isomers of trichlorobenzene	75
Atrazine	350*
Simazine	350*
Tributyltin compounds	4 (expressed as TBT)
Triphenyltin compounds	4 (expressed as TBT)
Trifluralin	20
Fenitrothion	2
Azinphos-methyl	2
Malathion	2
Endosulfan	0.5

Figure 7: LISTED SUBSTANCES

* Where both Altrazine and Simazine are released, the figure for both substances in aggregate is 350 grammes.

References to a substance listed in this paragraph are to any of the following substances:

- alkali metals and their oxides and alkaline Earth metals and their oxides
- organic solvents
- azides
- halogens and their covalent compounds
- metal carbonyls
- organo-metallic compounds
- oxidising agents
- polychlorinated dibenzofuran and any congener thereof
- polychlorinated dibenzo-p-dioxin and any congener thereof
- polyhalogenated biphenyls, terpehenyls and naphthalenes
- phosphorus
- pesticides

[Part 2: Pollution Prevention and Control (England and Wales) Regulations 2000]

Airborne particulates

Asbestos

Asbestos: activities involving

Carbon activities

Carbon monoxide

Chlorine

Dioxins

Dyestuffs, printing ink and coating materials

Environmental pollution

Exempt activity

Ferrous metals

Fluorides

Fluorocarbon

Inorganic chemical production

Isocyanates

Nitrogen fixation

Nitrogen oxides

Non-ferrous metals

Organic solvents

Other mineral activities

Pesticide

Pollution: definition

Pollution Prevention and Control Act 1999

Pollution Prevention and Control (England and Wales) Regulations 2000

Polychlorinated biphenyls (PCBs) and other dangerous substances

Phthalates

Relevant activities

Rubber: activities involving

Scheduled activities

Solvent emissions

Tar and bitumen activities

Timber activities

Litter

The term *litter* can relate to anything other than natural matter, such as fallen leaves, but which is on the ground sooner than in, for example, a waste receptacle or litter bin.

Section 87 of the EPA provides for the offence of "leaving litter" thus.

If any person throws down, drops or otherwise deposits in, into or from any place and leaves anything whosoever in such circumstances as to cause, or to contribute to, or to tend to lead to, the defacement by litter of any place to which this Section applies, he shall be guilty of an offence.

This Section applies to any public open place and, in so far as the place is not a public open place, also to the following places:

(a) any relevant highway or relevant road and any trunk road which is a special road;

(b) any place on relevant land of a principal Litter Authority;

(c) any place on relevant Crown land;

(d) any place on relevant land of any designated statutory undertaker;

(e) any place on relevant land of any designated educational institution; and

(f) any place on relevant land within a Litter Control Area of a local authority.

Section 88 brought in Fixed Penalty Notices for persons leaving litter.

Section 99 also gives local authorities the power to deal with abandoned shopping and luggage trolleys.

[Environmental Protection Act 1990]

Environmental Protection Act 1990

Litter Authorities

Litter Control Area

Litter Control Notice

Shopping and luggage trolleys

Litter Abatement Notice

Under Section 92 of the EPA, the principal Litter Authority is permitted to serve a Litter Abatement Notice upon a site which is defaced by litter or refuse, or where there is a possibility of such defacement recurring. The Notice may incorporate time limits for the improvement of the site.

The Notice must be served on the occupier of the land or, when the land is unoccupied, on the owner. Such a person on whom a Notice is served may appeal to the Magistrates' Court.

Failure to comply with a Litter Abatement Notice is an offence and any person may be liable to a fine not exceeding level 4 on the standard scale, and for one twentieth of this amount for every day the offence continues. A Litter Authority may undertake the work in default and recover the costs from the responsible person.

[Environmental Protection Act 1990]

Environmental Protection Act 1990

Litter

Litter Authorities

Litter Control Area

Litter Control Notice

Litter Authorities

The control of litter rests with the principal Litter Authorities namely, in England and Wales:

(a) a county council;

(b) a district council;

(c) a London borough council;

(d) the Common Council of the City of London; and

(e) the Council of the Isles of Scilly.

[Environmental Protection Act 1990]

Environmental Protection Act 1990

Litter

Litter Abatement Notice

Litter Control Area

Litter Control Notice

Litter Fixed Penalty Notice

Litter Control Area

The Litter Control Areas Order 1991 enables the Litter Control Authorities to designate certain land as Litter Control Areas if the presence of litter is detrimental to the amenities of the locality. Typical areas of land classed as Litter Control Areas include public car parks, industrial estates, inland beaches or seashores and shopping centres.

Land may also be designated by reference to its ownership or the activities carried out upon it.

[Environmental Protection Act 1990 and Litter Control Areas Order 1991]

Litter

Litter Abatement Notice

Litter Control Notice

Litter Fixed Penalty Notice

Litter Control Notice

Under Sections 93 and 94 of the EPA, the Litter Authority may issue a Street Litter Control Notice with the aim of preventing accumulations of litter or refuse in any street or open land.

Such a Notice could be served on the occupier of the premises associated with the street litter problems where:

(a) there is recurrent defacement by litter or refuse on any land, being part of the street or open land adjacent to the street, which is in the vicinity of the premises; or

(b) the condition of any part of the premises which is open land in the vicinity of the frontage and is detrimental to the amenities of the locality because of the litter or refuse; or

(c) the premises produces types and quantities of litter or refuse which is likely to cause the defacement of any part of the street.

A Litter Control Notice will specify requirements relating to the clearance of the litter or refuse from a specified area. Failure to comply with a Notice is an offence punishable by a fine not exceeding level 4 on the standard scale.

[Environmental Protection Act 1990]

Litter

Litter Abatement Notice

Litter Authorities

Litter Fixed Penalty Notice

Litter Fixed Penalty Notice

Where on any occasion an authorised officer of a Litter Authority finds a person who he has reason to believe has on that occasion committed an offence under Section 87 of the EPA (offence of leaving litter) in the area of that Authority, he may give that person a Notice offering him the opportunity of discharging any liability to conviction for that offence by payment of a fixed penalty.

[Environmental Protection Act 1990]

Litter

Local Air Pollution Control (LAPC)

This regulatory regime under the EPA was replaced by Pollution Prevention and Control (PPC) under the Pollution Prevention and Control (England and Wales) Regulations 2000.

Pollution Prevention and Control Act 1999

Pollution Prevention and Control (England and Wales) Regulations 2000

Pollution Prevention and Control (PPC)

Local exhaust ventilation (LEV) systems

In a process producing airborne particulates, a local exhaust ventilation system should remove the airborne contaminant at the point of, or close to, the site of production and before the contaminant can be inhaled. LEV systems may be fixed, as with, for instance, a laboratory fume cupboard, or portable, as in the case of a welding fume extraction unit. LEV systems largely take the form of receptor systems and captor systems.

Receptor systems and captor systems

Current HSE Guidance is provided in booklet HS(G)37 '*An Introduction to Local Exhaust Ventilation*' which draws the distinction between *receptor* systems and *captor* systems.

With a *receptor system*, which may take the form of a total enclosure, eg a laboratory fume cupboard, partial enclosure eg a welding booth, or receptor hood eg the canopy above a plating tank, the contaminant enters the system with inducement. Fundamentally, the contaminant is produced within the confines of the system and a fan is used to provide the necessary air flow, along with thermal currents, taking the contaminant through a system of ducting to a collection system. In many cases, the collection unit incorporates a filtration device.

In the case of *captor systems*, the contaminant is produced outside the confines of the system. Moving air entrains the contaminant at some point outside the capture hood and induces flow into the hood. On this basis, the rate of air flow into the hood must be great enough to capture the contaminant at the furthest point of origin.

Design factors for LEV systems

In most cases LEV systems incorporate the following features:

(a) a hood, enclosure or other inlet to collect and contain the contaminant close to the source of its generation or point of emission;

(b) ductwork to convey the contaminant away from the source;

(c) a filter or other cleaning device to remove the contaminant from the extracted airstream; (Note – The filter should normally be located between the hood and the fan);

(d) a fan or other air-moving device to provide the necessary airflow; and

(e) further ductwork to discharge the cleaned air to the outside atmosphere at a suitable point.

In particular, the design capture velocity should be appropriate to the aerosol contaminant in terms of particle size and weight.

Examination and testing

Regulation 9 of the COSHH Regulations stipulates that employers must ensure that all physical control measures provided to prevent or control exposure to substances hazardous to health are maintained in an efficient state, in efficient working order and in good repair. This implies the operation of a system of visual checks, inspection, testing and servicing of LEV systems. Manufacturers and suppliers of LEV systems must specify the means of testing and examination.

Where engineering controls are provided, the employer must ensure that thorough examination and tests of those engineering controls are carried out:

(a) in the case of LEV plant, at least once every 14 months; and

(b) in any other case, at suitable intervals.

In addition to the general duty to ensure effective preventive maintenance, there are specific requirements on employers to undertake formal examination and testing of LEV systems in certain industries, e.g. ceramics.

For effective examination and testing, it is helpful to have available comprehensive information on the system and the design specification. This information should have been provided at the commissioning stage of the LEV system. Employers must keep records of examination and testing of LEV systems, which must be kept available for inspection by employees, Employment Medical Advisers and inspectors of the relevant enforcing authority.

M

Maintenance requirements

Apart from the absolute duty on employers under the COSHH Regulations to maintain engineering controls, there is a similar duty on employers under the Provision and Use of Work Equipment Regulations 1998 to maintain any item of work equipment (including an LEV system) in an efficient state, in efficient working order and in good repair. By implication, all such systems should be incorporated in a formal planned preventive maintenance system.

Airborne particulates

Comfort ventilation

Control of Substances Hazardous to Health (COSHH) Regulations 2006

Hazardous substances: classification

Manures and slurries

As a result of recent case law, manures and slurries are not classed as waste when used as a fertiliser on agricultural premises, including those premises that did not produce same.

The Code of Good Agricultural Practice for the Protection of Water recommends that allowance should be made with respect to available nitrogen, total phosphate and total potash in manures and slurries when assessing fertiliser requirements. Manures and slurries should not be spread:

(a) within 10 metres of a ditch or watercourse;

(b) within 50 metres of a spring, well or borehole;

(c) when the land is frozen hard or snow covered; or

(d) when the land is waterlogged.

Groundwater Regulations 1998

Waste

Waste Management (England and Wales) Regulations 2006

Market instrument

A mechanism, other than a straightforward tax, by which government adjusts a market so that environmentally-desirable behaviour has lower costs associated with it.

Integrated Product Policy

Market transformation

Market transformation

This involves creating a situation whereby producers place less environmentally-damaging products on the market and consumers have sufficient information and incentives to reward them with their custom. For market transformation to be successful, both buyers and sellers may need to change their attitudes and differentiate their products from their competitors in new ways.

Integrated Product Policy

Market instrument

Mobile plant

Plant which is designed to move or to be moved whether on roads or otherwise and which is used to carry out one or more activities listed in Part 1 or Schedule 1.

[Pollution Prevention and Control (England and Wales) Regulations 2000]

Mobile radioactive source

This includes apparatus, equipment, appliances or other things that are radioactive material and that are either:

(a) constructed or adapted for being transported from place to place; or

(b) portable and used for releasing radioactive material into the environment or introducing it into organisms.

[High Activity Sealed Radioactive Sources and Orphan Sources Regulations 2005]

High activity sealed radioactive sources and orphan sources

Open radioactive sources

Radiation

Sealed radioactive sources

Montreal Protocol

An international agreement that set down timetables for the phasing out of the production and use of chlorofluorocarbons (CFCs) in order to slow down the destruction of ozone in the stratosphere resulting from the breakdown of these chemicals. Originally formulated in 1987, the agreement was later revised to accelerate the elimination of CFCs and to include other ozone-depleting products.

Chlorofluorocarbons (CFCs)

Ozone

Ozone depletion

Ozone-depleting substances

Ozone layer

Motor vehicle pollution

Emissions of, for example, benzene and carbon monoxide, from vehicles are a major source of air pollution. Vehicle emissions have further been associated with other pollutants, such as 1.3 butadiene, which has been linked to an increased risk of leukaemia or lymphoma.

Pollution from vehicles is regulated by:

(a) the Road Traffic Act 1988;

(b) various Regulations, such as the Motor Vehicles (Construction and Use) Regulations; and

(c) EC Directives on vehicle emissions.

Carbon monoxide

Emission

Mutagenic

Hazardous substances: classification

N

National air quality objectives

These are quality objectives for air pollution and comprise concentrations of pollutants, such as carbon monoxide, lead, nitrogen dioxide, ozone and sulphur dioxide, over a given period of time that are considered to be acceptable in the light of current knowledge about the effects of each pollutant on health and the environment.

Air

Air pollution

Air Quality Management Area

Air Quality Standard

Emission limit value

Environmental pollution

Greenhouse gases

Lead pollution

Nitrogen oxides

Ozone

Ozone depletion

Smoke

National Nature Reserves

These sites protect some of the best examples of habitat and geological formations in the UK. They are of national and often international importance. They are mainly managed by government conservation bodies but also by non-governmental organisations, such as the Royal Society for the Protection of Birds, Wildlife Trusts and the National Trust.

Conservation

Conservation Area

Habitat

National Parks

Special Areas of Conservation

Special Protection Areas

Wildlife

National Parks

These are sites chosen for their scenery as well as their wildlife. Their principal function is to conserve and enhance the landscape, buildings, plants and animals. Each National Park is managed by its own authority.

Environment Act 1995

Habitat

Special Areas of Conservation

Special Protection Areas

Wildlife

National Rivers Authority

The NRA is the main regulatory body with responsibility for controlling water pollution, although it shares responsibilities with HMIP in relation to those industrial processes that are governed by Integrated Pollution Control Regimes of the EPA. The constitution, functions and powers of the NRA are prescribed in the Water Resources Act 1991.

Water Resources Act 1991

National water classification system

Water Resources Act 1991

Natural environment

The natural environment comprises all living and non-living organisms, including human beings, that occur naturally on Earth. Many natural environments arise from the interaction between nature and human beings. The term *ecosystem* is used to describe an environment that incorporates nature, including people.

Ecosystems

Habitat

Natural Environment and Rural Communities Act 2006

This statute, among other measures, created a new integrated agency, *Natural England*, to act as a powerful champion for the natural environment, and established a *Commission for Rural Communities*, a national rural adviser, advocate and watchdog, charged with ensuring that government policies are making a real difference on the ground in tackling rural disadvantage.

The Act was designed to help achieve a rich and diverse natural environment and thriving rural communities through modernised and simplified arrangements for delivering government policy.

The objective of *Natural England* was to unite in a single organisation the responsibility for enhancing biodiversity and landscape in rural, urban and coastal areas with promoting access and recreation.

The *Commission for Rural Communities* has the task of ensuring that government policies make a real and tangible difference to people in rural areas, especially in tackling social and economic exclusion and disadvantage.

Biodiversity

Natural habitats

The Conservation (Natural Habitats, etc) Regulations 1994 (as amended) implemented the Council Directive 92/43/EEC on the conservation of natural habitats and of wild fauna and flora (the EC Habitats Directive) into national law. The Regulations provide for the designation and protection of *European sites*, the protection of *European protected species* and the adaptation of planning and other controls for the protection of European sites.

Under the Regulations, competent authorities, e.g. government departments, public bodies or persons holding public office, have a general duty in the exercise of their functions to have regard to the EC Habitats Directive.

The Regulations are concerned with three main aspects:

(a) conservation of natural habitats and habitats of species;

(b) protection of species; and

(c) adaptation of planning and other controls.

Habitat

Nature Conservancy Council

Nature conservation

Wildlife

Natural resources

These are naturally occurring substances classed as valuable in their natural or untreated form, such as fish, forestry, fossil fuels and oils. They can be classified as renewable and non-renewable sources.

Renewable resources take the form of living resources, such as animals, fish, forests and plants, which can renew themselves over a period of time if not threatened by over-harvesting of these resources. The rate of sustainable use of a renewable resource is determined by the replacement rate and the amount of standing stock of that resource.

Non-renewable resources are those resources which, once utilised, cannot be replaced, such as fossil fuels, natural gas and minerals.

Biodiversity

Nature Conservancy Council

This was established by the Nature Conservancy Council Act 1973. It was a former British government agency responsible for designating and managing national nature reserves and other such conservation areas.

Following the introduction of the Environmental Protection Act, the Nature Conservancy Council was regionalised by division into English Nature, Scottish National Heritage and the Countryside Council for Wales.

Nature conservation

Nature conservation

Nature conservation is the means for the protection of living species, habitats, geology and landforms and is organised through designated conservation sites. Certain rare or threatened species, such as bats, badgers, otters, water voles, greater crested newts and many wild birds, are classed as protected species regardless of where they are encountered.

The government bodies largely responsible for species and habitat conservation in the UK are:

(a) Natural England;

(b) Environmental and Heritage Service (Natural Heritage) in Northern Ireland;

(c) Scottish Natural Heritage; and

(d) Countryside Council for Wales.

These organisations are responsible for promoting nature conservation and for protecting and encouraging biodiversity.

Regulators:

(a) have a duty to conserve and enhance the natural environment;

(b) must consider the effects on species or habitats of any proposed work they undertake, for example, flood defence and land management;

(c) must consider the potential effects on species or habitats when considering any consent, licence or permit application, for example, water discharge or abstraction consents;

(d) must consult with the government's conservation bodies where their interests overlap, particularly when a proposal or application would affect Sites of Special and Scientific Interest, Areas of Special Specific Interest or European Natura nature conservation sites.

It is an offence to disturb or harm:

(a) protected species, or any structure that they use as shelter, unless holding a licence for this sort of activity;

(b) all wild birds, their nests and their eggs;

(c) all species of bats and their roosts.

It is further an offence to:

(a) capture, kill or disturb any animal or bird species, including taking or destroying eggs and damaging or disturbing breeding sites or resting places;

(b) pick, collect, cut, uproot or destroy any plant species; and

(c) keep, transport, sell, exchange or advertise for sale protected species of plants and animals.

Biodiversity

Conservation

Conservation Area

Conservation sites

Habitats

National Nature Reserves

National Parks

Nature Conservancy Council

Regulator

Special Areas of Conservation

Special Protection Areas

Negligence

"Negligence" is defined as "careless conduct injuring another".

In torts, negligence can mean:

(a) a state of mind in which a particular tort may be committed;

(b) an independent tort in which the claimant must prove the following:

  (i) the existence of a duty of care owed by the defendant to the claimant;

  (ii) breach of that duty; and

  (iii) damage, loss or injury resulting from or caused by that breach.

(Lochgelly Iron & Coal Co.Ltd. v M'Mullan [1934] AC1)

These three facts must be established by a claimant before he is entitled to bring a claim for damages though, in the case of breach of statutory duty, he merely has to show that the breach of that statutory duty was the material cause of his injury. It is essential that the breach of duty caused the injury or occupational disease. (Causation) Breach of duty need not be the exclusive cause, but it must be a substantial one, i.e. materially contribute to the injury or ill-health condition.

The legal process involving the tort of negligence is for a claimant to sue a defendant for damages. If the suit is successful, the claimant would be awarded such damages.

Breach of a statutory duty of care

Tort

Neighbour noise

Very few people are in a position to vet their neighbours when it comes to moving house, but the problem may rapidly become apparent after they have moved in. Noisy neighbours can be a curse, disturbing sleep and the normal enjoyment of home life. Over the last decade local authorities have experienced a rapid increase in complaints from residents in respect of excessive noise from a wide range of equipment, in particular stereo equipment, played late into the night.

The Noise Act 1996 was introduced to deal with this problem and gives significant powers to local authorities in dealing with these classic causes of noise.

Noise Abatement Zone

Noise Act 1996

Noise and Statutory Nuisances Act 1993

Noise nuisance

Statutory nuisances

Nitrate Sensitive Area

Where there may be a need to prevent or control the entry of nitrates into controlled waters as a result of, or in connection with, the use of land for agricultural purposes, that land may be designated a Nitrate Sensitive Area. Payments may be made to the landowner for securing the management of the land under an agreement.

In addition to the agreement, the designation may restrict specific agricultural activities and provide for payments to be made in return for the obligations imposed.

Controlled waters

Nitrate Vulnerable Zone

Nitrate Vulnerable Zone

This conservation designation is used by the Environment Agency to indicate areas of land that drain into nitrate polluted waters or waters which would become polluted by nitrates. They are areas of land identified as exceeding, or being at risk of exceeding, 50mg/NO_3/l of drinking water, the standard set by EU for nitrate in drinking water.

These Zones are subject to requirements on fertiliser application including:

(a) not applying fertiliser at certain times of the year, for example during the winter, when run off is greatest and uptake by plants at a minimum;

(b) reducing the amount of fertiliser used; and

(c) changing the times when animal waste is applied to the land.

Farmers are required to adhere to these restrictions and can be prosecuted for breaches of the restrictions.

Nitrate Sensitive Area

Nitrogen fixation

The conversion of atmospheric nitrogen to plant compounds by micro-organisms.

Nitrogen oxides

Nitrogen oxides include nitrogen dioxide, nitrous oxide and nitric oxide. Natural sources of nitrogen oxides include volcanoes and biological decay. They are further produced in the combustion of fossil fuels. Major sources of nitrogen oxides are road transport, power stations and industrial processes, particularly iron and steel processes.

Fossil fuels

Inorganic chemical production

Nitrogen fixation

Noise Abatement Notices

Where an environmental health office is satisfied that a statutory noise nuisance exists, or is likely to occur, then a Noise Abatement Notice must be served on the person responsible for the noise nuisance. This is the person by whose act, default or at whose sufferance the noise is attributable. Where the noise is emitted from a vehicle, the Notice must be served on the owner and driver. Where the noise comes from machinery or equipment, then it should be served on the person who is, for the time being, the operator.

Defences

The defences available are:

(a) Reasonable excuse

It will be a defence if the defendant can prove that there was a reasonable excuse for non-compliance. A birthday party or celebration will not constitute a reasonable excuse.

(b) Best practicable means

Where a noise nuisance has been alleged in relation to noise from a vehicle, machinery or equipment, then it is a defence to show that best practicable means were used to prevent or control the noise. The defence is only available where the machinery or equipment is used for industrial, trade or business purposes.

Noise Abatement Zone

Noise Act 1996

Noise and Statutory Nuisances Act 1993

Statutory nuisances

Noise Abatement Zone

A local authority may designate by order all or any part of its area as a Noise Abatement Zone in which specified classes of premises may not emit noise exceeding permitted sound pressure levels, except with the authority's consent.

A noise register recording the levels of noise permitted for each premises must be maintained by the local authority and made available for public inspection.

Environmental Protection Act 1990

Noise Abatement Notices

Noise Act 1996

Noise and Statutory Nuisances Act 1993

Noise Act 1996

This statute gives considerable powers to local authorities to take action in respect of noise nuisance.

Enforcement procedures

Section 2 fundamentally reiterates Section 79 of the EPA, placing a duty on local authority officers to investigate complaints made by persons present in dwelling houses during 'night hours', namely 11pm to 7am.

Some local authorities have established night time 'noise patrols' with a view to dealing with complaints quickly and efficiently. In such cases, where an investigating officer is satisfied that noise being emitted from a dwelling ('an offending dwelling') during night hours might, and if measured from inside the complainant's dwelling, exceed the permitted noise level, he is empowered to serve a Warning Notice on the offender. He need not necessarily measure the noise in this case. This Section also incorporates 'cross-border' powers, enabling investigating officers to apply powers in areas outside their own boundary, and similar to the powers in respect of statutory nuisances.

Warning Notices

The content of the Warning Notice is specified in Section 3. Its purpose is to warn any responsible person for the excessive noise emitted from the dwelling that he may be guilty of an offence if the noise continues. In this case, the investigating officer is free to state the actual time when the Notice will come into effect, subject to a minimum delay of 10 minutes.

Warning Notices must be served either by personal delivery to any person present at or near the offending dwelling and appearing to be a person to whose act, default or sufferance the noise emission is at least in part attributable or, where it is not practicable to identify anyone fitting this description, by leaving it at the dwelling.

Once the Warning Notice is served, anyone responsible for excessive noise emitted from the offending dwelling during the period specified in the Warning Notice commits a summary offence, for which the maximum fine is defined by level 3, i.e. £1000. In this case the noise must be physically measured using an approved measuring device. A statutory defence of 'reasonable excuse' is available to a person charged with this offence.

Permitted level of noise

Section 5 is concerned with the 'permitted level', namely the maximum level of noise permitted to be emitted from a dwelling during night hours, to be set by a 'direction' from the Secretary of State. Such a direction may specify conditions for measurement and 'permitted noise levels' for different circumstances.

Measuring devices

Section 6 covers the approval system for measuring devices by type. Evidence of measurements submitted in a prosecution is not admissible unless taken using an approved device and in accordance with any conditions to be set with regard to, for instance, the positioning of the device. In most cases, a signed statement as to the approved nature of the device and its use in accordance with any conditions set, would be satisfactory evidence for the purposes of prosecution. Such a statement would generally include a print-out from the device indicating clearly the measurements obtained. (Section 7)

Fixed Penalty Notices

The power of an authorised officer to serve a Fixed Penalty Notice on any person who he has reason to believe is committing, or has just committed, an offence of emitting excessive noise from a dwelling during the period specified in a Warning Notice, is incorporated in Section 8. Furthermore, in serious situations, a Fixed Penalty Notice may be 'given to', and not necessarily served on, a person committing an offence either by delivering it to him or, if it is not reasonably practicable to do so, by leaving the Notice, addressed to the offender, at the offending dwelling. Provided the penalty is paid within 14 days, the offender is not liable to conviction, nor can any information be laid.

Seizure of equipment

Section 10 concerns 'seizure of equipment used to make noise unlawfully'. Thus where excessive noise is emitted from a dwelling during the period specified in a Warning Notice, an authorised officer may enter the dwelling and seize and remove any equipment which it appears is being or has been used in the emission of the noise.

Refusal of entry

Where entry is refused or anticipated, a warrant may be applied for which remains in force as long as necessary. Wilful obstruction can result in a fine of up to £1000.

Seized equipment

Seized equipment must be retained for up to 28 days, unless it was used in the commission of an offence for which proceedings are commenced within that time or, where a Fixed Penalty Notice was given, the penalty is paid. Equipment not claimed after six months may be sold.

In addition, any person convicted of an offence may forfeit his rights in any seized equipment on an Order of the Court. In the case of organisations, such as hirers of equipment, they are protected provided they make a claim to the Court within six months of the Order being made. Where no claim is made, the local authority may dispose of the equipment. Local authorities must take reasonable steps to bring to the notice of persons, who may be entitled to reclaim equipment which has been seized or forfeited, their right to make such a claim.

Personal liability

Authorised officers are protected from personal liability for 'acts done in good faith' .

Neighbour noise

Noise and Statutory Nuisances Act 1993

Noise nuisance

Noise and Statutory Nuisances Act 1993

The provisions of the Environmental Protection Act (EPA) relating to noise nuisance were amended by the Noise and Statutory Nuisances Act 1993 (NSNA). In particular, the NSNA incorporated a new statutory nuisance in the EPA at Section 79(1)(ga).

Section 79(1)(g) and 79(1)(ga) provide that noise can be a statutory nuisance in the following circumstances:

- Section 79(1)(g) – noise emitted from premises so as to be prejudicial to health or a nuisance; and
- Section 79(1)(ga) – noise that is prejudicial to health or a nuisance and is emitted from or caused by a vehicle, machinery or equipment in a street.

The EPA does not provide any particular definition of 'noise' other than that it 'includes vibration'.

Common law principles

Since noise is more likely to interfere, as a nuisance, with enjoyment, rather than cause injury or be injurious to health, interpretation as to what is a statutory noise nuisance is based on common law principles. Thus, when a court is considering whether noise constitutes a nuisance, it may consider various matters including:

(a) the duration and time of the noise;

(b) the nature of the activity;

(c) the harm suffered by the person affected; and

(d) the neighbourhood in which the noise took place.

In practice, the environmental health officer who is making the evaluation, will take the above matters into consideration.

Noise control

In any strategy to reduce or control noise, two factors must be considered, that is:

(a) the actual source or sources of noise, e.g. machinery, ventilation systems; and

(b) the transmission pathway taken by the noise to the recipient.

The design stage

The first consideration must be that of tackling a potential noise hazard at the design stage of new projects, rather than attempting to control noise once the machinery or noise-emitting plant is installed.

Manufacturers, suppliers and importers of machinery and plant must be required to give an indication of anticipated sound pressure levels from their equipment once installed, and of the measures necessary to reduce noise emission, prior to the ordering of the equipment. Ensuring appropriate reduction of noise emission by manufacturers, suppliers and importers of plant and machinery should feature in any contract to supply.

Existing machinery and plant

In this case, a range of methods of noise control are suitable for dealing with identified sources of noise and the stages in the transmission pathway. These methods are summarized in the Table below: *Methods of noise control.*

Sources and pathways	Control measures
Vibration produced through machinery operation components; use of tapered tools on power presses	Reduction at source, e.g. substitution of metal components by nylon
Structure-borne noise (vibration)	Vibration isolation, e.g. use of resilient mounts and connections, anti-vibration mounts
Radiation of structural vibration	Vibration damping to prevent resonance
Turbulence created by air or gas flow	Reduction at source or the use of silencers
Airborne noise pathway	Noise insulation – reflection; use of heavy barriers
	Noise absorption – no reflection; use of porous lightweight barriers

Figure 8: METHODS OF NOISE CONTROL

Control of the main or primary pathway is the most important strategy in noise control and to ensure compliance with noise-related legislation.

Control of Noise at Work Regulations 2005

Noise Act 1996

Noise and Statutory Nuisances Act 1993

Noise in a street which is emitted from a vehicle, machinery or equipment

This particular statutory nuisance was incorporated in the EPA by the NSNA. The amendment was made largely because the EPA did not provide sufficient protection from noise in streets. (A street is defined as 'a highway and any other road, footway, square or court that is for the time being open to the public'.) A great deal of noise is generated in streets not only from vehicles but from people playing loud music, ice cream vans and car alarms. Certain exemptions are provided, however. It does not apply to noise created by traffic, the armed forces or by political demonstrations (or demonstrations supporting or opposing a campaign or cause. 'Traffic' is understood to mean vehicles in motion.

Noise nuisance

Noisy neighbours can be a curse, disturbing sleep and the normal enjoyment of home life. Over the last ten years, local authorities have experienced a great increase in complaints from residents in respect of excessive noise from a wide range of equipment, in particular stereo equipment, played late into the night.

Under the Noise Act 1996, local authorities have extensive powers in dealing with the causes of noise nuisance from dwellings.

Neighbour noise

Noise Act 1996

Noise and Statutory Nuisances Act 1993

Non-ferrous metals

These scheduled activities are:

Part A(1)

(a) Unless falling within Part A(2) of this Section, producing non-ferrous metals from ore, concentrates or secondary raw materials by metallurgical, chemical or electrolytic activities;

(b) Melting, including making alloys of non-ferrous metals, including recovered products (refining, foundry, casting, etc) where:

  (i) the plant has a melting capacity of more than 4 tonnes per day for lead or cadmium or 20 tonnes per day for all other metals; and

  (ii) any furnace, bath or other holding vessel used in the plant for the melting has a design holding capacity of 5 tonnes or more;

(c) Refining any non-ferrous metal or alloy, other than the electrolytic refining of copper, except where the activity is related to an activity described in paragraph (a) of Part A(2), or paragraph (a), (d) or (e) of Part B, of this Section;

(d) Producing, melting or recovering by chemical means or by the use of heat, lead or any lead alloy, if:

   (i) the activity may result in the release into the air of lead; and

   (ii) in the case of lead alloy, the percentage by weight of lead in alloy in molten form is more than 23 per cent if the alloy contains copper and 2 per cent in other cases;

(e) Recovering of any of the following elements if the activity may result in their release into the air: gallium, indium, palladium, tellurium, thallium;

(f) Producing, melting or recovering (whether by chemical means or by electrolysis or by the use of heat) cadmium or mercury or any alloy containing more than 0.05 per cent by weight of either of those metals or, in aggregate, of both;

(g) Mining zinc or tin bearing ores where the activity may result in the release into water of cadmium or any compound of cadmium in a concentration which is greater than the background concentration;

(h) Manufacturing or repairing involving the use of beryllium or selenium or an alloy containing one or both of those metals if the activity may result in the release into the air of any substances listed in paragraph 12 of Part 2 to this Schedule; but an activity does not fall within this paragraph by reason of it involving an alloy that contains beryllium if that alloy in molten form contains less than 0.1 per cent by weight of beryllium and the activity falls within paragraph (a) or (d) of Part B of this Section;

(i) Pelletising, calcining, roasting or sintering any non-ferrous metal ore or any mixture of such ore and other materials.

In paragraph (g), *background concentration* means any concentration of cadmium or any compound of cadmium which would be present in the release irrespective of any effect the activity may have had on the composition of the release and, without prejudice to the generality of the foregoing, includes such concentration of those substances as is present in:

(i) water supplied to the site where the activity is carried out;

(ii) water abstracted for use in the activity; and

(iii) precipitation onto the site on which the activity is carried out.

Part A(2)

(a) Melting, including making alloys, of non-ferrous metals, including recovered products (refining, foundry casting, etc) where:

(i) the plant has a melting capacity of more than 4 tonnes per day for lead or cadmium or 20 tonnes per day for all other metals; and

(ii) no furnace, bath or other holding vessel used in the plant for the melting has a design holding capacity of 5 tonnes or more.

Part B

(a) Melting, including making alloys, of non-ferrous metals (other than tin or any alloy which in molten form contains 50 per cent or more by weight of tin), including recovered products (refining, foundry casting, etc) in plant with a melting capacity of 4 tonnes or less per day for lead or cadmium or 20 tonnes or less per day for all other metals;

(b) The heating in a furnace or any other appliance of any non-ferrous metal alloy for the purpose of removing grease, oil or any other non-metallic contaminant, including such operations as the removal by heat of plastic or rubber covering from scrap cable, if not related to another activity described in this Part of this Section; but an activity does not fall within this paragraph if:

(i) it involves the use of one or more furnaces or other appliances, the primary combustion chambers of which have in aggregate a net rated thermal input of less than 0.2 megawatts; and

(ii) it does not involve the removal by heat of plastic or rubber covering from scrap cable or of any asbestos contaminant;

(c) Melting zinc or zinc alloy in conjunction with a galvanising activity at a rate of 20 tonnes or less per day;

(d) Melting zinc, aluminium or magnesium or an alloy of any one or more of these metals in conjunction with a die-casting activity at a rate of 20 tonnes or less per day;

(e) Unless falling within Part A(1) or A(2) of this Section, the separation of copper, aluminium, magnesium or zinc from mixed scrap by differential melting.

Net rated thermal input is the rate at which fuel can be burned at the maximum continuous rating of the appliance multiplied by the net calorific value of the fuel and expressed as megawatts thermal.

[Schedule 1: Part 1: Pollution Prevention and Control (England and Wales) Regulations 2000]

Ferrous metals

Global warming

Lead and lead poisoning

Lead pollution

Part A activities

Part B activities

Pollution Prevention and Control Act 1999

Pollution Prevention and Control (England and Wales) Regulations 2000

Scheduled activities

Non-renewable fuels

These are non-renewable sources of energy, namely coal, oil, natural gas and nuclear energy.

Coal is a fossil fuel formed from the decomposed remains of trees and other vegetation that were growing over 300 million years ago. It is essentially carbon and when burned, produces carbon dioxide, a colourless, odourless gas, one of the gases capable of trapping the Earth's heat and thereby contributing to global warming.

Oil, as with other fossil fuels, was formed from the remains of animals and vegetation that existed many million years ago in a marine environment. As a result of heat and pressure applied by layers of mud, these remains were eventually converted to crude oil which needs to be refined prior to use as a petroleum product, such as petrol, propane and heating oil. When oil is burned it produces air emissions of carbon dioxide, sulphur dioxide and various oxides of nitrogen. These pollutants contributed to smog, acid rain and global warming.

Natural gas is a combustible mixture of hydrocarbons, mostly methane, that is produced from wells drilled into underground reservoirs of porous rock. It is a "clean" fossil fuel, formed by the below ground decomposition of a wide range of matter, such as dead plants and animals. Natural gas is found in a variety of underground formations, such as shale formations and coal seams.

The by-products of the burning of natural gas in the generation of electricity include carbon dioxide and nitrogen oxides, together with some pollutants which contribute to acid rain, water pollution and global warming.

Nuclear fuel is a fuel derived from a source of heat, namely uranium, which has been mined and processed before it is suitable as a fuel. The process that produces the heat in a nuclear plant is the splitting of uranium atoms. The electricity generated from this heat is transmitted via lines to clients. The generation of nuclear energy produces nuclear wastes and hot water.

Acid rain

Fossil fuels

Global warming

Nitrogen oxides

Nuclear energy

Nuclear waste

Sulphur oxides

Nuclear energy

The production of nuclear energy entails the splitting of uranium atoms in a nuclear plant which produces heat. The heat generated boils water producing steam, which is used to drive turbine generators, thereby producing electricity.

Nuclear energy is released by two main processes:

(a) radioactive decay, where a radioactive nucleus decays spontaneously into a lighter nucleus by emitting a particle; and

(b) endothermic nuclear reactions where two nuclei merge to produce two different nuclei.

Nuclear energy generated electricity is a "clean" fuel in that it does not emit carbon dioxide or other forms of air pollution.

Non-renewable fuels

Nuclear waste

Radiation

Radioactive substances and wastes

Nuclear waste

The process of generating nuclear energy in a nuclear plant results in the production of radioactive waste. As such, this is the principal environmental concern with the use of nuclear energy as a source of fuel. Whilst most nuclear radioactive wastes are a relatively low-level nuclear waste, the irradiated fuel assemblies are highly radioactive and need to be stored in specially designed pools. Here, water cools the fuel acting as a radiation shield. In other cases, it may be stored in dry storage containers.

Non-renewable fuels

Nuclear energy

Nuisance

The law of nuisance is very much associated with the evolution of public health law which goes back to the Public Health Act 1848 and subsequent legislation. This Act required local Boards of Health to appoint "fit and proper persons" to be "inspectors of nuisances". (Inspectors of nuisances became "sanitary inspectors", then "public health inspectors" and, more recently, "environmental health officers".) However, this early legislation was more concerned with the concept of a nuisance as something creating discomfort or inconvenience to people, rather than its later association with the causes of epidemic disease. Subsequent legislation, the Public Health Acts 1936 and 1961 and, more recently, the Environmental Protection Act (EPA) 1990 have extended the whole concept of "statutory nuisances".

It is appropriate to distinguish, however, between the common law concept of the tort of nuisance and statutory nuisances. On this basis, the law of nuisance can be separated into two specific areas, namely nuisances at common law and statutory nuisances, the latter being defined in Part III of the EPA.

Environment Act 1995

Neighbour noise

Noise Act 1996

Noise and Statutory Nuisances Act 1993

Noise control

Noise nuisance

Nuisance at common law

Statutory nuisances

Tort

Nuisance at common law

This term has been defined in a number of ways over the last century, thus:

> "a common law nuisance is one which apart from statute, violates the principles which the common law lays down for the protection of the public and individuals in the exercise and enjoyment of their rights";
>
> "an act not warranted by law, or an omission to discharge a legal duty, which act or omission obstructs or causes inconvenience or damage to the public in the exercise of rights common to all Her Majesty's subjects".

A common law nuisance may also be a public or private nuisance, the distinction between the two lying more in the effect than in the kind of nuisance. In the case of a private nuisance there must be interference with the use of, or enjoyment of, or of rights, in land. Such interference is not necessary for a public nuisance to exist.

Private nuisances

Public nuisance

Statutory nuisances

Tort

O

Ocean acidification

An increased concentration of carbon dioxide in the atmosphere causes an increase in the amount of carbon dioxide dissolved in the oceans. Dissolved carbon dioxide reacts with water to form carbonic acid resulting in acidification of same.

Carbon dioxide

Offences

A number of principles underpin the framework of the law relating to protection of the environment. These principles are incorporated in the EC Treaty (Article 130) and form the basis for the majority of UK legislation.

A breach of environmental law can result in criminal proceedings being taken against the offender by an enforcement agency. The principal offences can be summarised thus:

(a) causing pollution;

(b) permitting pollution;

(c) breach of licence conditions;

(d) breach of statutory duty;

(e) breach of permit conditions; and

(e) failure to comply with Notices and Orders, e.g. an Enforcement Notice, Suspension Notice, Abatement Notice, Abatement Order, Noise Abatement Notice, Works Notice.

Abatement Notice

Anti-Pollution Works Regulations 1999

Breach of statutory duty

Causing pollution (offence)

Contaminated Land (England) Regulations 2000

Controlled Waste Regulations 1992

Enforcement Notice

Environmental Protection Act 1990

Environmental Protection (Duty of Care) Regulations 1991

Noise Abatement Notices

Noise Abatement Zone

Noise and Statutory Nuisances Act 1993

Permit

Permit conditions

Permitting pollution: offence

Pollution Prevention and Control Act 1999

Pollution Prevention and Control (England and Wales) Regulations 2000

Regulator

Suspension Notice

Waste electrical and electronic equipment

Water Act 2003

Water Resources Act 1991

Works Notice

Offshore installation

Any structure or other thing (but not a ship) in or under:

(a) United Kingdom territorial waters; or

(b) any waters mentioned in Section 7(9)(b) or (c),

which is used for the purposes of, or in connection with, the exploration, development or production of petroleum.

[Pollution Prevention and Control Act 1999]

Petroleum

Offshore platform

Any fixed or floating structure which:

(a) is used for the purposes of or in connection with the production of petroleum; and

(b) in the case of a floating structure, is maintained on a station during the course of production,

but does not include any structure where the principal purpose of the use of the structure is the establishment of the existence of petroleum or the appraisal of its characteristics, quality or quantity or the extent of any reservoir in which it occurs.

[Pollution Prevention and Control (England and Wales) Regulations 2000]

Petroleum

Off-site condition

A permit authorising the operation of an installation or Part A mobile plant may include a condition requiring an operator to carry out works or do other things in relation to land not forming part of the site of the installation or mobile plant notwithstanding that he is not entitled to carry out the works or do the things and any person whose consent would be required shall grant, or join in granting, the operator such rights in relation to that land as will enable the operator to comply with any requirements imposed on him by the permit.

[Pollution Prevention and Control (England and Wales) Regulations 2000]

Installation

Mobile plant

Permit conditions

Permit

Oil storage

Many pollution incidents arise from oil leaking from tanks either during the storage of oil or at the delivery stage.

The Control of Pollution (Oil Storage) (England) Regulations 2001 apply in the case where oil is stored:

(a) in containers greater than 200 litres above ground at an industrial, commercial or institutional site; and

(b) in quantities greater than 3,500 litres at a domestic premises.

The Regulations cover the storage of oil at a wide range of premises, such as factories, churches, village halls, hospitals, public buildings, restaurants and licensed premises.

Tank owners are required to provide a secondary containment facility, such as a bund or drip tray, to prevent oil entering the water environment.

The requirements are enforced by the Environment Agency who have the power to take action for non-compliance, including the service of a Notice requiring improvements to the oil storage facility.

The Regulations do not apply to:

(a) premises used for the refining or distribution of oils;

(b) oil stored in a building or entirely underground;

(c) the agricultural use of oil on farms;

(d) waste mineral oil; and

(e) premises used mainly as a single private dwelling where less than 3,500 litres of oil are stored.

Pollution incidents

Release to land: substances

Release into water

Open radioactive sources

This is radioactive material in a form that may be readily divided or diluted, including radioactive powders, gases, solutions or solids. There is a potential for contamination of other materials in the normal use of these materials.

High activity sealed radioactive sources and orphan sources

Mobile radioactive source

Radiation

Sealed radioactive sources

Operational plans

Any compliance scheme that proposes to register and take on the obligations of its members must have an operational plan and, under Regulation 12 and Schedule 4 Part IV of the Producer Responsibility Obligations (Packaging Waste) Regulations, this plan must demonstrate to the relevant Agency's satisfaction:

(a) that it has sufficient financial resources and the technical expertise to discharge the recovery and recycling obligations that its members would have had but for membership of the scheme;

(b) that the scheme's proposals for discharging the necessary recovery and recycling obligations will take account of any waste strategy that the Government may develop;

(c) that appropriate arrangements exist for the scheme to supply to the relevant Agency the necessary data, using the form shown in Schedule 4, Part II; and

(d) how the necessary recovery and recycling obligations will be performed, particularly in relation to each packaging material, including details of:

(i) the reprocessors that will be used (name and address);

(ii) the waste disposal authorities to be used (names);

(iii) how much packaging waste is to be obtained from, respectively, member businesses' own wastes, the commercial/industrial waste stream and the household waste stream;

(iv) the amount of packaging waste that the scheme proposes to recover in the three years following registration; and

(v) within that, the amounts of each material to be recycled; and

(vi) the steps that the scheme proposes to take to minimise, as far as possible, material cross-subsidy.

The relevant Agency can decide that the operational plan is unsatisfactory in relation to one or more of the above points and may, on those grounds, refuse to register a scheme. The scheme has a right of appeal against this decision.

The registration of a scheme can be cancelled if:

(a) the required information or the fee are not provided;

(b) the operator of the scheme knowingly provided false information to the relevant Agency; or

(c) the required data is not provided.

[Producer Responsibility Obligations (Packaging Waste) Regulations 1997 – 2005]

Packaging

Producer Responsibility Obligations (Packaging Waste) Regulations 2005

Recovery and recycling obligations

Recovery of waste

Recycling and disposal of waste

Reduction

Operator

In relation to an installation or mobile plant, the person who has control over its operations.

(a) Where an installation or mobile plant has not been put into operation, the person who will have control over the operation of the installation or mobile plant when it is put into operation shall be treated as the operator of the installation or mobile plant.

(b) Where an installation or mobile plant has ceased to be in operation, the person who holds the permit which applies to the installation or mobile plant shall be treated as the operator of the installation or mobile plant.

[Pollution Prevention and Control (England and Wales) Regulations 2000]

Installation

Mobile plant

Pollution Prevention and Control (England and Wales) Regulations 2000

Opinions and Directions

A developer may ask a local planning authority (LPA) for an *opinion* on whether an Environmental Statement is required for a proposed development. If the developer is not satisfied, he may ask the Secretary of State for a *Direction* on the matter.

The LPA must give its opinion within 3 weeks of the request, although this period may be extended in writing. The Secretary of State must give a Direction in three weeks or such longer periods as may be required.

Environmental Statement

Organic chemicals: manufacture and use

These scheduled activities are:

Part A(1)

(a) Producing organic chemicals such as:

(i) hydrocarbons (linear or cyclic, saturated or unsaturated, aliphatic or aromatic);

(ii) organic compounds containing oxygen, such as alcohols, aldehydes, ketones, carboxylic acids, esters, ethers, peroxides, phenols, epoxy resins;

(iii) organic compounds containing sulphur, such as sulphides, mercaptans, sulphonic acids, sulphonates, sulphates and sulphones and sulphur heterocyclics;

(iv) organic compounds containing nitrogen, such as amines, amides, nitrous-, nitro- or azo compounds, nitrates, nitriles, nitrogen heterocyclics, cyanates, isocyanates, di-isocyanates and di-isocyanate prepolymers;

(v) organic compounds containing phosphorus, such as substituted phosphines and phosphate esters;

(vi) organic compounds containing halogens, such as halocarbons, halogenated aromatic compounds and acid halides;

(vii) organometallic compounds, such as lead alkyls, Grignard reagents and lithium alkyls;

(viii) plastic materials, such as polymers, synthetic fibres and cellulose-based fibres;

(ix) synthetic rubbers;

(x) dyes and pigments;

(xi) surface-active agents;

(b) Producing any other organic compounds not described in paragraph (a);

(c) Polymerising or co-polymerising any unsaturated hydrocarbon or vinyl chloride (other than a pre-formulated resin or pre-formulated gel coat which contains any unsaturated hydrocarbon) which is likely to involve, in any period of 12 months, the polymerisation or co-polymerisation of 50 tonnes or more of any of those materials or, in aggregate, any combination of those materials;

(d) Any activity involving the use in any 12 months of one tonne or more of toluene di-isocyanate or other di-isocyanate of comparable volatility or, where partly polymerised, the use of partly polymerised di-isocyanates or prepolymers containing one tonne or more of those monomers, if the activity may result in a release into the air which contains such a di-isocyanate monomer;

(e) The flame bonding of polyurethane foams or polyurethane elastomers;

(f) Recovering:

(i) carbon disulphide;

(ii) pyridine or any substituted pyridine;

(g) Recovering or purifying acrylic acid, substituted acrylic acid or any ester of acrylic acid or substituted acrylic acid.

Part A(2)

Nil

Part B

(a) Unless falling within Part A(1) of this Section, any activity involving in any period of 12 months:

  (i) the use of less than one tonne of toluene di-isocyanate or other di-isocyanate of comparable volatility or, where partially polymerised, the use of partly polymerised di-isocyanates or prepolymers containing less than 1 tonne of these monomers; or

  (ii) the use of 5 tonnes or more of diphenyl methane di-isocyanate or other di-isocyanate of much lower volatility than toluene di-isocyanate or, where partly polymerised, the use of partly polymerised di-isocyanates or prepolymers containing 5 tonnes or more of these volatile monomers, where the activity may result in a release into the air which contains such a di-isocyanate monomer;

(b) Cutting polyurethane foams or polyurethane elastomers with heated wires;

(c) Any activity for the polymerisation or co-polymerisation of any pre-formulated resin or pre-formulated gel coat which contains any unsaturated hydrocarbon, where the activity is likely to involve, in any period of 12 months, the polymerisation or co-polymerisation of 100 tonnes or more of unsaturated hydrocarbon.

Pre-formulated resin or pre-formulated gel coat means any resin or gel coat which has been formulated before being introduced into polymerisation or co-polymerisation activity, whether or not the resin or gel coat contains a colour pigment, activator or catalyst.

[Schedule 1: Part 1: Pollution Prevention and Control (England and Wales) Regulations 2000]

Chemical fertiliser production

Explosives production

Inorganic chemical production

Isocyanates

Nitrogen oxides

Part A activities

Part B activities

Pharmaceutical production

Scheduled activities

Storage of chemicals in bulk

Sulphur oxides

Organic farming

Farming processes which do not involve the use of organic chemical substances and conforming to detailed production standards.

Hazardous substances: classification

Organic solvents

The term 'solvent' is applied to a large number of chemical substances which are used to dissolve or dilute other substances or materials. Many solvents are also used as chemical intermediates, fuels and as components of a wide range of products.

Typical solvents include acetone, dichloromethane, toluene, methanol, perchlorethylene, trichlorethylene, carbon tetrachloride, tetrachloroethane and methyl bromide. They are widely used in industrial processes and are incorporated in many products, such as cleaning and degreasing materials, paints, lacquers and varnishes, paint removers, adhesives, ink and ink removers.

Solvents can enter the body by inhalation of vapours and through the skin by direct contact. The symptoms of exposure to solvents depend very much on the particular solvent and the dose received. Acute symptoms include irritation of the eyes, lungs and skin, headache, nausea, dizziness and light headedness. In serious cases, unconsciousness and death may result from exposure to high concentrations of vapour. Long-term health effects may include dermatitis, damage to the central nervous system, the kidneys, liver or the blood and, in some cases, cancer.

Chlorine

Organic chemicals: manufacture and use

Solvent emissions

Organism

Organism means any acellular, unicellular or multicellular entity (in any form), other than humans or human embryos; and unless the context otherwise requires, the term also includes any article or substance consisting of biological matter.

[Genetically Modified Organisms (Contained Use) Regulations 2000]

Genetically Modified Organisms (Contained Use) Regulations 2000

Genetically modified organisms (GMO)

Genetic engineering

Other mineral activities

These scheduled activities are:

Part A(1)

Nil

Part A(2)

(a) Manufacturing cellulose fibre reinforced calcium silicate board using unbleached pulp;

Part B

(a) Unless falling within Part A(1) or Part A(2) of any Section in this Schedule, the crushing, grinding or other size reduction, other than the cutting of stone, or the grading, screening or heating of any designated mineral or mineral product except where the operation of the activity is unlikely to result in the release into the air of particulate matter;

(b) Any of the following activities unless carried on at an exempt location:

  (i) crushing, grinding or otherwise breaking up of coal or coke or any other coal product;

  (ii) screening, grading or mixing coal, or coke or any other coal product;

  (iii) loading or unloading coal, coke or any other coal product except unloading on retail sale;

(c) The crushing, grinding or other size reduction with machinery designed for that purpose of bricks, tiles or concrete;

(d) Screening the product of any activity described in paragraph (c);

(e) Coating road stone with tar or bitumen;

(f) Loading, unloading or storing pulverised fuel ash in bulk prior to further transportation in bulk;

(g) The fusion of calcined bauxite for the production of artificial corundum.

Coal includes lignite.

Designated mineral or mineral product means:

(a) clay, sand and any other naturally occurring mineral other than coal or lignite;

(b) metallurgical slag;

(c) boiler or furnace ash produced from the burning of coal, coke or any other coal product;

(d) gypsum which is a by-product of any activity.

Exempt location means:

(a) any premises used for the sale of petroleum coke, coal, coke or any coal product where the throughput of such substances at those premises in any period of 12 months is in aggregate likely to be less than 10,000 tonnes;

(b) any premises to which petroleum coke, coal, coke or any coal product is supplied only for use there.

[Schedule 1: Part 1: Pollution Prevention and Control (England and Wales) Regulations

2000 as amended]

Airborne particulates

Fossil fuels

Part A activities

Part B activities

Particulate matter

Pollution Prevention and Control Act 1999

Pollution Prevention and Control (England and Wales) Regulations 2000

Scheduled activities

Other mineral fibres

These scheduled activities are:

Part A(1)

(a) Unless falling within Part A(1) or A(2) of Section 3.3 (Manufacturing glass and glass fibre), melting mineral substances in plant with a melting capacity of more than 20 tonnes per day;

(b) Unless falling within Part A(1) of Section 3.3, producing any fibre from any material.

Part A(2)

Nil

Part B

Nil

[Schedule 1: Part 1: Pollution Prevention and Control (England and Wales) Regulations 2000]

Part A activities

Part B activities

Pollution Prevention and Control Act 1999

Pollution Prevention and Control (England and Wales) Regulations 2000

Scheduled activities

Ozone

Ozone is a form of oxygen (O_3) that can be created by electrical currents. Excessive releases of carbon dioxide and other compounds from vehicles and industrial processes produce ozone that can result in smog at ground level.

Carbon dioxide

Environmental Protection (Controls on Ozone-Depleting Substances) Regulations 2002

Ozone depletion

Ozone-depleting substances

Ozone layer

Ozone-depleting substances

These include emissions from vehicles and industrial processes which disrupt the creation of ozone.

The Environmental Protection (Controls on Ozone-Depleting Substances) Regulations 2002 apply controls over the production, importation, exportation, placing on the market, emission, recovery, recycling and destruction of substances that have an adverse impact on the ozone layer in the upper atmosphere.

Ozone-depleting substances include certain refrigerants, solvents, foam blowing agents and fire-fighting fluids.

Environmental Protection (Controls on Ozone-Depleting Substances) Regulations 2002

Organic solvents

Ozone

Ozone depletion

Ozone layer

Ozone depletion

When hydrocarbons and other man-made substances reach the ozone layer, the process that creates ozone is disrupted, resulting in ozone depletion.

Ozone

Ozone-depleting substances

Ozone layer

Ozone layer

This is a layer of air, rich in ozone (ozonosphere), which encircles the Earth at altitudes of six to thirty miles. In the ozone layer, ultraviolet and other short wavelength light from the sun convert oxygen into ozone, which prevents most of the shorter wavelengths from reaching Earth, where they can be lethal to living organisms.

Loss of the protective ozone layer in the upper atmosphere may be a faraway event but its significance to life on Earth is profound.

Ozone

Ozone depletion

Ozone-depleting substances

P

Packaging

Packaging means all products made of any materials of any nature to be used for the containment, protection, handling, delivery and presentation of goods from raw materials to processed goods, from the producer to the user or the consumer, including non-returnable items used for the same purposes but only where the products are:

(a) *sales packaging or primary packaging,* that is to say packaging conceived so as to constitute a sale unit to the final user or consumer at the point of purchase;

(b) *grouped packaging or secondary packaging,* that is to say packaging conceived so as to constitute at the point of purchase a grouping of a certain number of sales units whether the latter is sold as such to the final user or consumer or whether it serves only as a means to replenish the shelves at the point of sale; it can be removed from the product without affecting its characteristics; or

(c) *transport packaging or tertiary packaging,* that is to say packaging conceived so as to facilitate handling and transport of a number of sales units or grouped packaging in order to prevent physical handling and transport damage; for the purpose of these Regulations, transport packaging does not include road, rail, ship and air containers.

[Producer Responsibility Obligations (Packaging Waste) Regulations 1997 – 2005]

Packaging materials

Packaging waste

Producer Responsibility Obligations (Packaging Waste) Regulations 2005

Waste

Packaging: essential requirements

Under the Packaging (Essential Requirements) Regulations 1998 suppliers must ensure that any packaging placed on the market:

(a) is minimised with respect to weight and volume;

(b) is designed to be re-usable or recoverable;

(c) is designed to have minimum environmental impact when disposed of as waste; and

(d) contains less than the prescribed limits of certain heavy metals.

Environmental Impact Assessment

Heavy metal pollution

Producer Responsibility Obligations (Packaging Waste) Regulations 2005

Recovery and recycling obligations

Recovery of waste

Recycling and disposal of waste

Waste

Waste offences

Packaging materials

Packaging materials means materials used in the manufacture of packaging and includes raw materials and processed materials prior to their conversion into packaging.

[Producer Responsibility Obligations (Packaging Waste) Regulations 1997 – 2005]

Packaging

Packaging waste

Producer Responsibility Obligations (Packaging Waste) Regulations 2005

Waste

Packaging waste

This means any packaging or packaging materials covered by the definition of *waste* in Article 1 of Directive 75/442/EC (The Waste Directive). (See Schedule 3, Part I.)

[Producer Responsibility Obligations (Packaging Waste) Regulations 1997 – 2005]

Packaging

Packaging materials

Producer Responsibility (Packaging Waste) Regulations 2005

Waste

Paper, pulp and board manufacturing activities

These scheduled activities are:

Part A(1)

(a) Producing in industrial plant pulp from timber or other fibrous materials;

(b) Producing in industrial plant paper and board where the plant has a production capacity of more than 20 tonnes per day;

(c) Any activity associated with making paper pulp or paper, including activities connected with the recycling of paper such as de-inking, if the activity may result in the release into water of any substance listed in paragraph 13 of Part 2 of this Schedule in a quantity which, in any period of 12 months, is greater than the background quantity by more than the amount specified in that paragraph in relation to that substance.

Paper pulp includes pulp made from wood, grass, straw and similar materials and references to the making of paper are to the making of any product using paper pulp.

Part A(2)

(a) Manufacturing wood particleboard, oriented strand board, wood fibreboard, plywood, cement-bonded particleboard or any other composite wood-based board.

Part B

Nil

[Schedule 1: Part 1: Pollution Prevention and Control (England and Wales) Regulations 2000 as amended]

Part A activities

Part B activities

Pollution Prevention and Control Act 1999

Pollution Prevention and Control (England and Wales) Regulations 2000

Scheduled activities

Part A activities

These are installations and mobile plant carrying out any of the activities listed in Part 1 of Schedule 1 to the Pollution Prevention and Control (England and Wales) Regulations 2000 in terms of the implementation of Integrated Pollution Control (IPC) and the allocation for enforcement of the Regulations thus:

- Part A(1): Integrated Pollution Control – Environment Agency
- Part A(2): Integrated Pollution Control – local authorities.

Installation

Integrated Pollution Prevention and Control (IPPC)

Mobile plant

Pollution Prevention and Control (England and Wales) Regulations 2000

Scheduled activities

Part B activities

These are installations and mobile plant carrying out any of the activities listed in Part 1 of Schedule 1 to the Pollution Prevention and Control (England and Wales) Regulations 2000 in terms of the implementation of Air Pollution Control (APC) and the allocation of enforcement of the Regulations thus:

- Part B: Air Pollution Control – local authorities

Installation

Mobile plant

Pollution Prevention and Control (England and Wales) Regulations 2000

Scheduled activities

Partial transfer of permit

Regulation 18 of the Pollution Prevention and Control (England and Wales) Regulations 2000 deals with the transfer of permits. Where an operator wishes to retain part of his permit (a partial transfer), an application to the regulator shall:

(a) identify the installation or mobile plant to which the transfer applies (the transferred unit); and

(b) where the transfer applies to the operation of an installation or Part A mobile plant, contain a map or plan identifying the part of the site used for the operation of the installation or mobile plant (the identified part of the site).

[Pollution Prevention and Control (England and Wales) Regulations 2000]

Installation

Mobile plant

Permit

Particulate matter

Airborne particulates

Pathway

The means by which a hazardous substance comes into contact with a receptor (or target).

Conceptual Model

Pollutant linkage

Receptor

Source-Pathway-Receptor Model

Penalties

Offences under environmental protection law are classed as criminal offences. They are dealt with, in the first instance, by the Magistrates' Court or, in some cases, the Crown Court. Both courts have the power to impose a range of penalties but, principally, fines. The levels of fines are limited in the Magistrates' Court, whereas the Crown Court can impose unlimited fines.

In addition to imposing fines, the courts can impose custodial sentences. They can impose a prison sentence of up to two years on a person in relation to waste.

Courts also have the power:

(a) to confiscate the proceeds of offences;

(b) to order the effect of an offence to be remedied within a specific period;

(c) to make compensation orders;

(d) to enforce by injunction; and

(e) to deprive an offender of property.

Anti-Pollution Works Regulations 1999

Contaminated Land (England) Regulations 2000

Environment Act 1995

Environmental Protection Act 1990

Environmental Protection (Duty of Care) Regulations 1991

Groundwater Regulations 1998

Injunction

Producer Responsibility Obligations (Packaging Waste) Regulations 2005

Water Resources Act 1991

Permit

The issuing of permits by the Environment Agency is part of the direct Regulation process. It enables the Agency to control emissions or abstractions from processes in England and Wales that have the potential to pollute through various environmental permits.

Permits include licences, authorisations, consents, registrations and notices which are featured in specific Regulations.

Permitted processes include:

(a) complex process industries, such as chemical works, cement works and power stations;

(b) sewage treatment works;

(c) waste management facilities, such as landfill and incinerator sites;

(d) industries using radioactive material.

In some cases, permits set limits and stated conditions to control the level of pollutants that can be released to air, water and land from a specific site. Permits are reviewed on a regular basis by the Agency to ensure they are keeping pace with changing circumstances.

The Environment Agency is the regulator for the following permits.

(a) water abstraction licences;

(b) fishing licences;

(c) discharge consents;

(d) authorisations for industrial processes;

(e) waste licences;

(f) licences for solid waste disposal at sea;

(g) authorisations for the use, storage and disposal of radioactive materials at smaller sites that deal with radioactive material;

(h) authorisations for radioactive liquid and gaseous discharges form the major nuclear establishments.

Permits issued by other regulators are:

(a) mineral, oil and gas extraction licences – Department of Trade and Industry;

(b) dredging permits – Department for the Environment, Food and Rural Affairs;

(c) radioactive substances licences – Nuclear Installations Inspectorate and Health and Safety Executive.

Under the Pollution Prevention and Control (PPC) regime, a business may require a PPC permit if it carries out a *directly associated activity* that serves a site regulated by a PPC permit and could have an effect on pollution caused by that site. *Directly associated activities* could, for example, include the undertaking of the following activities at a PPC-regulated site:

(a) operating a landfill site;

(b) operating an effluent treatment plant; and

(c) storing or treating materials.

Those holding a PPC permit must comply with its conditions and contact the regulator in the event of any planned changes to operations. Where people plan to operate a new site or mobile plant, they must apply to the regulator for a PPC permit.

Part II (Regulations 9 to 22) of the Pollution Prevention and Control (England and Wales) Regulations deals with the requirements with respect to permits for the operation of installations and mobile plant for specified waste management activities.

Under Regulation 9, no person shall operate an installation or mobile plant after the prescribed date for that installation or mobile plant except under and to the extent authorised by a permit granted by the regulator.

A permit may authorise the operation of:

(a) more than one Part A installation or Part A mobile plant on the same site operated by the same operator;

(b) more than one Part B installation on the same site operated by the same operator; or

(c) more than one Part B mobile plant operated by the same operator, but may not authorise the operation of more than one installation or mobile plant.

A permit may include conditions:

(a) imposing limits on the amount or composition of any substance produced or utilised during the operation of the installation or mobile plant in any period;

(b) which are supplemental or incidental to other conditions contained in the permit.

Cement and lime production

Contaminated Land Regime

Discharge consent

Effluent

Emission limit value

Environmental Quality Standard

"Fit and proper person"

General binding rules

General binding rules condition

Hazardous waste

Installation

Landfill: disposal of waste

Landfill (England and Wales) Regulations 2002 – 2005

Mobile plant

Off-site condition

Oil storage

Part A activities

Part B activities

Partial transfer of permit

Permit conditions

Pollution Prevention and Control Act 1999

Pollution Prevention and Control (PPC)

Polychlorinated biphenyls (PCBs) and other dangerous substances

Radioactive substances and wastes

Regulator

Revocation of permit

Sewage effluent

Specified waste management activity

Variation Notice

Waste management facility (licensed site)

Waste Management Licences

Water abstraction

Permit conditions

A permit authorising the operation of a Part A installation or a Part A mobile plant shall include conditions:

(a) aimed at minimising long distance and trans-boundary pollution;

(b) ensuring, where necessary, appropriate protection of the soil and groundwater and appropriate management of waste generated by the installation or mobile plant;

(c) relating to the periods when the installation or mobile plant is not operating normally where there is a risk that the environment may be adversely affected during such periods, including, in particular, conditions relating to the start up of operations, leaks, malfunctions and momentary stoppages;

(d) setting out the steps to be taken prior to the operation of the installation or mobile plant and after the definitive cessation of operations;

(e) setting out suitable emission monitoring requirements, specifying the measurement methodology and frequency and the evaluation procedure, and ensuring that the operator supplies the regulator with the data required to check compliance with the permit;

(f) requiring the operator to supply the regulator regularly with the results of the monitoring of emissions and to inform the regulator, without delay, of any incident or accident which is causing or may cause significant pollution.

There is implied in every permit a condition that, in operating the installation or mobile plant, the operator shall use the Best Available Techniques for preventing or, where that is not practicable, reducing emissions from the installation of mobile plant.

Best Available Techniques (BAT)

Emission

Groundwater pollution

Hazardous waste

Incineration

Installation

Mobile plant

Off-site condition

Oil storage

Operator

Part A activities

Part B activities

Permit

Pollution: definition

Pollution incidents

Pollution Prevention and Control (England and Wales) Regulations 2000

Polychlorinated biphenyls (PCBs) and other dangerous substances

Radioactive substances and wastes

Soil pollution

Waste Management Licences

Permitting pollution: offence

Certain statutes, for example, the Water Resources Act, provide for a separate offence of "permitting pollution", such as knowingly permitting poisonous or polluting matter to enter controlled waters. Whilst "causing pollution" requires evidence of a positive act on the part of the offender, "permitting pollution" may apply in passive situations where the offender allowed the pollution to take place without taking preventive action.

Causing pollution (offence)

Environmental crimes

Water Resources Act 1991

Persistent organic pollutants

These are organic compounds, such as pesticides, industrial chemicals and waste products of industrial processes that are resistant to any form of environmental degradation through physical, chemical or biological processes. As such, they:

(a) persist in the environment, being capable of resisting degradation in environmental media (air, water and ground) for long periods;

(b) bio-accumulate, in that they can accumulate in living tissues at levels higher than those in the immediate environment; and

(c) have the potential for long-range transport enabling them to travel great distances from the source of release through air, water and migratory species.

Their effects include disruption of endocrine systems, suppression of immune system functions and induction of reproductive and developmental changes.

Well-established persistent organic pollutants are aldrin, chlordane, DDT, dieldrin, hexachlorbenzene and polychlorinated biphenyls (PCBs).

Hazardous substances: classification

Pesticide

Polychlorinated biphenyls (PCBs) and other dangerous substances

Persons aggrieved by statutory nuisances

Any person aggrieved by the existence of a statutory nuisance can make a formal complaint to a Magistrates' Court.

Complaint to a Magistrates' Court

Statutory nuisances

Pesticide

Any chemical substance or preparation prepared or used for destroying any pest, including those used for protecting plants or wood or other plant products from harmful organisms, regulating the growth of plants, giving protection against harmful creatures, rendering such creatures harmless, controlling organisms with harmful or unwanted effects on water systems, buildings or other structures, or on manufactured products, or protecting animals against ectoparasites.

[Pollution Prevention and Control (England and Wales) Regulations 2000]

Biocides

Hazardous substances: classification

Plant health products and biocides

Petroleum

Any mineral oil or relative hydrocarbon and natural gas existing in its natural condition in strata but does not include coal or bituminous shales or other stratified deposits from which oil can be extracted by destructive distillation.

[Pollution Prevention and Control (England and Wales) Regulations 2000]

Pharmaceutical production

These scheduled activities are:

Part A(1)

(a) Producing pharmaceutical products using a chemical or biological process;

(b) Formulating such products if this may result in the release into water of any substance listed in paragraph 13 of Part 2 of this Schedule in a quantity which, in any period of 12 months, is greater than the background quantity by more than the amount specified in that paragraph for that substance.

Part A(2)

Nil

Part B

Nil

[Schedule 1: Part 1: Pollution Prevention and Control (England and Wales) Regulations 2000]

Part A activities

Part B activities

Pollution Prevention and Control Act 1999

Pollution Prevention and Control (England and Wales) Regulations 2000

Scheduled activities

Phthalates

These are a group of chemicals used as plasticisers or softeners in polyvinyl chloride (PVC) products, including building products and toys, and as solvents and additives in many consumer products, such as personal care products, cosmetics, insecticides and wood treatments.

They vary from being mildly toxic to moderately toxic depending on the route of entry to the body.

Planning Contravention Notice

Conservation Area

Planning (Control of Major Accident Hazards) Regulations 1999

These Regulations cover sites where there are certain quantities of dangerous substances, including those harmful to the environment.

Operators must take all measures necessary to prevent major accidents and to limit their consequences to persons and the environment, including certain prescribed measures.

Control of Major Accident Hazards (COMAH) Regulations 1999

Hazardous substances: classification

Plans relating to emissions

The Secretary of State may make plans for:

(a) the setting of limits on the total amount, or the total amount in any period, of emissions from all or any description of source within England and Wales; or

(b) the allocation of quotas relating to such emissions.

Where the Secretary of State allocates a quota in a such a plan, he may also make a scheme for the trading or other transfer of the quota so allocated.

[Pollution Prevention and Control (England and Wales) Regulations 2000]

Emission

Emission limit value

Emission Trading Scheme

Plant health products and biocides

These scheduled activities are:

Part A(1)

(a) Producing plant health products or biocides;

(b) Formulating such products if this may result in the release into water of any substance listed in paragraph 13 of Part 2 of this Schedule in a quantity which, in any period of 12 months, is greater than the background quantity by more than the amount specified in that paragraph for that substance.

Part A(2)

Nil

Part B

Nil

[Schedule 1: Part 1: Pollution Prevention and Control (England and Wales) Regulations 2000]

Biocides

Part A activities

Part B activities

Pollution Prevention and Control Act 1999

Pollution Prevention and Control (England and Wales) Regulations 2000

Scheduled activities

Pollutant

This is any substance, vibration, heat or noise as a result of such an emission which may create pollution.

Schedule 5 to the Pollution Prevention and Control (England and Wales) Regulations lists the main polluting substances to be taken into account if they are relevant to fixing emission limit values:

Air

- Sulphur dioxide and other sulphur compounds
- Oxides of nitrogen and other nitrogen compounds
- Carbon monoxide
- Volatile organic compounds
- Metals and their compounds
- Dust
- Asbestos (suspended particulates, fibres)
- Chlorine and its compounds
- Fluorine and its compounds
- Arsenic and its compounds
- Cyanides
- Substances and preparations which have been proved to possess carcinogenic or mutagenic properties or properties which may affect reproduction via the air
- Polychlorinated dibenzodioxins and polychlorinated dibenzofurans

Water

- Organohalogen compounds and substances which may form such compounds in the aquatic environment
- Organophosphorus compounds
- Organotin compounds
- Substances and preparations which have been proved to possess carcinogenic or mutagenic properties or properties which may affect reproduction in or via the aquatic environment

- Persistent hydrocarbons and persistent and bio accumulable organic toxic substances
- Cyanides
- Metals and their compounds
- Arsenic and its compounds
- Biocides and plant health products
- Materials in suspension
- Substances which contribute to eutrophication (in particular, nitrates and phosphates)
- Substances which have an unfavourable influence on the oxygen balance (and can be measured using parameters such as BOD, COD, etc)

[Pollution Prevention and Control (England and Wales) Regulations 2000

Biochemical Oxygen Demand (BOD)

Biocides

Carcinogens

Chemical Oxygen Demand (COD)

Emission limit value

Environmental pollution

Eutrophication

Heavy metal pollution

Mutagenic

Nitrogen oxides

Plant health products and biocides

Pollutant linkage

Polluter Pays Principle

Pollution: definition

Pollution of the environment

Pollution Prevention and Control Act 1999

Pollution Prevention and Control (England and Wales) Regulations 2000

Sulphur oxides

Pollutant linkage

The relationship between a contaminant (source), a pathway and a receptor.

Contaminant

Receptor

Source-Pathway-Receptor Model

Polluter Pays Principle

The basis of this principle is that a person or organisation who create the pollution resulting in damage to the environment should bear the full cost for such pollution. This means that the polluter should pay for:

(a) the administration of the pollution prevention and control system; and

(b) the consequences of the pollution, such as compensation of affected parties and remedial measures to remove the pollution.

Defences: criminal proceedings

Environmental crimes

Environmental law

Waste offences

Pollution: definition

The introduction by Man into the environment of substances or energy liable to cause hazards to human health, harm to living resources and ecological systems, damage to structure or amenity, or interference with legitimate uses of the environment.

[Royal Commission on Environmental Pollution: Third Report]

Pollution is defined by the reference to the potential effect of the introduction of substances or energy into the environment rather than the fact of the introduction itself.

Pollution means emissions as a result of human activity which may be harmful to human health or the quality of the environment, cause offence to any human senses, result in damage to material property, or impair or interfere with amenities and other legitimate uses of the environment.

[Pollution Prevention and Control (England and Wales) Regulations 2000]

Environmental pollution

Pollutant

Pollution Control Regime

Pollution incidents

Pollution of controlled waters

Pollution of the environment

Pollution Control Regime

This is a regime which regulates certain types of business in terms of the environmental impacts from those businesses and through various forms of permit, for example, to operate a landfill site or an effluent treatment plant.

Local Air Pollution Control (LAPC)

Part A activities

Part B activities

Pollution Prevention and Control (PPC)

Pollution Prevention and Control Act 1999

Pollution Prevention and Control (England and Wales) Regulations 2000

Pollution incidents

These are categorised thus:

- Category 1 – incidents having persistent and extensive impact on land, air or water
- Category 2 – incidents having significant impact on land, air or water
- Category 3 – incidents having minimal impact on land, air or water

Pollution Control Regime

Pollution of controlled waters

Pollution of the environment

Pollution of controlled waters

Section 85 of the Water Resources Act 1991 incorporates the following offences relating to the pollution of controlled waters. A person contravenes Section 85 if he causes or knowingly permits:

(a) any poisonous, noxious or polluting matter to enter any controlled waters or discharges trade or sewage effluent into controlled waters;

(b) any matter, other than trade effluent or sewage effluent, to enter controlled waters by being discharged from a drain or sewer in contravention of a prohibition imposed under Section 86;

(c) any trade effluent or sewage effluent to be discharged into any controlled waters or from land (in England and Wales) through a pipe, into the sea outside the seaward limits of controlled waters;

(d) any trade effluent or sewage effluent to be discharged in contravention of any prohibition imposed under Section 86, from a building or from any fixed plant either onto or into any land or into any waters of a lake or pond that are not inland fresh waters;

(e) any matter whatever to enter any inland fresh waters so as to tend to impede the proper flow of the waters in a manner leading, or likely to lead, to substantial aggravation of pollution due to other causes or the consequences of that pollution.

Controlled waters

Effluent

Sewage effluent

Substance

Trade effluent

Water Resources Act 1991

Pollution of the environment

Pollution of the environment means pollution of the environment due to the release (into any environmental medium) from any process of substances which are capable of causing harm to man or any other living organisms supported by the environment.

[Environmental Protection Act 1990]

Harm

Pollution Prevention and Control (England and Wales) Regulations 2000

These extensive Regulations are made under the Pollution Prevention and Control Act 1999 and set out a Pollution Control Regime for the purpose of implementing the Integrated Pollution Prevention and Control Directive (96/61/EC) and for regulating other environmentally polluting activities not covered by the Directive.

The Regulations control the operation of any installations or mobile plant carrying out any of the activities listed in Part 1 of Schedule 1 to the Regulations.

Installations or mobile plant used to carry out activities listed under the heading "Part (A)1" in Part 1 of the Schedule are subject to integrated pollution control by the Environment Agency.

Those used to carry out activities listed under the heading "Part A(2)" are subject to integrated pollution control by local authorities.

Those used to carry out activities listed under the heading "Part B" are subject to air pollution control by local authorities.

- Part I of the Regulations sets out general provisions, in particular Regulation 8 which specifies those installations and mobile plant regulated by the Environment Agency and those by local authorities, and the procedure for service of Notices.
- Part II deals with a range of matters, including the need for a permit to operate an installation or mobile plant, the procedure for granting permits and the treatment of permits once granted. The basic requirement for the content of permits is to impose emission limit values based on the Best Available Techniques.
- Part III covers the enforcement powers and appeal provisions under the Regulations.
- Part IV provides for appeals to the Secretary of State.
- Part V sets out the information gathering powers and publicity requirements.
- Part VI deals with offences under the Regulations, providing for enforcement by the High Court and admissibility of evidence.
- Part VII enables the Secretary of State to give directions and guidance to regulators and to make plans relating to emissions.
- Part VIII deals with the consequential amendments required by the introduction of the Pollution Control Regimes in the Regulations.

Appeals

Background quantity

Best Available Techniques (BAT)

Change in operation

Directions to regulators

Emission

Emission limit value

Enforcement Notice

Enforcement by the High Court

Environment Agency

"Fit and proper person"

General binding rules

Guidance to regulators

Installation

Integrated Pollution Prevention and Control (IPPC)

Mobile plant

Offences

Off-site condition

Part A activities

Part B activities

Permit

Pollution Control Regime

Pollution Prevention and Control Act 1999

Publicity requirements

Public registers of information (various)

Regulator

Revocation of permit

Scheduled activities

Specified waste management activity

Substance

Suspension Notice

Variation Notice

Pollution Prevention and Control (PPC)

This is a regime which regulates certain types of businesses, such as those carrying out:

(a) manufacturing and other industrial activities;

(b) waste management activities;

(c) intensive farming;

(d) activities involving solvents.

Where a site is covered by the PPC regime, the operator must hold a permit issued by the regulator and comply with the conditions of the permit.

In England and Wales, PPC is divided into different categories, namely Part A(1), Part A(2) and Part B.

PPC Part A controls a broad range of environmental impacts from affected businesses, including:

(a) emissions to air, land and water;

(b) energy efficiency;

(c) waste reduction;

(d) raw materials consumption;

(e) noise, vibration and heat;

(f) accident prevention; and

(g) the condition of the site.

PPC Part B controls emissions to air from affected businesses, similar to that covered by its predecessor, Local Authority Air Pollution Control (LAAPC)

Part A activities

Part B activities

Permit

Permit conditions

Pollution Control Regime

Pollution Prevention and Control Act 1999

Pollution Prevention and Control (England and Wales) 2000

Regulator

Scheduled activities

Solvent emissions

Solvent Emissions (England and Wales) Regulations 2004

Waste activity

Waste minimisation: process or resource efficiency

Pollution Prevention and Control Act 1999

This statute was enacted with a view to enabling provision to be made for the Regulation of polluting activities by:

(a) implementing Council Directive 96/61/EC concerning integrated pollution prevention and control;

(b) regulating, otherwise than in pursuance of that Directive, activities which are capable of causing any environmental pollution; and

(c) otherwise preventing or controlling emissions capable of causing any such pollution.

In particular, this statute repealed Sections 1 to 28 (Integrated Pollution Control and Air Pollution Control by Local Authorities) of the Environmental Protection Act 1990

Environmental pollution

Harm

Integrated Pollution Prevention and Control (IPPC)

Pollution Prevention and Control (England and Wales) Regulations 2000

Pollution Prevention and Control (PPC)

Scheduled activities

Polychlorinated biphenyls (PCBs) and other dangerous substances

These are a class of organic compounds with 1 to 10 chlorine atoms attached to biphenyl and taking the form of colourless, odourless crystals. Commercial mixtures containing PCBs are clear viscous liquids. Although the physical and chemical properties vary widely across the class, they have low water solubility and vapour pressure. They are generally stable and do not degrade readily.

The hazard arises when, under specific conditions, PCBs oxidise to form dioxins and dibenzofurans. Whilst these may be destroyed by thermal, chemical and biochemical processes, it is very difficult to achieve full destruction and there is a risk of creating dioxins and furans through partial oxidation.

PCB mixtures have been used in the past for a variety of applications, including dielectric fluids for capacitors and transformers, heat transfer fluids, hydraulic fluids, cutting and lubricating oils, and as additives in adhesives, sealants, paints, pesticides, reactive flame retardants and plastics. As such, they are persistent organic pollutants and have entered the environment through both use and their disposal.

The toxicity of PCBs varies considerably. The most commonly observed health effects in people exposed to large amounts of PCBs are skin conditions, such as chloracne and rashes. Studies have also identified the potential for liver damage, effects on infant behaviour and reproduction problems in women. Several studies of workers indicate that PCBs are associated with specific forms of cancer, such as biliary and liver cancer.

In the past, large quantities of PCBs have been placed in landfill sites, mainly in the form of transformers and capacitors, permitting escape to the atmosphere and ground water.

The disposal of PCBs and other dangerous substances is regulated by the Environmental Protection (Disposal of Polychlorinated Biphenyls) (England and Wales) Regulations 2000 (as amended). These Regulations require that equipment containing PCBs is identified, registered, labelled and disposed of in specific ways. They must also be decontaminated in some cases.

PCB is defined as covering the following substances:

(a) polychlorinated biphenyls (PCBs);

(b) polychlorinated terphenyls (PCTs);

(c) monomethyl-dibromo-diphenyl methane;

(d) monomethyl-dichloro-diphenyl methane; and

(e) monomethyl-tetrachlorodiphenyl methane.

All holders of PCBs or PCB contaminated equipment are affected by the Regulations. They must:

(a) register all contaminated equipment with the Environment Agency;

(b) provide information to the Agency for inclusion in an inventory; and

(c) dispose of and/or decontaminate, in the case of transformers, all contaminated PCB equipment.

Contaminated equipment is defined as any equipment (including any transformer, capacitor or receptacle contained residual stocks) which:

(a) contains PCBs; or

(b) having contained PCBs, has not been decontaminated.

Anything of a type which may contain PCBs is treated as containing PCBs unless it is reasonable to assume the contrary. Types of equipment which may contain PCBs include:

(a) transformers and pole mounted transformers;

(b) power factor capacitors;

(c) heat transfer equipment;

(d) resistors;

(e) process heating equipment;

(f) vacuum pumps; and

(g) hydraulic equipment.

Chlorine

Dioxins

Landfill (England and Wales) Regulations 2002 – 2006

Power lines

The question of the health risks associated with overhead power lines has been the subject of much debate since the 1970s. A particular concern is that extremely low frequency electric and, in particular, magnetic fields may be associated with cancer. The International Agency for Research on Cancer classified extremely low magnetic fields as "possibly carcinogenic" on the basis of limited epidemiological evidence and inadequate evidence from animals.

Powers of inspectors

Section 17 provides inspectors appointed under the EPA with considerable powers relating to premises on which a prescribed process is, or is believed to be, carried on, and to premises on which a prescribed process has been carried on, the condition of which is believed to be such as to give rise to a risk of serious pollution of the environment.

Such powers include:

(a) power of entry at any reasonable time if there is reason to believe a prescribed process is such as to give rise to a risk of serious pollution;

(b) to take a constable where obstruction on entry is anticipated, plus any equipment or materials;

(c) to make such examinations and investigations as may be necessary;

(d) to direct that a premises or any part of a premises remain undisturbed;

(e) to take measurements and photographs and make such recordings as he considers necessary;

(f) to take samples of articles and substances, and of air, water or land;

(g) to cause any article or substance which has caused, or likely to cause, pollution to be dismantled or subjected to any process or test;

(h) to take possession of and detain any above article or substance for the purpose of examination, to ensure it is not tampered with before examination and to ensure it is available for use as evidence;

(i) to require any person to answer questions as the inspector thinks fit and to sign a declaration of truth of his answers;

(j) to require the production of written or computerised records and to take copies of same;

(k) to require any person to provide facilities and assistance to enable him to exercise his powers; and

(l) any other power conferred upon him by Regulations.

Environmental Protection Act 1990

Offences

Pollution Prevention and Control Act 1999

Pollution Prevention and Control (England and Wales) Regulations 2002

Waste offences

Practicable: definition

A requirement qualified by the term "so far as is practicable" implies that if, "in the light of current knowledge or invention", or in "the current state of the art", it is feasible to comply with this requirement then, irrespective of the cost or sacrifice involved, such a requirement must be complied with. [Schwalb v Fass H. & Son (1946) 175 LT 345]

Thus, "practicable" means more than physically possible and implies a higher duty of care than a duty qualified by the term "so far as is reasonably practicable".

Absolute duties

Reasonably practicable

Precautionary principle

This principle was introduced by the Treaty on European Union, which states that it is the basis for environmental protection in the EC, including the UK.

The essence of the principle is that, in the absence of firm scientific evidence as to the effect of a particular substance or activity, the protection of the environment should be the main concern. There is no need to wait for conclusive scientific proof before preventive action is taken. The environment as a whole should be given the benefit of the doubt.

Environmental crimes

Environmental law

Polluter Pays Principle

Preventive Principle

Pre-treatment of waste

Under the Hazardous Wastes (England and Wales) Regulations 2005, all wastes must be pre-treated before landfill. Any potential treatment must fulfil all of the following criteria, but need only meet one of the four objectives of point 3 below.

1. It must be a physical, thermal, chemical or biological process, including sorting.
2. It must change the characteristics of the waste.
3. It must do so in order to:
   (a) reduce its volume; or
   (b) reduce its hazardous nature; or
   (c) facilitate its handling; or
   (d) enhance its recovery.

Hazardous waste

Waste

Waste Acceptance Criteria

Preventive Principle

This concept was included in the Single European Act in 1986. The principle requires more forward thinking actions on the basis that 'prevention is better than cure' and measures should be taken to prevent or minimise the effects of pollution before the polluting process commences.

Environmental law

Polluter Pays Principle

Precautionary principle

Primary packaging

Packaging

Prior approval of industrial installations

Section 4 of the CAA provides that, before installing a furnace over a certain size i.e. larger than a typical domestic installation, the person seeking to make the installation must obtain prior approval of the local authority.

[Clean Air Act 1993]

Chimney heights

Private actions

Section 82 of the EPA provides that any *person aggrieved* by a statutory nuisance has the right to complain to the Magistrates' Court with a view to obtaining a court order to terminate the nuisance. Failure to comply with such an order is an offence.

There is no requirement that the complainant be a neighbour or occupier of land or premises. However, the person must be at least in some way affected by the alleged nuisance.

Injunction

Private nuisances

Statutory nuisances

Tort

Private nuisances

A private nuisance is defined as "an interference, for a substantial length of time, with the use or enjoyment of land". The term was further defined in *Read v Lyons & Co.Ltd (1947)* as "unlawful interference with a person's use or enjoyment of land or some right over, or in connection with it".

It is very much concerned with the relationship between adjacent owners and occupiers of land and their various rights. Examples of private nuisances are those associated with the keeping of animals, such as continually barking dogs; the use of equipment, for example, loudspeakers; or the use of land, for instance, the frequent burning of refuse, thereby creating a smoke nuisance to local householders, or the obstruction of an access by parking a vehicle across same. The act or omission which causes a private nuisance may be strictly legitimate except that it interferes with the rights of the adjacent landowner.

A person aggrieved by a private nuisance is entitled to take a civil action with a view to establishing liability and the provision of a remedy. This usually takes place by way of the person seeking damages and/or an injunction, an order from the High Court, preventing the nuisance or requiring the nuisance to be abated.

In certain circumstances, a complainant may enter land and abate the nuisance themselves, but only if other remedies have been exhausted and an emergency arises. Any action must, however, be reasonable in the circumstances.

Private nuisances, therefore, generally fall into three specific groups:

(a) those causing interference with the enjoyment of land;

(b) those resulting in some form of encroachment on to the land; and

(c) those causing actual damage to the land.

Duty of care

Injunction

Negligence

Nuisance

Nuisance at common law

Public nuisance

Statutory nuisances

Private prosecution

Whilst the enforcement of environmental protection law is largely undertaken by the pollution control authorities, an alternative course of action is for an aggrieved person or pressure group to bring a private prosecution, often using information from the public registers of information.

Private prosecutions are commonly brought with respect to statutory nuisances, in some cases where the statutory authority has failed to take action.

Private nuisances

Public registers of information: Integrated Pollution Control

Public registers of information: waste disposal

Public registers of information: water pollution

Statutory nuisances

Process

Process means any activities carried on in Great Britain, whether on premises or by means of mobile plant, which are capable of causing pollution of the environment and *prescribed process* means a process prescribed under Section 2(1).

[Environmental Protection Act 1990]

Process mapping

A logical step by step representation of business activities showing key inputs and outputs.

Producer

A producer is a legal person who does the following:

(a) performs an activity; and

(b) supplies packaging, which he owns, to another stage in the chain or to the final user of the packaging.

[Producer Responsibility Obligations (Packaging Waste) Regulations 1997 – 2005]

Packaging

Producer Responsibility Obligations (Packaging Waste) Regulations 2005

Producer responsibility

A concept that requires industry and commerce involved in the manufacture, distribution and sale of particular goods to take greater responsibility for the disposal and/or recovery of those goods at the end of their useful life. This is closely identified in the Producer Responsibility Obligations (Packaging Waste) Regulations 1997 – 2005, legislation which requires producers, converters, fillers and sellers of packed goods to pay towards the recovery and recycling of packaging materials.

Environment Act 1995

Packaging

Packaging materials

Packaging waste

Producer

Producer Responsibility Obligations (Packaging Waste) Regulations 2005

Recovery

Recovery and recycling obligations

Recycling and disposal of waste

Producer Responsibility Obligations (Packaging Waste) Regulations 2005

These Regulations implemented a revised Packaging Directive and replaced the original 1997 Regulations. The Regulations have a number of objectives, namely:

- (a) to achieve a more sustainable approach in dealing with packaging waste;
- (b) to reduce the amount of packaging waste being deposited in landfills;
- (c) to implement targets established in the Directive; and
- (d) to:
  - (i) respond to the UK's need to have a legislative underpinning for recovery and recycling operations;
  - (ii) have a business-led scheme; and
  - (iii) share the recovery and recycling obligations between all parties in the packaging chain.

The *packaging chain* involves those who:

(a) manufacture the raw materials for packaging;

(b) convert packaging raw materials into packaging;

(c) pack and fill the packaging material;

(d) sell packaged products;

(e) supply transport packaging;

(f) provide some form of service; and

(g) import packaging, packaged materials and packaged goods for any of the above activities.

The Regulations apply to:

(a) any business forming part of the packaging chain; and

(b) who has a turnover in excess of £2,000,000 per annum; and

(c) handles more than 50 tonnes of packaging per annum.

Producers are required to take steps to recover and recycle specific tonnages of packaging waste. These are based on the amount of packaging handled, the producer's part in the packaging chain and on nationally set targets.

Any producer that comes within the above criteria must register with the environmental regulator and show that they have met their recovery and recycling targets. This may be achieved through:

(a) joining a compliance scheme which undertakes these obligations on behalf of the organisation;

(b) an organisation calculating its own recovery and recycling requirements and registering individually; or

(c) in the case of small producers, namely:

  (i) those handling more than 50 tonnes of packaging per annum; and

  (ii) with a turnover between £2,000,000 and £5,000,000 per annum, follow the allocation method.

At the end of each year, producers who are not part of a scheme must confirm by means of a certificate to the Environment Agency that the required amounts of packaging have been recovered and recycled. Producers must maintain records for at least four years in order to prove compliance.

These Regulations place an obligation on some businesses for the first time, or extend existing business obligations, to ensure that packaging is, as far as possible, picking up a 100% obligation. Provisions are made for the Regulations to obligate:

(a) lessors, which are businesses that lease or hire out packaging;

(b) franchisors and other licensors, companies operating public houses and companies operating under similar business models; and

(c) all imported transit packaging.

A *licensor* is a person who is party to a licence agreement in or under which he grants a licence to use a trade mark to another.

Where an operator produces packed products or places packaging or packaged goods on the market, he must comply with the Packaging (Essential Requirements) Regulations.

Under the Regulations, it is an offence to:

(a) fail to register;

(b) fail to meet the recycling or recovery obligations;

(c) fail to certify;

(d) falsify information on a certificate; and

(e) delay or obstruct an authorised officer.

Heavy metal pollution

Packaging

Packaging: essential requirements

Packaging materials

Packaging waste

Producer responsibility

Regulator

Prohibition Notice

Section 14 of the EPA makes provision for the service of Prohibition Notices. If the enforcing authority is of the opinion, in respect of the carrying on of a prescribed process under an authorisation, that the continuing to carry it on, or the continuing to carry it on in a particular manner, *involves an imminent risk of serious pollution of the environment* the authority shall serve a Prohibition Notice on the person carrying on the process.

A Prohibition Notice may be served whether or not the manner of carrying on the process in question contravenes a condition of the authorisation and may relate to any aspects of the process, whether regulated by the condition of the authorisation or not.

A Prohibition Notice shall -

(a) state the authority's opinion;

(b) specify the risk involved in the process;

(c) specify the steps that must be taken to remove it and the period in which they must be taken; and

(d) direct that the authorisation shall, until the Notice is withdrawn, wholly or to the extent specified in the Notice cease to have effect to authorise the carrying on of the process;

and where the direction applies to part only of the process it may impose conditions to be observed in carrying on the part which is authorised to be carried on.

Genetically modified organisms (GMOs)

Section 110 empowers the Secretary of State to serve a Prohibition Notice on any person he has reason to believe -

(a) is proposing to import or acquit, release or market GMOs; or

(b) is keeping any such organisms,

if he is of the opinion that doing any such act to those organisms or continuing to keep them would involve a risk of causing damage to the environment.

Genetically modified organism (GMO)

Offences

Water Resources Act 1991

Prohibition Order

Complaint to a Magistrates' Court

Public nuisance

This has been defined as "an act or omission which materially affects the comfort, safety, health, quality of life or property of a class of Her Majesty's subjects". "A class of Her Majesty's subjects" could be a group of neighbours in a street or the residents of a particular city area.

Where a public nuisance exists, legal action is taken by the Attorney General in the public interest. Local authorities are also empowered by the Local Government Act 1972 to take such action. Thus, in addition to being a tort under civil law, a public nuisance can be a criminal offence punishable by a fine and/or imprisonment. Much will depend on individual circumstances.

Duty of care

Negligence

Nuisance at common law

Private nuisances

Statutory nuisances

Public registers of contaminated land

Under the EPA, a local authority has a duty to maintain a public register of contaminated land. The register must be open to members of the public who can obtain copies of the entries.

Contaminated land

Contaminated Land (England) Regulations 2000

Contaminated Land Regime

Public registers of information: installations and mobile plant

It shall be the duty of each regulator, in respect of installations or mobile plant for which it is the regulator, to maintain a register containing the particulars described in paragraph 1 of Schedule 1.

The register maintained by a local authority regulator shall also contain any particulars contained in any register maintained by the Environment Agency relating to the operation of an installation or Part A mobile plant in the area of the local authority in relation to which the Environment Agency has functions under these Regulations.

[Pollution Prevention and Control (England and Wales) Regulations 2000]

Installation

Mobile plant

Regulator

Public registers of information: Integrated Pollution Control

Registers of Integrated Pollution Control information are available for inspection free of charge at Environment Agency and local authority offices.

Regulation 15 of the Environmental Protection (Applications, Appeals and Registers) Regulations 1991 provides more detail on the information that must be contained on the register.

Information must be placed on the register as soon as possible. This is particularly important where the information is relevant to an application etc. on which the public are being given the opportunity to comment.

Part A activities

Part B activities

Public registers of information: waste disposal

Waste Regulatory Authorities (WRA) are required by virtue of Section 64 of the Act to maintain a register containing details of:

(a) current or recently current licences granted by the authority;

(b) applications made to the authority for licences;

(c) applications for modification of licences;

(d) notices issued by the WRA effecting the modification, revocation or suspension of a licence or imposing requirements on a licence holder;

(e) appeals against decisions of the WRA under Section 43 of the Act;

(f) certificates of completion issued by the WRA;

(g) any offence on the part of the licence holder;

(h) any action taken by the WRA under Sections 42 or 61 of the Act;

(i) directions issued by the Secretary of State;

(j) such matters relating to the treatment, keeping or disposal of waste in the authority's area or any pollution of the environment caused thereby; and

(k) where any information is excluded by virtue of Section 66, a statement indicating the existence of that information.

Public registers of information: water pollution

Waste

Waste Collection Authorities (WCAs)

Waste Disposal Authorities (WDAs) and Companies

Waste Disposal Plans by Waste Regulation Authorities

Waste holders' duties

Waste Local Plans

Waste Management Licences

Waste Management Licensing Regulations 1994 – 2006

Waste Minimisation Act 1998

Waste offences

Waste on land

Waste planning and recycling

Waste Recycling Plans

Waste Regulatory Authorities

Waste Regulation Authorities (WRAs)

Waste transfer

Waste unlawfully deposited

Public registers of information: water pollution

The Water Resources Act 1991 makes specific provision for the maintenance of public registers relating to water pollution. The National Rivers Authority (NRA) is under a duty to keep public registers which must be available for inspection by the public at all reasonable times.

Where an application for a discharge consent is made, the NRA must enter the details on the register within 28 days. The following information should be provided in the register:

(a) details of any notice of water quality objectives or other notices served under Section 83 of the WRA;

(b) details of applications for discharge consents;

(c) details of the consent, plus any conditions attached;

(d) the maximum levels of substances to be contained in the effluent;

(e) any notices served on the consent holder and any time limits;

(f) details of any samples of water or effluent taken by the NRA;

(g) the steps taken as a result of any sample taken;

(h) details of any discharges into controlled water which are controlled by HMIP under the system of Integrated Pollution Control; and

(i) details of any directions issued by the Secretary of State.

Controlled waters

Discharge consent

Water quality objectives and standards

Water Resources Act 1991

Publicity requirements

An important element of an environmental assessment is the emphasis placed upon public participation and consultation. The preparation of an Environmental Statement must be a collaborative exercise involving communication with the local planning authority, the statutory consultees e.g. the National Rivers Authority, Health and Safety Executive, HMIP, and the public. Once a planning authority has determined that an environmental assessment is required to support a planning application, it must make this determination known on the public register, thereby enabling the public to be aware of the application.

An applicant is further required to publish a notice in a local newspaper and to post notices around the site with information about where and when the Environmental Statement can be inspected or purchased.

Following publication of the Environmental Statement, the public has 21 days to inspect it before it is formally submitted with the application for planning permission.

Environmental Assessment and Planning

Environmental Statement

Public registers of information (various)

R

Radiation

Radiation is a form of energy and can be a source of danger in uncontrolled situations.

Radiation energy is released in the form of waves, the length and frequency of the wave depending upon how much energy the atom is releasing. The length and frequency of the waves control the form of energy and its effects on the human body.

Energy types can be listed in increasing wavelength.

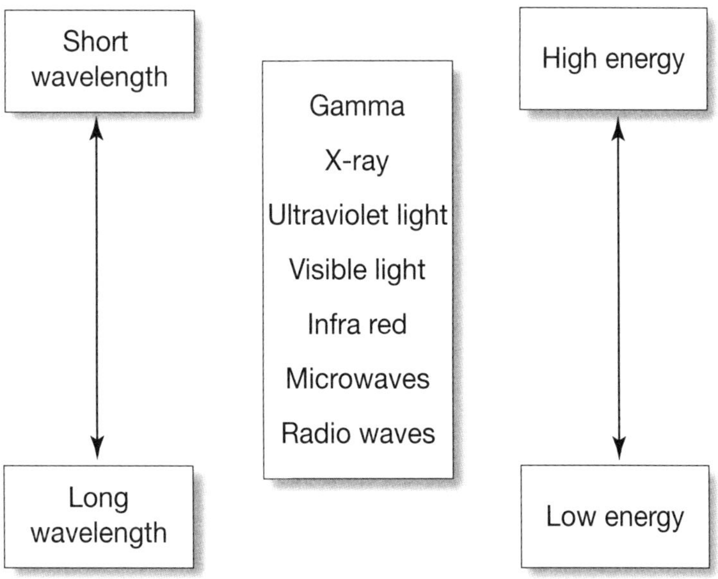

Figure 9: THE ELECTRO-MAGNETIC SPECTRUM

The most important division in the spectrum is between ionising and non-ionising radiation. (An *ion* is a charged atom or group of atoms.)

Ionising radiation can produce chemical changes as a result of ionising molecules upon which it is incident. Non-ionising radiation does not, however, have this effect and is usually absorbed by the molecules upon which it is incident, with the result that the material will heat up, as in the case of microwaves.

Radiation hazards

To assess the hazard associated with radiation, it is necessary to consider:

(a) the type of radiation;

(b) the energy;

(c) the extent of penetration of tissue; and

(d) the duration of exposure.

Exposure to radiation

Effects on the human body may vary according to the type of exposure, i.e. local or general, and the duration of exposure.

The most common form of *local exposure* results in reddening of the skin with ulceration. Where there is a small dose but of long duration, loss of hair, atrophy and fibrosis of the skin can occur.

Acute general exposure can have variable results from mild nausea to severe illness, with vomiting, diarrhoea and collapse, leading ultimately to death. Where exposure is in small doses, chronic anaemia and leukaemia can result. The ovaries and testes are vulnerable and this can lead to reduced fertility and sterility.

Radiological protection

In considering radiological protection strategies, it is necessary to distinguish between sealed and unsealed sources of radiation.

Sealed sources

The source is contained in such a way that the radioactive material cannot be released, e.g. X-ray machines. The source of radiation can be a piece of radioactive metal, such as cobalt, which is sealed in a container or held in another material which is not radioactive. It is usually solid and the container and any bonding material are regarded as the source.

Unsealed sources

Unsealed sources may take a variety of forms – gases, liquids and particulates. Because they are unsealed, entry into the body is comparatively easy.

Criteria for radiological protection

The basic criteria for radiological protection rest on three specific considerations – *time, distance* and *shielding*. The principle is to ensure that no one receives a harmful dose of radiation.

Radiation workers may be protected on a time basis by limiting the duration of exposure to certain predetermined limits.

Alternatively, they may be protected by ensuring that they do not come within certain distances of radiation sources. This may be achieved by the use of restricted areas, barriers and similar controls. The Inverse Square Law applies in this case.

They may be shielded by the use of absorbent material, such as lead or concrete, between themselves and the source to reduce the level of radiation to below the maximum dose level. The quality and quantity (thickness) of shielding varies for the radiation type and energy level and varies from no shielding through lightweight shielding (e.g. 1 cm thick Perspex) to heavy shielding (e.g. centimetres of lead or metres of concrete).

Further protection procedures

Radiological protection procedures may also include:

(a) pre-employment and subsequent medical examinations;

(b) appointment of a responsible trained person;

(c) maintenance of individual dose records;

(d) full training and employee awareness;

(e) continuous and spot-check radiation (dose) monitoring by the use of personal dosemeters, such as film badges;

(f) adherence to maximum permissible dose levels.

Additionally, for unsealed sources -

(g) provision and use of appropriate protective clothing;

(h) efficient ventilation;

(i) enclosure of sources (containment);

(j) use of impervious working surfaces;

(k) immaculate working techniques; and

(l) the use of remote control facilities.

The central objective is the avoidance of radioactive contamination.

High activity sealed radioactive sources and orphan sources

Mobile radioactive source

Open radioactive sources

Radioactive contaminated land

Radioactive substances and wastes

Sealed radioactive sources

Radioactive contaminated land

The keeping and use of radioactive materials and the accumulation and disposal of radioactive wastes on or from premises in England and Wales is covered by the Radioactive Substances Act 1993.

In 2006, Part 2A of the EPA Contaminated Land Regime was extended by DEFRA and the Welsh Assembly to include radioactive contaminated land in order to implement certain requirements of Directive 96/29/EURATOM (the Basic Standards Directive). The extended regime takes account of the special nature of radioactive contamination and the specific requirements of this Directive.

The extension allows radioactive contaminated land to be identified and remediated. This is land that is causing harm or posing a significant possibility of harm to human health as a result of radioactivity. It only applies in circumstances where radioactivity is the result of a past practice or work activity, or the after-effects of a radiological emergency. This includes substances containing artificial radionuclides or processed natural radionuclides.

For land to be classed as "radioactive contaminated land", a significant pollution linkage must be present. A pollutant linkage comprises a radioactive contaminant and a human receptor with a pathway or route capable of linking the two. All three elements must occur on a site for a pollution linkage to exist. The pollution linkage becomes "significant" if it results in harm to human health or there is a *significant possibility of harm* occurring.

A *significant possibility of harm* refers to the possibility or frequency of a situation or event occurring which could lead to exposure to the following levels of radioactivity:

(a) an effective dose of 3 mSv or more per year;

(b) an equivalent dose to the lens of the eye of 15 mSv or more per year; or

(c) an equivalent dose to the skin of 50 mSv or more per year.

Local authorities have a duty to inspect land under the Part 2A regime and to determine whether land is radioactively contaminated. Once contamination is established, the land becomes a special site with the Environment Agency as the regulator.

Radioactive contaminated land may be subject to remediation and various forms of intervention. Intervention includes any action taken on any component of the pollution linkage that results in reducing the exposure of the receptor.

Intervention may only be taken where it is justified and optimised. Intervention is *justified* when the benefits of reducing the detriment outweigh the harm and costs, including social costs, of taking a specific action. Intervention is *optimised* where the chosen action maximises the difference between the benefit produced by the reduction and the harm or costs, including social costs, of any intervention.

Contaminated Land Regime

Environmental Protection Act 1990

Pollutant linkage

Radioactive substances and wastes

Radiation

Receptor

Regulator

Remediation

Radioactive substances and wastes

The Radioactive Substances Act 1993 imposes controls on the keeping and use of radioactive materials and the accumulation and disposal of radioactive waste.

The Act applies to those who:

(a) keep or use, or cause or permit to be kept or used, radioactive material at premises used for the purposes of an undertaking; or

(b) dispose of solid, liquid or gaseous radioactive waste (or accumulate such waste with a view to its disposal) on or from such premises.

Premises include any land, whether covered by buildings or not, including any place underground and any land covered by water.

Radioactive material is categorised thus:

(a) *Open radioactive sources*

- Radioactive material in a form that may be readily divided or diluted, including radioactive powders, gases, solutions or solids. There is potential for contamination of other materials in the normal use of these materials.

(b) *Sealed radioactive sources*

- Sources whose structure prevents the dispersion of any radioactive material in normal conditions of use. Sealed sources include foil and electro-deposited materials.

(c) *Mobile radioactive apparatus*

- Apparatus, equipment, appliances or other things that are radioactive material and that are either:

  (i) constructed or adapted for being transported from place to place; or

  (ii) portable and used for releasing radioactive material into the environment or introducing it into organisms.

Mobile radioactive apparatus must be registered for use by the relevant regulator.

Certificates of Registration and/or Authorisation

Where an operator holds a Certificate of Registration and/or Authorisation, he must:

(a) comply with the conditions in any Certificate of Registration or Authorisation;

(b) pay the relevant application fees and registration fees;

(c) ensure any radioactive materials are stored securely and any radioactive wastes are disposed of safely;

(d) make provision for the costs of their disposal and for managing the sources when they become disused;

(e) in the case of high activity sealed sources, apply to the regulator for those registration or authorisations to be amended to include the additional requirements of the HASS Regulations.

Import and export of radioactive material or waste

Where an operator is involved in the import or export of radioactive material or waste across national boundaries, he must also refer to the requirements of the European Council Regulation (Euratom) 1493/93 and the Transfrontier Shipment of Radioactive Waste Regulations 1993.

Radiation

Radon

Radon is a gas associated with ionising radiation. Exposure to radon in the home and workplace is one of the main risks of ionising radiation, causing many thousands of deaths each year from lung cancer.

Radiation

Reasonable excuse

A person who contravenes or fails to comply with the terms of an Abatement Notice, without reasonable excuse, is guilty of an offence. (Section 80(7) of the EPA)

Reasonable excuse can include special difficulties in complying with the Notice, such as ill-health. On the other hand, lack of finance to comply with the Notice would not constitute reasonable excuse.

Abatement Notice

Reasonableness

In any action based on nuisance, a court must decide whether the defendant was using his property reasonably. In *Saunders-Clark v Grosvenor Mansions and D'Allesandrai* (1900), the importance of this requirement within the tort of nuisance was specified thus:

> '....the court must consider whether the defendant is using his property reasonably or not. If he is using it reasonably, there is nothing which at law can be considered a nuisance: but if he is not using it reasonably...then the plaintiff must be entitled to relief.'

In determining the reasonableness of a defendant's conduct, a court should consider the following factors:

(a) locality;

(b) duration;

(c) sensitivity of the claimant;

(d) intention of the claimant; and

(e) the utility of the defendant's conduct.

Nuisance

Private nuisances

Reasonably practicable

A duty qualified by the term "so far as is reasonably practicable" implies a lower or lesser level of duty than one which is qualified by "so far as is practicable".

"Reasonably practicable" is a narrower term than "physically possible" (i.e. "practicable"), and implies that a computation must be made in which the quantum of risk is placed in one scale and the sacrifice involved, (financial, organisational, etc.) in terms of the measures necessary for averting that risk, is placed in the other. If it can be shown that there is a gross disproportion between these two factors, i.e. the risk being insignificant in relation to the sacrifice, then a defendant discharges the onus upon himself. [Edwards v National Coal Board (1949) 1 AER 743]

Duties under some Regulations made under the EPA are qualified by the term "so far as is reasonably practicable".

Absolute duties

Practicable: definition

Receptor

The entity, e.g. an individual, animal, property, environment, which is vulnerable to the potential adverse effects of a contaminant.

Contaminant

Recommendations and opinions

In addition to Regulations, Directives and Decisions, the Treaty of Rome makes provisions for recommendations and opinions, which are not legally binding.

Decisions

Directives

Regulations

Recovery

Recovery means any of the applicable operations provided for in Annex IIB of the Waste Directive. (See Schedule 3, Part II.)

[Producer Responsibility Obligations (Packaging Waste) Regulations 1997 – 2005]

Recovery, when used in a waste management context, means the extraction of some kind of value (other than by recycling or re-use) from end-of-life products. It nearly always results in energy recovery for which the material is used as fuel in some form of incineration process, whether this is a dedicated waste-to-energy plant, an iron making process or a kiln.

Recovery entails recycling, namely collecting materials from waste products and processing them to produce marketable products.

Recovery as a strategy:

- (a) can result in significant energy savings;
- (b) depends upon the relative costs and impacts on the environment; and
- (c) is dependant on the availability of a market.

Other recycling elements are:

- (a) composting, such as:
  - (i) collecting 'green' waste separately; and
  - (ii) household composting;
- (b) spreading sewage sludge on land (50% currently); and
- (c) producing energy from waste, which has significant future potential.

Composting

End-of-life vehicles (ELVs)

Energy recovery

Recovery

Recovery and recycling obligations

Re-use

Recovery and recycling obligations

These obligations require producers to take reasonable steps to recover and recycle specific tonnages of packaging waste calculated on the basis of three factors:

(a) the tonnage of packaging handled by the producer in the previous year;

(b) the activities that the producer performs and the percentage obligation attached to each obligation; and

(c) the national recovery and recycling targets.

The activity obligations are:

Raw material manufacturing	6%
Converting	11%
Packing/filling	36%
Selling	47%

[Producer Responsibility Obligations (Packaging Waste) Regulations 1997]

Recovery

Recovery of waste

Recovery of waste

These scheduled activities include:

Part A(1)

(a) Recovering by distillation of any oil or any organic solvent;

(b) Cleaning or regenerating carbon, charcoal or ion exchange resins by removing matter which is, or includes, any substance listed in paragraphs 12 to 14 of Part 2 of this Schedule;

(c) Unless carried out as part of any other Part A activity, recovering hazardous waste in plant with a capacity of more than 10 tonnes per day by means of the following operations:

   (i) the use principally as a fuel or other means to generate energy (R1);

   (ii) solvent reclamation/regeneration (R2);

   (iii) recycling/reclamation of inorganic materials other than metals and metal compounds (R5);

   (iv) regeneration of acids or bases (R6);

   (v) recovering components used for pollution abatement (R7);

   (vi) recovery of components from catalysts (R8);

   (vii) oil re-refining or other reuses of oil (R9).

Nothing in paragraphs (a) and (b) of this Part applies to:

(a) distilling oils for the production or cleaning of vacuum pump oil; or

(b) an activity which is ancillary to and related to another activity, whether described in this Schedule or not, which involves the production or use of the substance which is recovered, cleaned or regenerated,

   except where the activity involves distilling more than 100 tonnes per day.

Nothing in this Part applies to the treatment of waste soil by means of mobile plant.

The reference to a R paragraph number in brackets at the end of paragraphs (c)(i) to (vii) is to the number of the corresponding paragraph in Annex IIB of Council Directive 75/442/EEC on waste (recovery operations).

Part A(2)

Nil

Part B

Nil

[Schedule 1: Part 1: Pollution Prevention and Control (England and Wales) Regulations 2000]

Fuel from waste

Incineration

Part A activities

Part B activities

Pollution Prevention and Control Act 1999

Pollution Prevention and Control (England and Wales) Regulations 2000

Prescribed activities

Recovery

Recycling and disposal of waste

Scheduled activities

Recycling and disposal of waste

Recycling involves the reprocessing of wastes, either into the same material (closed loop recycling) or a different material (open loop recycling). It is commonly applied to non-hazardous wastes such as paper, glass, cardboard, plastics and metals. Hazardous wastes, such as solvents, can also be recycled by specialist organisations or through the use of in-house equipment.

Recycling means the reprocessing in a production process of the waste materials for the original purpose or for other purposes, including organic recycling, but excluding energy recovery.

[Producer Responsibility Obligations (Packaging Waste) Regulations 1997 – 2005]

In relation to waste electrical and electronic equipment means the reprocessing in a production process of the waste materials for the original purpose or for other purposes, but excluding energy recovery which means the use of combustible waste as a means of generating energy through direct incineration with or without other waste but with recovery of heat.

[Waste Electrical and Electronic Equipment (Waste Management Licensing) (England and Wales) Regulations 2006]

Incineration

Packaging waste

Producer Responsibility Obligations (Packaging Waste) Regulations 2005

Re-use

Waste electrical and electronic equipment

Reduction

This implies reducing the quantity or the hazardous nature of a waste produced by a process. It generally results in reduced raw material and energy demands, thereby reducing costs.

Waste

Waste Acceptance Criteria

Waste Acceptance Procedures

Refractory material

Material (such as fireclay, silica, magnesite, chrome-magnesite, sillimanite, sintered alumina, beryllia and boron nitride) which is liable to withstand high temperatures and to function as a furnace lining or in other similar temperature applications.

[Pollution Prevention and Control (England and Wales) Regulations 2000]

Registration, Evaluation, Authorisation and Restriction of Chemicals (REACH)

REACH is the outcome of an EU Regulation directed at improving current EU legislation dealing with chemicals. Under the system, organisations that manufacture or import more than one tonne of a chemical substance per year are required to register information relating to that chemical on a central database. The REACH Regulation aims to improve the protection of human health and the environment through better and earlier identification of the properties of chemical substances. It is an integrated strategy to gather hazard information, assess risks, classify, label and restrict the marketing and use of individual substances and preparations.

Implementation of REACH is managed by the European Chemical Agency whose task is to ensure a strong involvement by Member States in the evaluation and authorisation process.

The principal requirements of the Regulation are:

Registration

Manufacturers and importers are required to gather comprehensive information on the properties of substances they produce or import in volumes over one tonne per year. They are required to submit to a European Chemical Register the necessary information to demonstrate the safe use of these substances. Failure to register could mean that the substance cannot be manufactured or imported in the EU market.

Evaluation

Competent public authorities, such as, in the UK, the Health and Safety Executive, are required to examine registration dossiers and substances of concern to determine hazards and risks.

Authorisation

Use-specific authorisations are required for chemicals that cause cancer, mutations or reproductive risks, or that accumulate in humans and in the environment. Authorisations are granted only to organisations that can demonstrate that risks are adequately controlled or if social and economic benefits outweigh the risks and suitable alternatives do not exist.

Chemicals (Hazard Information and Packaging for Supply) (CHIP) Regulations 1994 – 2002

Hazardous substances: classification

Regulations

Regulations have general application, are binding in their authority and directly applicable to all Member States. They can be used to ensure that the law is exactly the same throughout the Community. Regulations take effect within Member States either on the date specified in the Official Journal of the European Communities or, in the absence of a specified date, 20 days after publication.

Directives

Regulator

In relation to the exercise of functions under the Regulations, the authority by whom the functions are exercisable (i.e. Environment Agency, local authorities).

[Pollution Prevention and Control (England and Wales) Regulations 2000]

Part A activities

Part B activities

Pollution Prevention and Control (England and Wales) Regulations 2000

Scheduled activities

Relative humidity

This is defined as:

(a) the amount of moisture present in air expressed as a percentage of that which would produce saturation; for ideal comfort conditions, relative humidity should be between 30% and 70%;

(b) the ratio of the partial pressure of water vapour in a gaseous mixture of air and water vapour to the saturated vapour pressure of water at a given temperature.

For ideal comfort conditions, relative humidity should be between 30% and 60%. Low levels of relative humidity produce discomfort due to drying of the throat and nasal passages. High levels, on the other hand, result in a feeling of stuffiness. It reduces the rate at which body moisture (sweat) evaporates and can reduce the efficiency of the body's thermoregulatory system.

Humidity

"Released" and "release"

A substance is *released* into any environmental medium whenever it is released directly into that medium whether it is released into it within or outside Great Britain and *release* includes -

(a) in relation to air, any emission of the substance into the air;

(b) in relation to water, any entry (including any discharge) of the substance into water;

(c) in relation to land, any deposit, keeping or disposal of the substance in or on land.

Environmental Protection Act 1990

Release into the air: substances

- Oxides of sulphur and other sulphur compounds
- Oxides of nitrogen and other nitrogen compounds
- Oxides of carbon
- Organic compounds and partial oxidation products
- Metals, metalloids and their compounds
- Asbestos (suspended particulate matter and fibres), glass fibres and mineral fibres
- Halogens and their compounds
- Phosphorus and its compounds
- Particulate matter

[Environmental Protection Act 1990, Schedule 4]

Release into water

The release into water of aldrin, dieldrin, mercury and its compounds, cadmium and its compounds, polychlorinated biphenyls, dichlorvos, all isomers of DDT and fenitrothion. The accidental release of toxic wastes and sewage discharges to rivers, lakes or into the sea can cause deposition of poisonous sediments and the dispersal of toxins in currents.

Release into water: substances

Reference to the release into water of a substance or to its release in a quantity which, in any period of 12 months, is greater than the background quantity by an amount specified in this paragraph is to the following substances and amounts:

Substance	*Amount greater than the background quantity (in grammes) in any period of 12 months*
Mercury and its compounds	200 (expressed as metal)
Cadmium and its compounds	1,000 (expressed as metal)
All isomers of hexachlorocyclohexane	20
All isomers of DDT	5
Pentachlorphenol and its compounds	350 (expressed as PCP)
Hexachlorobenzene	5
Hexachlorobutadiene	20
Aldrin	2
Dieldrin	2
Endrin	1
Polychlorinated Biphenyls	1
Dichlorvos	0.2
1,2 – Dichloroethane	2,000
All isomers of trichlorobenzene	75
Atrazine	350*
Simazine	350*
Tributyltin compounds	4 (expressed as TBT)
Triphenyltin compounds	4 (expressed as TBT)
Trifluralin	20
Fenitrothion	2
Azinphos-methyl	2
Malathion	2
Endosulfan	0.5
*Where both Altrazine and Simazine are released, the figure for both substances in aggregate is 350 grammes.	

Figure 10: RELEASES INTO WATER: SUBSTANCES

[Pollution Prevention and Control (England and Wales) Regulations 2000]

Animal and vegetable matter and food industries

Coating activities, printing and textile treatment

Inorganic chemical production

Non-ferrous metals

Paper, pulp and board manufacturing activities

Pesticide

Release to land: substances

Land may become contaminated as a result of crude tipping or dumping of industrial wastes, the actual burial of wastes and through leakages from plant installed on land.

The contamination of soil and groundwater follows, and various chemical reactions or microbial degradation may take place over a long period of time. In some cases, the products of these reactions will leach out through natural or man-made features of the land.

Schedule 6 of the EPA lists the following prescribed substances.

- Organic solvents
- Azides
- Halogens and their covalent compounds
- Metal carbonyls
- Organo-metallic compounds
- Oxidising agents
- Polychlorinated dibenzofuran and any congener thereof
- Polychlorinated dibenzo-p-dioxin and any congener thereof
- Polychlorinated biphenyls, terphenyls and naphthalenes
- Phosphorus
- Pesticides, that is to say, any chemical substance or preparation for destroying any organism harmful to plants or to wood or other plant products, any undesired plant or any harmful creature
- Alkali and alkaline Earth metals and their oxides

"Damage to the environment"

Land pollution

Leaching

Permitting pollution: offence

Pesticide

Pollution incidents

Recycling and disposal of waste

Soil pollution

Unauthorised or harmful deposits

Waste: duty of care

Waste offences

Waste on land

Waste unlawfully deposited

Relevant activities

In relation to a licence, are:

(a) any activities authorised by the licence or, in the case of an expired licence, any which would have been authorised by it had it not expired; and

(b) any precautions or works required by a licence to be taken or carried out in connection with or in consequence of those activities or in the case of an expired licence, any which would have been so required had the licence not expired.

[Pollution Prevention and Control Act 1999]

Permit

Permit conditions

Relevant approval

This means any of the following:

(a) a permit;

(b) an authorisation;

(c) a Waste Management Licence granted under Section 36 of the EPA; or

(d) an exemption registered under Regulation 18 of the Waste Management Licensing Regulations 2006 and the entry in the register under Regulation 18 of those Regulations shall be treated as the grant of relevant approval for the purposes of the definition of "existing waste incineration installation".

[Waste Incineration (England and Wales) Regulations 2002]

Incineration

Waste Management Licences

Waste Management Licensing Regulations 1994 – 2006

Relevant lake or pond

Any lake or pond, including reservoirs, which, whether it is natural, artificial, above or below ground, discharges into a relevant river or watercourse or into another lake or pond which is itself a relevant lake or pond.

[Water Resources Act 1991]

Coastal waters

Controlled waters

Fresh water limit

Inland fresh waters

Ground waters

Relevant river or watercourse

Watercourse

Water Resources Act 1991

Relevant offences

These pollution-related offences are laid down in the Waste Management Licence Regulations 1994.

Competent person

"Fit and proper person"

Waste offences

Relevant river or watercourse

Any river or watercourse, including an underground river and an artificial river or watercourse, which is neither a public sewer nor a sewer or drain which drains into a public sewer.

[Water Resources Act 1991]

Coastal waters

Controlled waters

Fresh water limit

Inland fresh waters

Ground waters

Relevant lake or pond

Watercourse

Water Resources Act 1991

Remediation

This term is defined in Part IIa, Section 78(a)(7) of the EPA as:

(a) the doing of anything for the purpose of assessing the condition of:

 (i) the contaminated land in question;

 (ii) any controlled waters affected by that land; or

 (iii) any land adjoining or adjacent to that land;

(b) the doing of any works, the carrying out of any operations or the taking of any steps in relation to any such land or waters for the purpose:

 (i) of preventing or minimising, or remedying or mitigating the effects of any significant harm, or any pollution of controlled waters, by reason of which the contaminated land is such land; or

 (ii) of restoring the land or waters to their former state; or

(c) the making of subsequent inspections from time to time for the purpose of keeping under review the condition of the land or waters.

[Environmental Protection Act 1990]

Contaminated land

Contaminated Land (England) Regulations 2000

Controlled waters

Remediation Notice

Remediation Notice

Under both the EPA and the Contaminated Land (England) Regulations, local authorities are empowered to serve a Remediation Notice on any person with respect to contaminated land. Under the Regulations, a Remediation Notice shall state (in addition to the matters required by Section 78(e)(1) and (3)):

(a) the name and address of the person on whom the Notice is served;

(b) the location and extent of the contaminated land to which the Notice relates, sufficient to enable it to be identified whether by reference to a plan or otherwise;

(c) the date of any Notice which was given under Section 78(b) (EPA) to the person on whom the Remediation Notice is served identifying the contaminated land in question as contaminated land;

(d) whether the enforcing authority considers the person on whom the Notice is served is an appropriate person by reason of:

  (i) having caused or knowingly permitted the substances, or any of the substances, by reason of which the contaminated land in question is contaminated land, to be in, on or under that land;

  (ii) being the owner of the contaminated land in question; or

  (iii) being the occupier of the contaminated land in question;

(e) particulars of the significant harm or pollution of controlled waters by reason of which the contaminated land in question is contaminated land;

(f) the substances by reason of which the contaminated land in question is contaminated land and, if any of the substances have escaped from other land, the location of that other land;

(g) the enforcing authority's reasons for its decisions as to the things by way of remediation that the appropriate person is required to do, which shall show how any guidance issued by the Secretary of State under Section 78(e)(5) has been applied.

Further items which may be included in a Remediation Notice relate to:

(a) situations of joint ownership of contaminated land;

(b) provisions for apportionment of costs; and

(c) situations where there is imminent danger of serious harm or serious pollution of controlled waters.

A person on whom a Remediation Notice is served may be guilty of an offence for failure, without reasonable excuse, to comply with any requirements of the Notice. Such a person has the right of appeal to a Magistrates' Court and to the Secretary of State.

Contaminated land

Contaminated Land (England) Regulations 2000

Controlled waters

Remediation

Special sites

Renewable energy

Renewable energy is energy derived from sources that are regenerative and which cannot be depleted. Traditional sources of renewable energy are wind, water and solar energy.

The prime source of renewable energy is solar radiation, i.e. sunlight. Other sources are biofuels and geothermal energy.

Biofuels

Geothermal energy

Solar energy

Water power

Wind power

Respiratory diseases

Adverse environments are associated with a range of respiratory diseases. These diseases may be classified physiologically as obstructive conditions, which impede normal lung function and restrictive conditions, which cause a reduction in the functional volume of the lung.

Obstructive lung diseases

These include emphysema, bronchitis, asthma, chronic obstructive pulmonary diseases, bronchiectasis, byssinosis (cotton workers' disease) and asbestosis.

Restrictive lung diseases

These include fibrosis, alveolar damage, pleural effusion, hypersensitivity pneumonitis, asbestosis, pleurisy and lung cancer.

Airborne particulates

Asbestos

Asbestos: activities involving

Legionnaires' disease

Re-use

Re-use means any operation by which packaging, which has been conceived and designed to accomplish within its life cycle a minimum number of trips or rotations, is refilled or used for the same purpose for which it was conceived, with or without the support of auxiliary products present on the market enabling the package to be refilled; such re-used packaging will become packaging waste when no longer subject to re-use.

[Producer Responsibility Obligations (Packaging Waste) Regulations 1997 – 2005]

This entails using materials or products again, for the same or a different purpose, without material reprocessing as with glass bottles or returnable plastic containers.

In relation to waste electrical and electronic equipment means any operation by which waste electrical and electronic equipment or components thereof are used for the same purpose for which they were conceived, including the continued use of the equipment or components thereof which are returned to collection points, distributors, recyclers or manufacturers.

[Waste Electrical and Electronic Equipment (Waste Management Licensing) (England and Wales) Regulations 2006]

Packaging

Producer Responsibility (Packaging Waste) Regulations 2005

Waste

Waste electrical and electronic equipment

Waste offences

Revocation of permit

The regulator may at any time revoke a permit, in whole or in part, by serving a Notice (a Revocation Notice) on the operator.

Without prejudice to the generality of the above paragraph, the regulator may serve a Notice in relation to a permit where:

(a) the permit authorises the carrying out of a specified waste management activity and it appears to the regulator that the operator of the installation or mobile plant has ceased to be a fit and proper person to carry out that activity by reason of having been convicted of a relevant offence or by reason of the management of that activity having ceased to be in the hands of a technically competent person;

(b) the holder of the permit has ceased to be the operator of the installation or mobile plant covered by the permit.

A Revocation Notice may:

(a) revoke a permit entirely;

(b) revoke a permit only in so far as it authorises the operation of some of the installations or mobile plant to which it applies;

(c) revoke a permit only in so far as it authorises the carrying on of some of the activities which may be carried out in an installation or by means of mobile plant to which it applies.

A Revocation Notice shall specify:

(a) in the case of a revocation mentioned in sub-paragraph (b) or (c) above (a partial revocation), the extent to which the permit is being revoked;

(b) in all cases, the date on which the revocation shall take effect, which shall be at least 28 days after the date on which the Notice is served.

[Pollution Prevention and Control (England and Wales) Regulations 2000]

Competent person

"Fit and proper person"

Permit

Relevant offences

Specified waste management activity

Ringelmann Chart

The Ringelmann Chart indicates differing shades of darkness of smoke. It features a card with cross-hatching of black on a white background so that a known percentage of white is obscured. The chart is used by an observer some distance from a smoke source who notes the different shades of smoke from grey to black.

The different shades are numerically categorised thus:

Ringelmann 0	–	White
Ringelmann 1	–	20% black on white
Ringelmann 2	–	40% black on white – Dark smoke
Ringelmann 3	–	60% black on white
Ringelmann 4	–	80% black on white – Black smoke
Ringelmann 5	–	100% black.

Figure 11: RINGELMANN CHART

Air pollution

Authorised fuels

Clean Air Act 1993

"Dark smoke"

Dark smoke defences

Dark smoke offences

Riparian rights

The owners or occupiers of land and property adjacent to a river (riparian owners or occupiers) have the right to "the ordinary use of water flowing past their land", their riparian rights.

In *Miner v Gilmore(1859)*, Lord Kingsdown stated:

> "By the general law applicable to running streams, every riparian proprietor has a right to what may be called the ordinary use of water flowing past his land; for instance, to the reasonable use of the water for his domestic purposes and for his cattle, and this without regard to the effect which such use may have, in case of a deficiency, on a proprietor lower down the stream."

This ruling clearly took no account of the environmental consequences of upstream pollution for those further down the stream. The judgement was modified in *Rugby Joint Water Board v Walters (1967)* where the court stated that, in the case of water abstracted for "extraordinary use", such abstraction must either have no effect on the river or it must be returned to it substantially undiminished in terms of both quantity or quality.

Water abstraction

Watercourse

Water pollution

Water Resources Act 1991

Risk

The probability or likelihood of injury, damage or loss.

The likelihood that harm from a particular hazard is realised.

Harm

Hazard

Risk assessment

The identification of the hazards present, whether arising from work activities, industrial processes or other potential sources of pollution, the measurement and evaluation of the risks arising from those hazards, and the specification of preventive and protective measures directed at preventing or controlling exposure to the hazards, taking into account current legal requirements.

The process by which the various risks associated with a site or group of sites are assessed.

Rubber: activities involving

These scheduled activities are:

Part A(1)

Nil

Part A(2)

(a) Manufacturing new tyres (but not remoulds or retreads) if this involves the use in any period of 12 months of 50,000 tonnes or more of the following:

(i) natural rubber;

(ii) synthetic organic elastomers;

(iii) other substances mixed with them.

Part B

(a) Unless falling with Part A(1) or A(2) of any Section in this Schedule, the mixing, milling or blending of:

(i) natural rubber;

(ii) synthetic organic elastomers,

if carbon black is used;

(b) Any activity which converts the product of an activity falling within paragraph (a) into a finished product if related to any activity falling within that paragraph.

[Schedule 1: Part 1: Pollution Prevention and Control (England and Wales) Regulations 2000 as amended]

Part A activities

Part B activities

Pollution Prevention and Control Act 1999

Pollution Prevention and Control (England and Wales) Regulations 2000

Scheduled activities

Rylands v Fletcher

This case, going back to 1868, established a rule imposing strict liability on anyone who brings onto, or keeps on, their property anything which is likely to create mischief or harm if it escapes.

There are numerous examples of dangerous things, such as chemicals, oil, hazardous fumes and explosive materials which, if brought on to land or property, could cause mischief or harm. In determining "a dangerous thing", the courts have generally considered the potential for mischief if it escapes. The damage must be also foreseen as a result of the escape and the escape itself must be foreseeable.

Environmental law

Negligence

Tort

S

Safety data

Under the Chemicals (Hazard Information and Packaging for Supply) Regulations, a safety data sheet must contain the following obligatory headings:

1. Identification of the substance/preparation
2. Composition/information on ingredients
3. Hazards identification
4. First aid measures
5. Fire fighting measures
6. Accidental release measures
7. Handling and storage
8. Exposure controls/personal protection
9. Physical and chemical properties
10. Stability and reactivity
11. Toxicological information
12. Ecological information
13. Disposal considerations
14. Transport information
15. Regulatory information
16. Other information

Chemicals (Hazard Information and Packaging for Supply) (CHIP) Regulations 1994 – 2002

Hazardous substances: classification

Sales packaging

Packaging

Scheduled activities

Activities referred to are:

(a) manufacturing and packaging of raw materials;

(b) converting materials into packaging;

(c) packing and filling packaging; and

(d) selling packaging to the final user.

[Producer Responsibility Obligations (Packaging Waste) Regulations 1997 – 2005]

Activities of any nature, whether:

(a) industrial or commercial or other activities; or

(b) carried on on particular premises or otherwise,

and includes (with or without other activities) the depositing, keeping or disposal of any substance.

[Pollution Prevention and Control Act 1999]

Part I of Schedule 1 to the Pollution Prevention and Control (England and Wales) Regulations 2000 provides the following classification of *activities* to which the Regulations apply:

Chapter 1: Energy Industries

1.1 Combustion Activities

1.2 Gasification, Liquefaction and Refining Activities

Chapter 2: Production and Processing of Metals

2.1 Ferrous Metals

2.2 Non-Ferrous Metals

2.3 Surface Treating Metals and Plastic Materials

Chapter 3: Mineral Industries

3.1 Production of Cement and Lime

3.2 Activities Involving Asbestos

3.3 Manufacturing of Glass and Glass Fibre

3.4 Production of Other Mineral Fibres

3.5 Other Mineral Activities

3.6 Ceramic Production

Chapter 4: Chemical Industry

4.1 Organic Chemicals

4.2 Inorganic Chemicals

4.3 Chemical Fertiliser Production

4.4 Plant Health Products and Biocides

4.5 Pharmaceutical Production

4.6 Explosives Production

4.7 Manufacturing Activities Involving Carbon Disulphide and Ammonia

4.8 The Storage of Chemicals in Bulk

Chapter 5: Waste Management

5.1 Disposal of Waste by Incineration

5.2 Disposal of Waste by Landfill

5.3 Disposal of Waste Other Than by Incineration or Landfill

5.4 Recovery of Waste

5.5 The Production of Fuel from Waste

Chapter 6: Other Activities

6.1 Paper, Pulp and Board Manufacturing Activities

6.2 Carbon Activities

6.3 Tar and Bitumen Activities

6.4 Coating Activities, Printing and Textile Treatments

6.5 The Manufacture of Dyestuffs, Printing Ink and Coating Materials

6.6 Timber Activities

6.7 Activities Involving Rubber

6.8 The Treatment of Animal and Vegetable Matter and Food Industries

6.9 Intensive Farming

(See individual entries)

Section 5.1 was amended to *Incineration and Co-Incineration of Waste* by the Waste Incineration (England and Wales) Regulations 2002.

Environmental pollution

Harm

Incineration and co-incineration of waste

Packaging

Packaging materials

Packaging waste

Part A activities

Part B activities

Pollution Prevention and Control Act 1999

Pollution Prevention and Control (England and Wales) Regulations 2000

Producer

Producer Responsibility Obligations (Packaging) Waste Regulations 2005

Relevant activities

Sealed radioactive sources

These are sources whose structure prevents the dispersion of any radioactive material in normal conditions of use. Sealed sources include, for example, foil or electro-deposited materials.

[High Activity Sealed Radioactive Sources and Orphan Sources Regulations 2005]

Mobile radioactive source

Open radioactive sources

Radiation

Secondary packaging

Packaging

Service of Notices

Arrangements for the service of Notices are identified in Section 160 of the EPA and in specific Regulations, such as the Pollution Prevention and Control (England and Wales) Regulations. The principal requirements for the service of Notices are:

(a) any Notice served or given shall be in writing;

(b) any Notice may be served on or given to a person by leaving it at his proper address or by sending it by post to him at that address;

(c) any Notice may:

  (i) in the case of a body corporate, be served on the secretary or clerk of that body;

  (ii) in the case of a partnership, be served on or given to a partner or person having the control or management of the partnership business.

Abatement Notice

Breach of Conditions Notice

Litter Abatement Notice

Litter Control Notice

Noise Abatement Notices

Planning Contravention Notice

Prohibition Notice

Remediation Notice

Street Litter Control Notice

Variation Notice

Warning Notice

Works Notice

Sewage effluent

Includes any effluent from the sewage disposal or sewerage works of a sewerage undertaker but does not include surface water.

[Water Resources Act 1991]

Sewage effluent

Sewerage

Sewerage

Under Section 101(a) of the Water Industry Act 1991, two or more property owners can request their water company that serves their area to provide effective foul sewerage for their properties, subject to certain conditions.

The Environment Act 1995 introduced an amendment to the Water Industry Act 1991. If the owners of two or more properties require the provision of mains sewerage to their properties, and there are environmental problems with the existing systems, they can make an application to the water company that serves their area.

Costs

If the properties are then connected to a public sewer, the only costs for the property owner are:

(a) the infrastructure (approximately £200);

(b) the physical costs of amending his own system; and

(c) the annual water company charges.

Shopping and luggage trolleys

Section 89, together with Schedule 4, of the EPA gives powers to local authorities to deal with shopping and luggage trolleys which have been abandoned.

Section 89 applies to trolleys found on any land in the open air by an authorised officer of the authority which appear to him to be abandoned. Trolleys to which the Schedule applies may be seized and removed to a place under the control of the authority. The power of removal is subject to consent or notification requirements where the trolley is found on land which appears to be occupied. Trolleys seized must be kept for six weeks and may then be sold or otherwise disposed of. This is subject to the obligation to serve notice on any person believed to be the owner and to make reasonable enquiries as to who owns it. Owners have the right to delivery of their trolleys subject to payment of a charge. The authority may agree a scheme for collection with owners of trolleys and in such cases no charge may be demanded.

Devon County Council v Gateway Foodmarkets [1990] LMELR Issue 3, Vol. 2, p 96 is a case which deals with the obstruction of the highway by supermarket trolleys.

Environmental Protection Act 1990

Sick Building Syndrome

The reputedly high incidence of sickness amongst people who work in sealed buildings, especially offices, has attracted considerable attention over the last 30 years. Various terms have been used to describe the phenomenon – "building sickness", "sick building syndrome", "sick office syndrome", "tight building syndrome" and "office eye syndrome".

There is still much speculation as to whether the condition actually exists and its nature, prevalence, causes and even its existence are open to debate. The term is ill-defined, one definition used being "a building in which complaints of ill-health are more common than might reasonably be expected".

Most reports of outbreaks detail a common list of symptoms. These are summarised by the World Health Organisation (WHO) as:

(a) ear, nose and throat irritation;

(b) sensation of dry mucous membranes and skin;

(c) erythema (skin rash);

(d) mental fatigue;

(e) headaches, high frequency of airway infections and cough;

(f) hoarseness, wheezing, itching and unspecified hypersensitivity; and

(g) nausea, dizziness.

Some investigations have produced more extensive lists of symptoms including, for example, high blood pressure and miscarriages. However, these are not mentioned as occurring amongst staff in sick buildings; they are not specifically attributed to "sick building syndrome".

Studies in the UK show a number of patterns:

(a) symptoms are most common in air conditioned buildings but they also occur in buildings that are naturally ventilated;

(b) clerical staff are more likely than managerial staff to suffer, and complaints are more frequent in the public than the private sector; complaints are more frequent in offices housing many staff;

(d) people with most symptoms have least perceived control over their environment; and

(e) symptoms are more frequent in the afternoon than in the morning.

Common features of sick buildings

The WHO identifies a number of features common to sick buildings, namely:

(a) they are often forced ventilated;

(b) they are often of light construction;

(c) indoor surfaces are often covered in light textiles (carpets, furnishing fabrics, etc.);

(d) they are energy efficient, kept relatively warm and have a homogeneous thermal environment; and

(e) they are airtight, i.e. windows cannot be opened.

The possible causes

Many causes have been suggested for sick building syndrome, including airborne pollutants, such as:

(a) chemical pollutants from the building occupants, fabric and furnishings, office machinery and from outside;

(b) airborne dusts and fibres; and

(c) microbiological contaminants from carpets, furnishings, building occupants or from the ventilation or air conditioning system.

These may have a directly toxic, pathogenic or irritant effect on occupants or they may have an allergenic effect, i.e. once the occupants are sensitised, subsequent very small changes may cause illness.

Some outbreaks of illness among workers have been attributed to psychological causes. One report (Guidotti) describes an outbreak of illness in a telephone exchange when 81 members of staff were taken ill. Air sampling results were negative and the outbreak was eventually attributed to an employee with "a military history of involvement in psychological operations".

Whilst the evidence is largely circumstantial, it is useful to summarise the factors that may contribute towards symptoms associated with building sickness. These are:

(a) ventilation rates;

(b) temperature and air movement;

(c) humidity;

(d) lighting standards;

(e) airborne pollution;

(f) airborne organic matter from the air conditioning system; and

(g) low morale and general dissatisfaction.

Airborne particulates

Air pollution

Hazardous substances: classification

Humidity

Temperature control in the workplace

Ventilation of buildings

Work environment

Single European Act 1986

This Act fundamentally identified the need to eliminate technical barriers to trade, one of which was the varying legal standards for health and safety requirements throughout the Community. It introduced the "new approach" to technical harmonisation and standards, the development of the "essential safety requirements" philosophy, and of harmonisation Directives which establish these essential safety requirements. The Act further recognised the need to encourage improvements in the working environment.

Directives

Sites of Special and Scientific Interest

Sites of Special and Scientific Interest represent the best sites for wildlife and geology. They are notified throughout Great Britain and English Nature is responsible for identifying and protecting these sites. This takes place through a partnership with site owners and managers.

Notification of a site is primarily a legal mechanism to protect sites that are of particular conservation interest because of the wildlife they support, or because of the geological features that are found there.

Areas of Outstanding Natural Beauty

Conservation Area

Countryside and Rights of Way Act 2000

Smoke

Smoke includes soot, ash, grit and gritty particles emitted in smoke.

Clean Air Act 1993

"Dark smoke"

Dark smoke defences

Dark smoke offences

Ringelmann Chart

Smoke Control Areas

Smoke Control Areas

The establishment of Smoke Control Areas provides local authorities with measures to control, in particular, smoke from domestic premises. As such, a local authority may declare all or part of its area a Smoke Control Area by means of a Smoke Control Order.

The Smoke Control Order may designate certain classes of buildings, and exempt specific buildings or classes of buildings. Once the area has been designated a Smoke Control Area, then an occupier of a building in the area is guilty of an offence if smoke (not necessarily dark smoke) is emitted from a chimney of that building.

The following defences are available if:

(a) the emission resulted from the use of an authorised fuel; or

(b) the emission resulted from the use of a fireplace exempted from the Regulations.

[Clean Air Act 1993]

Authorised fuels

Clean Air Act 1993

Smoke

Smoke Control Areas (Authorised Fuels) (England) Regulations 2002 – 2006

These Regulations define the fuels authorised for use in Smoke Control Areas.

Smoke Control Areas (Exempted Fireplaces) (England) Order 2000 – 2006

These Regulations exempt certain classes of fireplace from the requirements for fireplaces in Smoke Control Areas.

Smoke-free premises and vehicles

Legal requirements relating to smoke-free premises and vehicles are incorporated in Part 1 Chapter 1 of the Health Act 2006. Because of the significance of this legislation, the principal elements of this Chapter are shown below.

1. Introduction

1. This Chapter makes provision for the prohibition of smoking in certain premises, places and vehicles which are smoke-free by virtue of this Chapter.

2. In this Chapter:
   (a) smoking refers to smoking tobacco or anything which contains tobacco, or smoking any other substance, and

   (b) smoking includes being in possession of lit tobacco or anything lit which contains tobacco, or being in possession of any other lit substance in a form in which it could be smoked.

3. In this Chapter, *smoke* and other related expressions are to be read in accordance with subsection 2.

2. Smoke-free premises

1. Premises are smoke-free if they are open to the public. But unless the premises also fall within subsection 2, they are smoke-free only when open to the public.

2. Premises are smoke-free if they are used as a place of work:
   (a) by more than one person (even if the persons who work there do so at different times, or only intermittently), or

   (b) where members of the public might attend for the purposes of seeking or receiving goods or services from the person or persons working there (even if members of the public are not always present).

   They are smoke-free all the time.

3. If only part of the premises is open to the public or (as the case may be) used as a place of work mentioned in subsection 2, the premises are smoke-free only to that extent.

4. In any case, premises are smoke-free only in those areas which are enclosed or substantially enclosed.

5. The appropriate national authority may specify in Regulations what *enclosed* and *substantially enclosed* mean.
6. Section 3 provides for some premises, or areas of premises, not to be smoke-free despite this Section.
7. Premises are *open to the public* if the public or a section of the public has access to them, whether by invitation or not, and whether on payment or not.
8. *Work*, in subsection 2, includes voluntary work.

2. Smoke-free premises: exemptions

1. The appropriate national authority may make Regulations providing for specified descriptions of premises, or specified areas within specified descriptions of premises, not to be smoke-free despite Section 2.
2. Descriptions of premises which may be specified under subsection 1 include, in particular, any premises where a person has his home, or is living whether permanently or temporarily (including hotels, care homes, and prisons and other places where a person may be detained).
3. The power to make Regulations under subsection 1 is not exercisable so as to specify any description of:
   (a) premises in respect of which a premises licence under the Licensing Act 2003 authorising the sale by retail of alcohol for consumption on the premises has effect;
   (b) premises in respect of which a club premises certificate (within the meaning of Section 60 of that Act) has effect.
4. But subsection 3 does not prevent the exercise of that power so as to specify any area, within a specified description of premises mentioned in subsection 3, where a person has his home, or is living whether permanently or temporarily.
5. For the purpose of making provision for those participating as performers in a performance, or in a performance of a specified description, not to be prevented from smoking if the artistic integrity of the performance makes it appropriate for them to smoke,
   (a) the power in subsection 1 also includes power to provide for specified descriptions of premises or specified areas within such premises not to be smoke-free in relation only to such performers; and
   (b) subsection 3 does not prevent the exercise of that power as so extended.

6. The Regulations may provide, in relation to any description of premises or areas of premises specified in the Regulations, that the premises or areas are not smoke-free;

   (a) in specified circumstances;

   (b) if specified conditions are satisfied; or

   (c) at specified times,

   or any combination of those.

7. The conditions may include conditions requiring the designation in accordance with the Regulations, by the person in charge of the premises, of any rooms in which smoking is to be permitted.

8. For the purposes of subsection 5, the references to a *performance*:

   (a) include, for example, the performance of a play, or a performance given in connection with the making of a film or television programme; and

   (b) if the Regulations so provide, include a rehearsal.

4. Additional smoke-free places

1. The appropriate national authority may make Regulations designating as smoke-free any place or description of place that is not smoke-free under Section 2.

2. The place, or places falling within the description, need not be enclosed or substantially enclosed.

3. The appropriate national authority may designate a place or description of place under this Section only if in the authority's opinion there is a significant risk that, without designation, persons present there would be exposed to significant quantities of smoke.

4. The Regulations may provide for such places, or places falling within the description, to be smoke-free only:

   (a) in specified circumstances;

   (b) at specified times;

   (c) if specified conditions are satisfied;

   (d) in specified areas,

   or any combination of those.

5. Vehicles

1. The appropriate national authority may make Regulations providing for vehicles to be smoke-free.
2. The Regulations may in particular make provision:
   (a) for the descriptions of vehicle which are to be smoke-free;
   (b) for the circumstances in which they are to be smoke-free;
   (c) for them to be smoke-free only in specified areas, or except in specified areas;
   (d) for exemptions.
3. In this Chapter, *vehicle* means every type of vehicle, including train, vessel, aircraft and hovercraft.

6. No-smoking signs

1. It is the duty of any person who occupies or is concerned in the management of smoke-free premises to make sure that no-smoking signs complying with the requirements of this Section are displayed in those premises in accordance with the requirements of this Section.
2. Regulations made by the appropriate national authority may provide for a duty corresponding to that mentioned in subsection 1 in relation to:
   (a) premises which are smoke-free by virtue of Section 4;
   (b) vehicles which are smoke-free by virtue of Section 5.

   The duty is to be imposed on persons, or on persons of a description, specified in Regulations.
3. The signs must be displayed in accordance with any requirements contained in Regulations made by the appropriate national authority.
4. The signs must conform to any requirements specified in Regulations made by the appropriate national authority (for example, requirements as to content, size, design, colour, or wording).
5. A person who fails to comply with a duty in subsection 1, or any corresponding duty in Regulations under subsection 2 commits an offence.
6. It is a defence for a person charged with an offence under subsection 5 to show:
   (a) that he did not know, or could not reasonably have been expected to know, that the premises were smoke-free (or, as the case may be, that the place or vehicle was smoke-free); or

(b) that he did not know, and could not reasonably have been expected to know, that no-smoking signs complying with the requirements of this Section were not being displayed in accordance with the requirements of this Section; or

(c) that on other grounds it was reasonable for him not to comply with the duty.

7. If a person charged with an offence under subsection 5 relies on a defence in subsection 6, and evidence is adduced which is sufficient to raise an issue with respect to that defence, the court must assume that the defence is satisfied unless the prosecution proves beyond reasonable doubt that it is not.

8. A person guilty of an offence under subsection 5 is liable on summary conviction to a fine not exceeding a level on the standard scale specified in Regulations made by the Secretary of State.

7. Offence of smoking in a smoke-free place

1. In this Section, a *smoke-free place* means any of the following:

   (a) premises, so far as they are smoke-free under or by virtue of Sections 2 and 3 (including premises which by virtue of Regulations under Section 3(5) are smoke-free in relation to performers);

   (b) a place, so far as it is smoke-free by virtue of Section 4;

   (c) a vehicle, so far as it is smoke-free by virtue of Section 5.

2. A person who smokes in a smoke-free place commits an offence.

3. But a person who smokes in premises which are not smoke-free in relation to performers by virtue of Regulations under Section 3(5) does not commit an offence if he is such a performer.

4. It is a defence for a person charged with an offence under subsection 2 to show that he did not know, and could not reasonably have been expected to know, that it was a smoke-free place.

5. If a person charged with an offence under this Section relies on a defence in subsection 4, and evidence is adduced which is sufficient to raise an issue with respect to that defence, the court must assume that the defence is satisfied unless the prosecution proves beyond reasonable doubt that it is not.

6. A person guilty of an offence under this Section is liable on summary conviction to a fine not exceeding a level on the standard scale specified in Regulations made by the Secretary of State.

8. Offence of failing to prevent smoking in a smoke-free place

1. It is the duty of any person who controls or is concerned in the management of smoke-free premises to cause a person smoking there to stop smoking.

2. The reference in subsection 1 to a person smoking does not include a performer in relation to whom the premises are not smoke-free by virtue of Regulations made under Section 3(5).

3. Regulations made by the appropriate national authority may provide for a duty corresponding to that mentioned in subsection 1 in relation to:

   (a) places which are smoke-free by virtue of Section 4;

   (b) vehicles which are smoke-free by virtue of Section 5.

   The duty is imposed on persons, or on persons of a description, specified in the Regulations.

4. A person who fails to comply with the duty in subsection 1, or any corresponding duty in Regulations under subsection 3, commits an offence.

5. It is a defence for a person charged with an offence under subsection 4 to show:

   (a) that he took reasonable steps to cause the person in question to stop smoking; or

   (b) that he did not know, and could not reasonably have been expected to know, that the person in question was smoking; or

   (c) that on other grounds it was reasonable for him not to comply with the duty.

6. If a person charged with an offence under this Section relies on a defence in subsection 5, and evidence is adduced which is sufficient to raise an issue with respect to that defence, the court must assume that the defence is satisfied unless the prosecution proves beyond reasonable doubt that it is not.

7. A person guilty of an offence under this Section is liable on summary conviction to a fine not exceeding a level on the standard scale specified in Regulations made by the Secretary of State.

9. Fixed penalties

1. An authorised officer of an enforcement authority who has reason to believe that a person has committed an offence under Section 6(5) or 7(2) on premises, or in a place or vehicle, in relation to which the authorised officer has functions may give him a Penalty Notice in respect of the offence.
2. A Penalty Notice is a Notice offering a person the opportunity to discharge any liability to conviction for the offence to which the Notice relates by paying a penalty in accordance with this Chapter.
3. Schedule 1 makes further provision about fixed penalties.

10. Enforcement

1. The appropriate national authority may make Regulations designating the bodies or descriptions of body which are to be enforcement authorities for the purposes of this Chapter.
2. The Regulations:
   (a) must specify the descriptions of premises, place or vehicle in relation to which an enforcement authority has enforcement functions;
   (b) may provide for a case being dealt with by one enforcement authority to be transferred (or further transferred, or transferred back) to, and taken over by, another enforcement authority.
3. It is the duty of an enforcement authority to enforce, in respect of premises, places and vehicles in relation to which it has enforcement functions, the provisions of this Chapter and Regulations made under it.
4. The appropriate national authority may direct, in relation to cases of a particular description or a particular case, that any duty imposed on an enforcement authority by subsection 3 is to be discharged instead by the appropriate national authority.
5. In this Chapter, *authorised officer*, in relation to an enforcement authority, means any person (whether or not an officer of the authority) who is authorised by it in writing, either generally or specially, to act in matters arising under this Chapter.
6. If Regulations under this Section so provide, no person is to be so authorised unless he has such qualifications as are prescribed by the Regulations.
7. Schedule 2 makes provision about powers of entry, etc.

11. Obstruction, etc of officers

1. Any person who intentionally obstructs an authorised officer of an enforcement authority, acting in the exercise of his functions under or by virtue of this Chapter, commits an offence.
2. Any person who without reasonable cause fails to give an authorised officer of the enforcement authority, acting in the exercise of his function under or by virtue of this Chapter, any facilities, assistance or information which the authorised officer reasonably requires of him for the performance of those functions commits an offence.
3. A person commits an offence if, in purported compliance with any requirement of an authorised officer mentioned in subsection 2:
   (a) he makes a statement which is false or misleading; and
   (b) he either knows that it is false or misleading or is reckless as to whether it is false or misleading.

   False or misleading means false or misleading in a material particular.
4. A person guilty of an offence under this Section is liable on summary conviction to a fine not exceeding level 3 on the standard scale.

Smoke-free (Premises and Enforcement) Regulations 2006

Ventilation of buildings

Smoke-free (Premises and Enforcement) Regulations 2006

These Regulations are made under the Health Act 2006 and apply to England only. (Scotland and Wales have separate Regulations.) The Regulations clarify the distinction between 'enclosed' and 'substantially enclosed' premises and specify the enforcement authorities for the purpose of these Regulations.

Enclosed and substantially enclosed premises

1. For the purposes of Section 2 of the Act, premises are *enclosed* if they:
   (a) have a ceiling or roof; and
   (b) except for doors, windows and passageways, are wholly enclosed either permanently or temporarily.
2. For the purposes of Section 2 of the Act, premises are *substantially enclosed* if they have a ceiling or roof but there is:
   (a) an opening in the walls; or

(b) an aggregate area of opening in the walls,

which is less than half of the area of the walls, including other structures that serve the purpose of walls and constitute the perimeter of the premises.

3. In determining *an area of opening* or *an aggregate area of openings* for the purpose of paragraph 2, no account is to be taken of openings in which there are doors, windows or other fittings that can be opened or shut.

4. In this Regulation, *roof* includes any fixed or moveable structure or device which is capable of covering all or part of the premises as a roof, including, for example, a canvas awning.

Enforcement

Each of the following authorities is designated as an enforcement authority for the purposes of Chapter 1 of Part 1 of the Act:

(a) a unitary authority;

(b) a district council;

(c) a London borough council;

(d) a port health authority, etc

Smoke-free premises and vehicles

Soil erosion

Soil erosion implies the displacement of solids, such as soil, rock and mud by the actions of wind, water, ocean currents and ice, as a result of gravity or by the actions of living organisms (bioerosion). Whilst erosion is an on-going natural process, it can be increased or accelerated by human activities, such as construction operations, overgrazing by domestic animals, overpopulation of areas, deforestation and road building, and excessive erosion, for example, the rapid movement of gravels downstream in rivers, can result in water sedimentation, damage to the ecosystem and direct loss of soil.

Soil erosion is affected by factors such as the texture of the soil, the slope of the land, the amount of ground cover in terms of vegetation, rocks and stones, and the actual use of the land. The amount of rainfall in an area is significant in the potential for soil erosion.

'Slash and burn' treatments of tropical forests have been a significant cause of soil erosion where the total ground surface is stripped of vegetation and then seared of all living organisms making the land sterile. This makes the immediate soil surfaces vulnerable to water and wind erosion.

Soil erosion takes a number of forms:

Water erosion

Erosion as a result of the impact of raindrops and heavy rainfall, together with water forming depressions as it runs off sloping surfaces.

Shoreline erosion

Erosion caused by the action of currents and waves, together with changes in sea level.

Wind erosion

The movement of particles of soil arising from wind currents which abrade surfaces and cause drifting of soil.

Gravity erosion

The downward movement of rock and sediments due to the force of gravity created by wasting of the surrounding soil.

Ice erosion

Ice erosion is associated with the movement of large quantities of ice, such as glaciers, which cause fragmentation of rocks and eventual moving of these fragments to a lower level.

Deforestation

Ecosystems

Soil Guideline Values (SGVs)

In the case of potentially contaminated sites, it may be necessary to assess the soil concentration of a contaminant in terms of its risk to human health and the environment. Soil Guideline Values represent 'intervention values' which, if exceeded, indicate potentially unacceptable risks to users. Where an SGV is exceeded, this may indicate the need for further investigation of a site and remedial action may be required to protect human health.

Soil Guideline Values were derived using the Contaminated Land Exposure Assessment (CLEA) model for three land uses:

(a) residential (with or without vegetable growing);

(b) allotments; and

(c) commercial/industrial purposes.

SGVs can be used in support of the application of the statutory regimes addressing land contamination, especially Part IIA of the EPA (the Contaminated Land Regime) and development control under the Town and Country Planning Acts. Contaminated Land Advice Note (CLAN) 2/05 published by DEFRA provides advice on the use of Soil Guideline Values in the determination of land as contaminated land under Part IIA.

Contaminated land

Contaminated Land Regime

Health Criteria Values

Soil pollution

Soil pollution (contamination) implies the presence of man-made chemical substances or some other alteration of the natural soil environment. Soil pollution can arise from:

(a) the application of pesticides and herbicides;

(b) leaching of wastes from landfill sites;

(c) leakage of transformers;

(d) leaking underground and above ground storage tanks, including those storing petroleum hydrocarbons (benzene, toluene, etc);

(e) the percolation of contaminated surface water to sub-surface strata;

(f) the direct discharge or tipping of wastes to land;

(g) deposition of dust from industrial processes, such as smelting operations; and

(h) spillage or leakage of solvents, such as acetone and trichloroethylene.

Many chemical substances can be involved in land pollution, such as solvents, lead and other heavy metals, pesticides and petroleum hydrocarbons.

Soil pollution can lead to both risks to the health of the immediate community and pollution of water supplies.

Groundwater pollution

Hazardous substances: classification

Landspreading

Leaching

Organic solvents

Pesticide

Petroleum

Polychlorinated biphenyls (PCBs) and other dangerous substances

Remediation

Soil remediation

Waste

Waste offences

Soil remediation

This is the process which prevents chemically contaminated land from harming the environment and restores the land to safe and usable condition. It is a process which entails the assessment, monitoring and verification of contaminant conditions before, during and after remediation.

Contaminated land

Contaminated Land (England) Regulations 2000

Contaminated Land Regime

Remediation

Soil pollution

Solar energy

Solar energy is the form of energy derived either directly or indirectly from the sun in the form of solar radiation. There is a balance between heat radiation into space and incoming solar radiation (the Earth-atmosphere system), and the resulting level of energy within this system accounts for the Earth's climate in the broadest sense. A large amount of incoming radiation is absorbed by the hydrosphere (water).

Solar energy is applied in many ways:

(a) to generate electricity by:

(i) using photovoltaic solar cells;

(ii) using concentrated solar power;

(iii) heating trapped air which rotates turbines in a solar updraft tower;

(b) to heat buildings directly through passive solar design.

Renewable energy

Water power

Wind power

Solvent emissions

A solvent is a liquid that has the ability to dissolve another substance. Water is the most common solvent. Industrial solvents, however, take the form of organic liquid hydrocarbons, such as toluene, white spirit, methyl alcohol, ethyl acetate, trichloroethylene, carbon tetrachloride and carbon disulphide. Solvents are extremely volatile substances and are heavier than air. This means that they can settle at ground level. Solvents vary widely in their toxicological properties but exposure to solvent emissions can be dangerous to human health and the environment.

Solvents are used extensively in a range of industrial processes including the manufacture of paints, printing inks and adhesives, and in the application of these products in processes, such as printing, cleaning and in the coating of surfaces. These volatile organic compounds can also undergo chemical reactions when emitted to the atmosphere resulting in the formation of ground level ozone which is hazardous to human health, vegetation and crops in addition to causing surface damage to building materials.

Where solvents are used in a business operation, the Solvent Emissions (England and Wales) Regulations 2004 may apply.

Organic solvents

Ozone

Ozone-depleting substances

Ozone depletion

Solvent Emissions (England and Wales) Regulations 2004

Solvent Emissions (England and Wales) Regulations 2004

The Regulations are directed at preventing or reducing the direct and indirect effects of emissions of volatile organic compounds (VOCs) from the users of organic solvents. The Regulations cover both releases to air and the control of fugitive releases to land and water.

The Regulations apply where an operator operates a listed activity and uses solvents above the stated threshold limit for those solvents. Operators are required to implement measures to reduce and control VOC emissions in accordance with requirements of the Regulations.

Where an operator has a Pollution Prevention and Control permit, or an Integrated Pollution Control or Local Authority Air Pollution Control authorisation, that operator may already meet the requirements of the Regulations. However, much will depend upon the conditions attached to the permit or authorisation. In certain cases, the permit or authorisation may need to be amended by the regulator. Where an operator does not have a permit or authorisation, he is required to apply to the regulator for same.

Where activities fall within the scope of the Regulations, an operator must limit solvent emissions by one of the following methods:

(a) *Meeting an emission limit for VOCs in waste gases and fugitive emissions*

- Concentration limits may be imposed on specific substances and collectively for all substances at individual discharge points. The fugitive emissions are controlled by a limit that is set as a percentage of solvent input into the process.

(b) *Meeting a total emission limit value for VOCs*

- A limit relating to a unit of production is used, e.g. 25g VOCs released per item manufactured.

(c) *Implementing a solvent reduction scheme*

- This allows an operator to meet an equivalent emissions reduction via other means. It involves calculating an annual reference limit and complying with a target emission.

  Operators are required to undertake appropriate monitoring of VOC emissions in accordance with permit or authorisation requirements. If a reduction scheme is not being used, any new VOC abatement equipment installed must immediately meet the requirements of the Regulations.

Where an operator is covered by the Regulations, he must submit a Solvent Management Plan to the regulator. This plan must indicate annual solvent consumption and demonstrate compliance with emission limits.

Where the following harmful substances or preparations are used:

(a) halogenated VOCs which have been assigned the risk phrase R40; or

(b) VOCs that have been classified as *carcinogenic, mutagenic* or *toxic to reproduction*, and which carry the risk phrase R45, R49, R60 or R61,

there are additional requirements under the Regulations. Where the above VOCs are used, they must either be replaced (in the shortest possible time), contain and control them, or limit their use and/or the quantities used. (The requirement to replace VOCs with less harmful alternatives does not apply in the case of halogenated hydrocarbons with the risk phrase R40.)

Risk phrases must be incorporated in the safety data provided by a supplier under the Chemicals (Hazard Information and Packaging for Supply) (CHIP) Regulations.

Chemicals (Hazard Information and Packaging for Supply) (CHIP) Regulations 1994 – 2002

Emission limit value

Hazardous substances: classification

Pollution Prevention and Control (PPC)

Permit

Offences

Regulator

Safety data

Source-Pathway-Receptor Model

The accepted model by many environmental specialists for the assessment of the potential effects of contamination. The model is based on the premise that in order for contamination to create a hazard, it must be present at a *source*, and have a *pathway* to a *receptor* or target which is vulnerable to that contamination.

Contaminant

Pathway

Receptor

Special Areas of Conservation

These are sites which provide protection for natural habitats and rare and threatened species.

Conservation Area

Conservation sites

Habitat

National Parks

Special Protection Areas

Wildlife

Special Protection Areas

These are sites which provide protection for wild bird species and their habitats.

Conservation Area

Conservation sites

Habitat

National Parks

Special Areas of Conservation

Wildlife

Special sites

Land, where there is the potential for pollution of controlled waters from that land by any of the substances listed in Schedule 1 to the Contaminated Land (England) Regulations 2000, must be designated as a special site. These families and groups of substances are:

(a) organohalogen compounds and substances which may form such compounds in the aquatic environment;

(b) organophosphorus compounds;

(c) organotin compounds;

(d) substances which possess carcinogenic, mutagenic or teratogenic properties in or via the aquatic environment;

(e) mercury and its compounds;

(f) cadmium and its compounds;

(g) mineral oil and other hydrocarbons; and

(h) cyanides.

Contaminated land

Contaminated Land (England) Regulations 2006

Controlled waters

Hazardous substances: classification

Heavy metal pollution

Specified waste management activity

Means any one of the following activities:

(a) the disposal of waste in a landfill, whether or not the disposal falls with Section 5.2 of Part 1 of Schedule 1;

(b) the disposal of waste falling within Section 5.3 of that Part of that Schedule;

(c) the recovery of waste falling within paragraphs (i), (ii), (v) or (vii) of paragraph (c) of Part A(1) of Section 5.4 of that Part of that Schedule.

[Pollution Prevention and Control (England and Wales) Regulations 2000]

Landfill sites

Waste disposal contractor

Waste Recycling Plans

Static fields

Static electric fields are created by the attraction and repulsion of electric charges that are fixed in space, i.e. static electricity. They occur naturally in the atmosphere, particularly under thunderclouds, and can lead to lightning strikes. The use of direct current in some rail systems can produce static electric fields. Static electric fields can be generated from certain types of carpet leading to sparks. Static electric fields do not enter the body.

Static magnetic fields, on the other hand, are force fields created by a magnet or by the steady flow of electricity, for example in electrical appliances using direct current. Static magnetic fields have medical application in magnetic resonance imaging (MRI) which provides three dimensional images of soft tissues, including the brain. They can interact with the human body by:

(a) generating electric fields and currents around the heart and slightly impede the blood flow;

(b) affecting metallic implants and possibly certain molecules and cell structures; and

(c) possibly interfering with some chemical reactions in the body.

Statutory nuisances

Section 79 of the EPA replaced the various provisions of the Public Health Act (PHA) 1936 and the Public Health (Recurring Nuisances) Act 1969 and defines a "statutory nuisance" as:

(a) any premises in such a state as to be prejudicial to health or a nuisance;

(b) smoke emitted from premises so as to be prejudicial to health or a nuisance;

(c) fumes or gases emitted from premises so as to be prejudicial to health or a nuisance;

(d) any dust, steam, smell or other effluvia arising on industrial, trade or business premises and being prejudicial to health or a nuisance;

(e) any accumulation or deposit which is prejudicial to health or a nuisance;

(f) any animal kept in such a place or manner as to be prejudicial to health or a nuisance;

(g) noise emitted from premises so as to be prejudicial to health or a nuisance; and

(h) any other matter declared by any enactment to be a statutory nuisance.

Section 79 further requires every local authority to cause its area to be inspected from time to time to detect any statutory nuisances which ought to be dealt with under Section 80, and where a complaint of statutory nuisance is made to it by a person living within its area, to take such steps as are reasonably practicable to investigate the complaint.

The following matters should be considered with regard to Section 79 and its various subsections.

(a) "Any premises in such a state as to be prejudicial to health or a nuisance"

The term "premises", which also appears in (b), (c), (d) and (g), includes land and any vessel (other than a vessel powered by steam reciprocating machinery).

This clearly extends the term "premises" to include vessels, i.e. boats and ships. Section 79(11) makes it clear that where a local authority's area includes part of a seashore, that authority's area shall also include territorial sea lying off the shore, and the term "occupier" should be read as "master of a vessel".

(b) "Smoke emitted from premises so as to be prejudicial to health or a nuisance"

There are several qualifications to this definition. It does not apply to the Crown's defence premises or to premises occupied by a visiting force. Further, it does not apply to smoke from the chimney of a private house in a designated Smoke Control Area, dark smoke in certain circumstances or to smoke emitted from a steam locomotive.

(c) "Fumes or gases emitted from premises so as to be prejudicial to health or a nuisance"

Fumes are defined as meaning any airborne solid matter smaller than dust, and *gas* as including vapour and moisture precipitated from vapour. These two definitions should be compared with the definitions in (d) below. The local authority must take care to ensure the correct term for the form of airborne particulate is used when taking action against an offender.

(d) "Any dust, steam, smell or other effluvia arising on industrial, trade or business premises and being prejudicial to health or a nuisance"

The term *dust* is defined as not including dust emitted from a chimney as an ingredient of smoke. This form of nuisance would be dealt with as a statutory nuisance, whether or not the premises from which the nuisance arises are industrial, trade or business premises.

(e) "Any accumulation or deposit which is prejudicial to health or a nuisance"

There are no qualifications covering this subsection.

(f) "Noise emitted from premises so as to be prejudicial to health or a nuisance"

Noise is defined as including vibration. This type of statutory nuisance refers to noise emitted from premises and could be used by the local authority to deal with problems where the noise emanates from a premises and affects other people, for instance, local residents.

(g) "Any other matter declared by any enactment to be a statutory nuisance"

These statutory nuisances include:

(i) Any well, tank, cistern or water butt used for the supply of water for domestic premises which is so placed, constructed or kept as to render the water therein liable to contamination prejudicial to health. (Sec 141 PHA 1936)

(ii) Any pond, pool, ditch, gutter or watercourse which is so foul or in such a state as to be prejudicial to health or a nuisance; and

(iii) Any part of a watercourse, not being a part ordinarily navigated by vessels employed in the carriage of goods by water, which is so choked or silted up as to obstruct or impede the proper flow of water and thereby to cause a nuisance, give rise to conditions prejudicial to health. (Sec 259 PHA 1936)

A tent, van or shed, or similar structure used for human habitation:

(a) which is in such a state, or so overcrowded, as to be prejudicial to the health of the inmates; or

(b) the use of which, by reason of the absence of proper sanitary accommodation or otherwise, gives rise, whether on the site or on other land, to a nuisance or to conditions prejudicial to health. (Sec 268 PHA 1936)

In the case of any building:

(a) any cesspool or other such work or appliance provided for the building is in such a condition as to be prejudicial to health or a nuisance; or

(b) any cesspool, private sewer or drain formerly used for the drainage of the building, but no longer used therefore, is prejudicial to health or a nuisance. (Sec 39 PHA 1936)

Under Section 151 of the Mines and Quarries Act 1954, the following are deemed to be statutory nuisances for the purposes of Part III of the Public Health Act 1936:

(a) a shaft or outlet of certain abandoned or disused mines where it is not provided with a properly maintained device designed and constructed to prevent persons from accidentally falling down the shaft or accidentally entering the outlet;

(b) a shaft or outlet of certain abandoned or disused mines where by reason of its accessibility from a highway or place of public resort it constitutes a danger to the public; and

(c) a quarry which is not provided with an efficient and properly maintained barrier so designed and constructed as to prevent persons from accidentally falling into it and which by reason of its accessibility from a highway or place of public resort constitutes a danger to the public.

A fence made with barbed wire adjoining a highway may also be a nuisance. (Section 143 Highways Act 1959)

Storage of chemicals in bulk

These scheduled activities are:

Part A(1)

Nil

Part A(2)

Nil

Part B

(a) The storage in tanks, other than in tanks for the time being forming part of a powered vehicle, of any of the substances listed below except where the total storage capacity of the tanks installed at the location in question in which the relevant substance may be stored is less than the figure specified below in relation to the substance:

any one or more acrylates	20 tonnes (in aggregate)
acrylonitrile	20 tonnes
anhydrous ammonia	100 tonnes
anhydrous hydrogen fluoride	1 tonne
toluene do-isocyanate	20 tonnes
vinyl chloride monomer	20 tonnes
ethylene	8,000 tonnes

Figure 12: STORAGE OF CHEMICALS IN BULK

[Schedule 1: Part 1: Pollution Prevention and Control (England and Wales) Regulations 2000]

Isocyanates

Part A activities

Part B activities

Pollution Prevention and Control Act 1999

Pollution Prevention and Control (England and Wales) Regulations 2000

Scheduled activities

Strategic Environmental Assessment

European Directive 2001/42/EC "on the assessment of the effects of certain plans and programmes on the environment" was implemented in UK law by the Environmental Assessment of Plans and Programmes Regulations 2004. The Regulations require a formal environmental assessment of certain plans and programmes which are likely to have significant effects on the environment.

Authorities which prepare and/or adopt such a plan or programme must prepare a report on its likely significant environmental effects, consult environmental authorities and the public, and take the report and the results of the consultation into account during the preparation process and before the plan or programme is adopted. They must also make information available on the plan or programme as adopted and how the environmental assessment was taken into account.

Stray dogs

Section 149 of the EPA places a direct duty on local authorities to appoint an officer for the purpose of discharging their functions for dealing with stray dogs. Those functions are:

(a) the seizure and detention, if practicable, of dogs which appear to be strays;

(b) notification of the owner, if known, or of the person whose name and address appears on the dog's collar, if any;

(c) the owner may claim the dog within 7 days clear of notification on payment of expenses and a sum prescribed by Regulations;

(d) if not claimed, the dog may be disposed of by sale or gift, either to a person who will care properly for it or to a stray dogs' home, or by destroying it;

(e) keeping a public register of dogs seized;

(f) properly feeding and maintaining dogs detained after seizure; and

(g) destroying any detained dog where necessary to avoid suffering.

Street Litter Control Notice

Litter arising from commercial premises, such as fish and chip shops, takeaway food shops and supermarkets, increases the costs of street cleaning by local authorities. Under the Street Litter Control Notices Order 1991 a local authority may issue a Street Litter Control Notice in respect of commercial and retail premises of the following descriptions:

(a) premises used wholly or partly for the sale of food or drink for consumption off the premises;

(b) premises used wholly or partly for the sale of food or drink for consumption on part of the premises forming open land adjacent to the street;

(c) service stations and other premises on which fuel for motor vehicles is sold to the public;

(d) premises used wholly or partly as a cinema, theatre, concert hall, bingo hall, casino, dance hall, swimming bath, skating rink, gymnasium or area for other indoor or outdoor sports or recreations, or as an amusement arcade or centre; or

(e) banks, building society offices or other premises with the automated teller machines located on an outside wall of the premises.

This type of Notice requires owners of land which forms part of the premises to maintain it free from litter if the land, which is part of a street, is within 10 metres of the premises.

Litter

Litter Abatement Notice

Litter Control Area

Litter Control Notice

Litter Fixed Penalty Notice

Substance

Includes micro-organisms and any natural or artificial substance or other matter, whether it is in solid or liquid form or in the form of a gas or vapour.

[Water Resources Act 1991]

Includes any chemical element and its compounds and any biological entity or micro-organism, with the exception of radioactive substances within the meaning of Council Directive 80/836/Euratom, genetically modified micro-organisms within the meaning of Council Directive 90/219/EEC and genetically modified organisms within the meaning of Council Directive 90/220/EEC.

[Pollution Prevention and Control (England and Wales) Regulations 2000]

Substantial change in operation

In relation to an installation or mobile plant, a change in operation which, in the opinion of the regulator, may have significant negative effects on human beings or the environment.

[Pollution Prevention and Control (England and Wales) Regulations 2000]

Change in operation

Regulator

"Suitable for use"

The accepted government guidelines on which the redevelopment and remediation of contaminated land is based. Within this framework, it is accepted that the level of 'clean up' of any contamination needs only to conform to the applicable statutory conditions and best practice for the proposed or current end use of a site.

Contaminated land

Contaminated Land (England) Regulations 2000

Contaminated Land Regime

Sulphur oxides

Sulphur dioxide is a greenhouse gas. Natural sources include volcanoes, biological decay, the oceans and forest fires, particularly arising from deforestation processes. Sulphur dioxide emissions also result from the combustion of fossil fuels whose sulphur content varies considerably.

Deforestation

Fossil fuels

Greenhouse gases

Summary proceedings for statutory nuisances

Section 80 of the EPA gives local authorities powers for dealing with statutory nuisances. Thus, where a local authority is satisfied that a statutory nuisance exists, or is likely to occur or recur, in the area of the authority, the local authority shall serve a Notice (an Abatement Notice) imposing all or any of the following requirements:

(a) requiring the abatement of the nuisance or prohibiting or restricting its occurrence or recurrence;

(b) requiring the execution of such works, and the taking of such other steps, as may be necessary for any of those purposes,

and the Notice shall specify the times or times within which the requirements of the Notice are to be complied with (e.g., 21 days or 28 days).

The Abatement Notice should be served:

(a) except in a case falling within (b) or (c) below, on the person responsible for the nuisance;

(b) where the nuisance arises from any defect of a structural nature, on the owner of the premises;

(c) where the person responsible for the nuisance cannot be found or the nuisance has not yet occurred, on the owner or occupier of the premises.

A person served with an Abatement Notice may appeal to a Magistrates' Court within 21 days from the date of service of the Notice. The grounds for appeal are laid down in the Statutory Nuisances (Appeals) Regulations 1990 (as amended). These grounds are summarised below:

(a) no statutory nuisance exists;

(b) the Notice has been served incorrectly;

(c) the local authority has acted unreasonably in refusing to accept alternative schemes for ensuring compliance;

(d) the requirements of the Notice are unreasonable;

(e) the time specified for compliance is unreasonable; and

(f) best practicable means have been used in the particular trade or business premises.

In most cases, notice of appeal to the court will result in the suspension of the Abatement Notice until that appeal is heard.

In addition to the grounds for appeal, there are two statutory defences laid down in the EPA, namely "reasonable excuse" and "best practicable means". "Reasonable excuse" is very much based on the test of reasonableness in the particular circumstances. This defence may stand if it can be shown that a reasonable person would consider the action taken to be consistent with a reasonable standard of conduct. A reasonable excuse might be a lack of resources to comply with the Notice.

Failure to comply with an Abatement Notice without reasonable excuse is an offence. A person who fails to comply with any requirement or prohibition imposed by the Notice is liable on summary conviction to a fine not exceeding level 5 on the standard scale together with a further fine of an amount equal to one-tenth of that level for each day that the offence continues after the conviction. A person who commits a similar offence on industrial, trade or business premises is liable on summary conviction to a fine not exceeding £20,000. Furthermore, the local authority may carry out the works or take the action necessary in default to abate a nuisance and recover the costs incurred.

Persons aggrieved by statutory nuisances

Section 82 of the EPA makes separate provision for people to formally complain to a Magistrates' Court in respect of statutory nuisances. Thus, a Magistrates' Court may act under this Section on complaint made by any person on the ground that he is aggrieved by the existence of a statutory nuisance. Where the court is satisfied that the alleged nuisance exists, or that, although abated, it is likely to recur on the same premises, the court may make an Order (Abatement Order) for either or both of the following purposes:

(a) requiring the defendant to abate the nuisance, within a time specified in the Order, and execute any works necessary for that purpose;

(b) prohibiting a recurrence of the nuisance and requiring the defendant, within a time specified in that Order, to execute any works necessary to prevent the recurrence,

and may also impose on the defendant a fine not exceeding level 5 on the standard scale.

Where a court is satisfied that the nuisance exists and is such as, in the opinion of the court, to render premises unfit for human habitation, an Order may be made prohibiting the use of the premises for human habitation until the premises are, to the satisfaction of the court, rendered fit for that purpose.

In conclusion, the law of nuisance is well established in the UK and has developed over the last century or more. As with health and safety law, common law decisions have formed the framework for subsequent statute law.

The concept of "nuisance" is very broad. Experience indicates that even the best-managed organisations can create nuisances (noise, odours, smoke, dust and gas emission, etc.) to the surrounding community without even realising their existence.

In the planning of new processes it is essential, therefore, to consider the potential for nuisance. The potential for some form of nuisance should also be taken into account in the design and specification of planned maintenance systems, waste disposal procedures, fuel-burning equipment and drainage systems. Failure to do so can have serious implications under the EPA.

Abatement

Abatement Order

Environment Act 1995

Environmental Protection Act 1990

Nuisance at common law

Nuisance

Offences

Statutory nuisances

Surface treating metals and plastic materials

These scheduled activities are:

Part A(1)

(a) Surface treating metals and plastic materials using an electrolytic or chemical process where the aggregated volume of the treatment vats is more than 30 m^3.

Part A(2)

Nil

Part B

(a) Any process for the surface treatment of metal which is likely to result in the release into air of any acid-forming oxide of nitrogen and which does not fall within Part A(1) of this Section.

[Schedule 1: Part 1: Pollution Prevention and Control (England and Wales) Regulations 2000]

Nitrogen oxides

Part A activities

Part B activities

Pollution Prevention and Control Act 1999

Pollution Prevention and Control (England and Wales) Regulations 2000

Scheduled activities

Surface Water Classification Regulations 1989

These Regulations implement the EC Abstraction Directive and prescribe a system for classifying waters according to their suitability for abstraction as drinking water.

Water classification

Surface Water (Dangerous Substances) (Classification) Regulations 1989 & 1992

These Regulations implement the EC Dangerous Substances Directive by prescribing a system for classifying inland, estuarine and coastal waters according to the presence in them of concentrations of certain dangerous substances. The Regulations list a number of dangerous substances and state the concentrations of each which should not be exceeded in fresh or marine waters.

Suspension Notice

If the regulator is of the opinion, as regards an installation or mobile plant authorised under these Regulations, that the operation of the installation or mobile plant, or the operation of it in a particular manner, involves an imminent risk of serious pollution, it shall, unless it intends for steps to be taken under Regulation 26(1) (taking of steps by regulator to remove the risk), serve a Notice (a Suspension Notice) on the operator of the installation or mobile plant.

If the regulator is of the opinion, as regards the carrying out of specified waste management activities under a permit, that the operator carrying out the activities has ceased to be a fit and proper person in relation to those activities by reason of their management having ceased to be in the hands of a technically competent person, it may serve a Suspension Notice on that operator.

[Pollution Prevention and Control (England and Wales) Regulations 2000]

"Fit and proper person"

Installation

Mobile plant

Permit

Regulator

Specified waste management activities

Sustainability

The process of maintaining, bearing, supporting, providing for, prolonging and supporting the life of man, animals and other living organisms.

Sustainable agriculture

The application of husbandry experience and scientific knowledge of natural processes to create integrated, resource-conserving farming systems, based on respect for the people and animals involved which reduce environmental degradation and which promote agricultural productivity and economic viability in both the short-term and long-term.

Sustainable development

Sustainable development is defined as "development which meets the needs of the present without compromising the ability of future generations to meet their own needs".

[Report of the World Commission on the Environment and Development (Bruntland Commission) 1987]

In 1990 the UK Government, in response to this Report, published a White Paper, *This Common Inheritance*, which introduced the concept of stewardship of the environment.

The issue of sustainable development was further considered at the United Nations Conference on Environment and Development, 'The Earth Summit', held in Rio de Janeiro in 1992. The most significant outcome was Agenda 21. This is a global action plan setting out what nations should do to achieve sustainable development. Local government has a key role in pursuing this agenda.

A report by the UK Local Government Management Board (LGMB) in 1993 on Local Agenda 21 further clarified the meaning of sustainable development and its practical application at the local level both in terms of the process of decision making and its substance and direction.

Sustainable decision making

The requirements for sustainable decision making include the following key principles and tools:

(a) partnership and participation between communities and the government;

(b) freedom of access to environmental information;

(c) environmental assessment and appraisal; and

(d) the selection and monitoring of sustainable indicators.

Key policy issues which need to be addressed in working towards sustainability include:

(a) consumption of natural resources, including energy, needs to be reduced;

(b) where possible, renewable resources should be substituted for non-renewable resources;

(c) fewer wastes should be produced and recycling should be encouraged where appropriate;

(d) wastes should as far as possible be bio-degradable and cause minimum pollution;

(e) bio-diversity should be preserved and enhanced where possible; and

(f) valuable natural and physical assets and other amenities should be preserved and managed for long-term protection.

Sustainability implies more than just giving the above environmental factors extra weight in decision making. It means accepting that there are limits to the capacity of the environment to support human activities.

The most central sustainability issues are those which affect the future viability of life on the plant, which include global warming, ozone depletion, global species and habitat diversity, resource depletion and deforestation. To this list may be added a number of issues which are important for human welfare and which, once damaged, may be difficult or even impossible to reverse. Examples are pollution of soil and water, local habitat diversity, damage to the landscape and townscape of urban and rural areas.

Sustainability and planning

Many of the above issues are relevant to planning. Some, such as the protection of landscape, townscape and important habitats are well established.

Related policy responses include:

(a) the control of siting and design of buildings;

(b) resisting urban sprawl (green belts);

(c) designation of areas of wildlife and landscape value; and

(d) conservation areas.

Other important issues include the need to:

(a) reduce energy consumption and carbon dioxide emissions;

(b) reduce the consumption of natural resources; and

(c) encourage the recycling of resources.

Planning Policy Guidance Notes (PPGNs)

The Government explicitly recognises the role of planning with respect to sustainable development and now issue revised guidance to planning authorities in the form of PPGNs. These form a framework of national and regional policy guidance which must be taken into account when formulating planning policy or making planning decisions.

Principal features of Department of Environment Planning Guidance

1. Conservation of land as a resource

Emphasis is placed on:

(a) recycling of urban land (especially where contaminated or under-used);

(b) resisting the development of green field sites;

(c) increasing the density of development and maintaining current ones;

(d) resisting the loss of high grade agricultural ground; and

(e) placing continued importance on green belt policy to resist urban sprawl and protect open land.

2. Protection of the physical (urban/rural) environment

This includes:

(a) protection of the built heritage;

(b) protecting the countryside;

(c) protecting areas of high landscape and wildlife value;

(d) encouraging good design; and

(e) resisting the loss of urban open space.

3. Conservation of energy and reduction in pollution

This includes:

(a) discouraging development in locations which would add to congestion;

(b) encouraging trip generating development at nodes in the public transport system;

(c) sustaining and enhancing the role of town centres as accessible locations and places where trip functions may be combined e.g. shopping, leisure, employment;

(d) sustaining the role of neighbourhood and local shopping areas to reduce the need to travel longer distances by car;

(e) encouraging walking and cycling;

(f) constraining the expansion of small settlements, especially if poorly served by public transport;

(g) seeking to limit decentralisation pressure especially to small new settlements;

(h) aiming for a balanced (self-contained) structure of land uses within urban areas/settlements;

(i) considering the relaxation of rigid zoning policies and providing for the juxtaposition of employment, service and residential land uses;

(j) planning at a strategic level to integrate transport and land use decisions;

(k) encouraging energy conservation, e.g. Combined Heat and Power.

Many of the above concepts are not new but planning authorities may well be faced with a series of policy choices which will significantly affect planning policy in relation to sustainable development. For example:

(a) cities and towns are likely to be more 'sustainable' than smaller dispersed communities in the countryside;

(b) central places, such as town centres, are generally to be preferred over peripheral or dispersed locations;

(c) higher density (urban) development has energy efficiency advantages over lower density (suburban) development;

(d) the re-use of open land is to be preferred over the use of green field sites;

(e) the creation of self-contained or multi-use land-use zones is preferable to the rigid separation of single land uses;

(f) policies encouraging public transport, cycling and walking are preferable to those which facilitate car use.

The Fifth Action Programme placed emphasis on sustainable development. This is defined in the Bruntland Report, *Our Common Future,* which established the agenda for discussion about the relationship between economic growth and protection of the environment. According to the Report, sustainable development is "economic development which meets the needs of the present generation without compromising the ability of future generations to meet their own needs".

The principle of sustainability was introduced by the Treaty on European Union for incorporation in the EC Treaty.

Environment Act 1995

Sustainability

Travel implications (Planning)

Sustainable use

This implies the use of resources at a rate which will meet the needs of the present without impairing the ability of future generations to meet their needs. This concept was put forward by the Brundtland Commission in 1987.

Sustainability

Sustainable agriculture

Sustainable development

Sustainable waste management

Sustainable waste management

This is the efficient use of materials to cut down on the amount of waste produced. Where waste is generated, it entails dealing with it in a way that actively contributes to the economic, social and environmental goals of sustainable development.

Sustainable waste management entails:

(a) eliminating waste at source;

(b) undertaking a waste minimisation programme;

(c) reusing and recycling materials in house; and

(d) sending waste for recovery, e.g. oils and solvents, or composting (for biodegradable wastes only) rather than for disposal.

Composting

Sustainable development

Waste management strategies and policies

Waste Minimisation Act 1998

Waste minimisation: process or resource efficiency

T

Tar and bitumen activities

These scheduled activities are:

Part A(1)

(a) The following activities:

(i) distilling tar or bitumen in connection with any process or manufacture; or

(ii) heating tar or bitumen for the manufacture of electrodes or carbon-based refractory materials,

where the carrying out of the activity by the person concerned at the location in question is likely to involve the use in any period of 12 months of 5 tonnes or more of tar or bitumen or, in aggregate, both.

Tar and *bitumen* include pitch.

Part A(2)

Nil

Part B

(a) Any activity not falling within Part A(1) of this Section or of Section 6.2 (Carbon Activities) involving:

(i) heating, but not distilling, tar or bitumen in connection with any manufacturing activity; or

(ii) oxidising bitumen by blowing air through it, at a plant where no other activities described in any Section in this Schedule are carried out,

where the carrying out of the activity is likely to involve the use in any period of 12 months of 5 tonnes or more of tar or bitumen or, in aggregate, both.

[Schedule 1: Part 1: Pollution Prevention and Control (England and Wales) Regulations 2000]

Part A activities

Part B activities

Pollution Prevention and Control Act 1999

Pollution Prevention and Control (England and Wales) Regulations 2000

Scheduled activities

Temperature control in the workplace

Regulation 7(1) of the Workplace (Health, Safety and Welfare) Regulations 1992 requires that during working hours, the temperature in all workplaces inside buildings shall be reasonable.

The ACOP qualifies the requirement thus:

> "The temperature in workrooms should provide reasonable comfort without the need for special clothing. Where such a temperature is impractical because of hot or cold processes, all reasonable steps should be taken to achieve a temperature which is as close as possible to comfortable.
>
> The temperature in workrooms should normally be at least 16°C unless much of the work involves severe physical effort in which case the temperature should be at least 13°C. These temperatures may not, however, ensure reasonable comfort, depending upon other factors such as air movement and relative humidity."

A temperature of 16°C, however, does not provide reasonable comfort conditions in, for instance, an office, and the following temperatures are recommended:

Offices	18-21°C (65-70°F)
Production areas (sedentary work)	18°C (65°F)
Production areas (active work)	16°C (60.8°F)
Amenity areas	18-21°C (65-70°F)

Figure 13: RECOMMENDED TEMPERATURES

In certain workplaces, e.g. depots, stores, which are sparsely or spasmodically occupied, localised space heating points should be provided for use during excessively cold periods of weather.

Central heating should operate independently of the hot water or steam installation so that central heating can be turned off in summer months. Individual control of radiators and heaters should be provided, together with the installation of thermostat control switches where central heating is by electrical means.

Where excessive heat is produced by processes, the adequacy of control and removal of this heat must be considered. Local exhaust ventilation (LEV) will, in many cases, solve this problem.

Heating units with exposed electrical elements should not be used, nor heating appliances producing gases as a result of combustion, unless efficient flues are installed. The use of privately-owned heating appliances, particularly those of the open radiant type, should be prohibited in view of the fire risk associated with such appliances.

Temperature effects

Work environment

Temperature effects

A number of occupational conditions are associated with exposure to, particularly, high temperatures in the workplace. These include heat cataract, heat stroke and heat cramps.

Heat cataract

Cataracts of the eye, caused by excessive exposure to heat and microwaves, have been common in many industries, e.g. glass blowing, chain making and others requiring the operation of furnaces. Continuous exposure to radiant heat results in the opacity of the lens of the eye. Such radiations, it is thought, disturb the nutrition of the lens and cause localised coagulation of the protein.

Heat stroke

This condition is occasionally encountered in workers in hot processes. The symptoms are due to a defect in thermoRegulation – the ability of the body to vary its temperature according to external factors. The onset is usually abrupt; the patient falls unconscious and could have a temperature of 40.6°C or more. Emergency treatment is aimed at reducing the body temperature to 40.0°C within one hour by all possible means, thus minimising the risk of damage to the central nervous system.

Heat cramps

Heat cramps may be encountered by workers engaged in the heat treatment of metals, e.g. forging or casting, as a result of heat from microwave radiation. Most cases occur during summer months. Cramps take the form of pain in the muscles beginning in the calves and spreading to the arms and abdomen. The pains are of an intermittent nature, occurring with increasing severity every few minutes. Generally, taking a drink containing common salt (saline) is the only treatment necessary, and it is normal in many industries to have stocks of salt tablets available.

Temperature control in the workplace

Work environment

Tertiary packaging

Packaging

Timber activities

These scheduled activities are:

Part A(1)

(a) Curing or chemically treating, timber or products made of wood if any substance listed in paragraph 13 of Part 2 of this Schedule is used.

Part A(2)

Nil

Part B

(a) Manufacturing products wholly or mainly of wood at any works if the process involves the sawing, drilling, shaping, turning, planing, curing or chemical treatment of wood (*relevant activities)* and the throughput of the works in any period of 12 months is likely to be more than:

(i) 10,000 cubic metres, in the case of works at which wood is sawed but at which wood is not subjected to any other relevant activities which are exempt activities; or

(ii) 1,000 cubic metres in any other case.

Relevant activities other than sawing are "exempt activities" where, if no sawing were carried out at the works, the activities carried out there would be unlikely to result in the release into the air of any substances listed in paragraph 12 of Part 2 of this Schedule in a quantity which is capable of causing significant harm.

Throughput shall be calculated by reference to the amount of wood which is subjected to any of the relevant activities, but where, at the same works, wood is subjected to two ore more relevant activities, no account shall be taken of the second or any subsequent activity.

[Schedule 1: Part 1: Pollution Prevention and Control (England and Wales) Regulations 2000]

Part A activities

Part B activities

Pollution Prevention and Control Act 1999

Pollution Prevention and Control (England and Wales) Regulations 2000

Release into water: substances

Scheduled activities

Tort

The term 'tort' is derived from the French 'avoir tort', to be wrong, and the Latin 'tortus', meaning bent, twisted or crooked. It is generally defined as 'a civil wrong other than a breach of contract or a breach of trust'.

The late Professor Winkfield defined tort more closely, thus:

> 'Tortious liability arises from a breach of duty primarily fixed by the law. Such duty is towards persons generally and its breach is redressible by an action for unliquidated damages'.

An action for unliquidated damages is where the amount of damages awarded to a successful claimant is fixed by the court.

Fundamentally, it concerns the legal relationship between parties generally in the everyday course of their affairs, the duties owed by one to the other and the legal effect of a wrongful act of one party causing harm to the person, property, reputation or economic interests of another.

Torts are of universal application compared with the law of contract, which applies only to the specific parties involved. The torts of particular significance in environmental protection are those of negligence, nuisance, trespass and breach of statutory duty.

Breach of statutory duty of care

Negligence

Nuisance

Trespass

Trade effluent

Includes any effluent which is discharged from premises used for carrying on any trade or industry, other than surface water and domestic sewage. For the purposes of this definition, any premises wholly or mainly used (whether for profit or not) for agricultural purposes, fish farming, scientific research or experiment, are to be deemed to be premises used for carrying on a trade.

[Water Resources Act 1991]

Effluent

Sewage effluent

Water Resources Act 1991

Trade effluent consents

Section 118 of the EPA requires that a consent be given by the National Rivers Authority prior to the disposal of a trade effluent into a sewer through a drain or sewer. It is an offence to discharge any trade effluent from trade premises otherwise than in accordance with the conditions of a consent from the sewerage undertaker.

Authorised discharge consent

Authorised discharges

Consents: controlled waters

Permit

Permit conditions

Transfer Note

Where waste is transferred it must be accompanied by a written description of the waste. This is to enable every person involved in the handling of waste to be certain as to the exact nature of the waste and to ensure that the waste is finally deposited at a suitably licensed site.

In addition to a written description of the waste, the transferer and transferee must also complete a Transfer Note in accordance with the Environmental Protection (Duty of Care) Regulations. A written Transfer Note must state:

(a) the waste to which it relates;

(b) the quantity of the waste;

(c) the time and place of transfer;

(d) the name and address of the transferer and the transferee;

(e) the capacity of both parties, i.e. if one is the producer or importer;

(f) if the transfer is to a person for authorised transport purposes; and

(g) whether the transferer or transferee falls within any of the categories of persons listed in column 1 of the Table to the Environmental Protection (Duty of Care) Regulations and provide, where appropriate, the information listed in column 2.

Environmental Protection (Duty of Care) Regulations 1991

Hazardous waste

Trans-frontier shipment of waste

This is the shipment of waste across national boundaries and is subject to a number of controls directed at protecting the environment and human health and to preventing the unauthorised disposal of international waste shipments and unregulated recovery of hazardous wastes. Operators must comply with international agreements, Regulations and policies.

Waste

Waste Management Licences

Waste Management Licensing Regulations 1994 – 2006

Waste management strategies and policies

Waste offences

Waste transfer

Transport of dangerous goods

The Transport of Dangerous Goods (Safety Advisers) Regulations 1999 implemented Council Directive 96/35/EC on the appointment and vocational qualifications of safety advisers for the transport of dangerous goods by road, rail and inland waterway. The Regulations apply both to employers and self-employed persons.

In these Regulations, 'transport of dangerous goods' means the transport, the related loading or unloading of these goods.

The Regulations:

- prohibit the transport of dangerous goods by road, rail and inland waterway by the employer unless he has appointed a safety adviser;
- require an employer to make arrangements for ensuring adequate co-operation between the safety advisers he appoints, impose requirements with respect to the number of safety advisers to be appointed and ensure any such safety adviser has adequate time and means to fulfil his functions and duties, and require an employer to provide any adviser with adequate information and facilities to perform his functions and duties;
- require a safety adviser to have the functions necessary to advise the employer who appointed him as to health, safety and environmental matters in connection with the transport of dangerous goods, to include specified functions (including the preparation of annual reports);
- require a safety adviser to prepare a report on specified accidents;
- require the keeping of reports;
- prohibit the appointment of an individual as a safety adviser unless he holds a vocational training certificate appropriate to the modes of transport used by the employer and to all dangerous goods or one or more of the groups of dangerous goods specified and transported by the employer, and impose ancillary requirements with regard to the issue, form, validity and renewal of such certificates;
- provide for the mutual recognition of vocational training certificates issued in other Member States of the Community or in Northern Ireland;
- impose requirements to provide the Secretary of State or any goods vehicle examiner on request with the name of any safety adviser, a copy of any accident and annual reports, and any vocational training certificate;
- provide that the Executive and Secretary of State for Defence may grant exemptions from any requirement or prohibition of the Regulations in specified circumstances;
- make minor amendments to the Carriage of Dangerous Goods (Classification, Packaging and Labelling) and Use of Transportable Pressure Receptacles Regulations 1996, the Carriage of Dangerous Goods by Road Regulations 1996 and the Carriage of Explosives by Road Regulations 1996; and
- provide, by amendment of the Health and Safety (Fees) Regulations 1997, for payment of fees for the issues of vocational training certificates.

Functions of safety advisers

Schedule 2 to the Regulations outlines the functions of safety advisers as including:

- monitoring compliance with the rules governing the transport of dangerous goods;
- advising the employer on the transport of dangerous goods;
- ensuring that an annual report to the employer is prepared on the activities of the employer concerning the transport of dangerous goods;
- monitoring the following practices and procedures relating to the activities of the employer which concern the transport of dangerous goods:
  - the procedures for compliance with the rules governing the identification of dangerous goods being transported;
  - the practice of the employer in taking into account, when purchasing means of transport, any special requirements in connection with the dangerous goods to be transported;
  - the procedures for checking the equipment used in connection with the transport of dangerous goods;
  - proper training of the employer's employees and the maintenance of records of such training;
  - the implementation of proper emergency procedures in the event of any accident or incident that may affect safety during the transport of dangerous goods;
  - the investigation of and, where appropriate, preparation of reports on serious accidents, incidents or serious infringements recorded during the transport of dangerous goods;
  - the implementation of appropriate measures to avoid the recurrence of accidents, incidents or serious infringements;
  - the account taken of the legal prescriptions and special requirements associated with the transport of dangerous goods in the choice and use of sub-contractors or third parties;
  - verification that employees involved in the transport of dangerous goods have detailed operational procedures and instructions;
  - the introduction of measures to increase awareness of the risks inherent in the transport of dangerous goods;
  - the implementation of verification procedures to ensure the presence, on board the means of transport, of the documents and safety equipment which must accompany transport and the

compliance of such documents and safety equipment with health and safety Regulations; and

- the implementation of verification procedures to ensure compliance with legislation governing loading and unloading of dangerous goods.

Transport packaging

Packaging

Travel implications (Planning)

Research by the Department of the Environment, *Reducing Transport Emissions through Planning* [1993], has shown that the spatial distribution of land use has significant implications for travel. Of particular relevance are population density, population size and regional/urban structure.

Population density

High population densities have been found to:

(a) reduce the average distance travelled to work;

(b) reduce the total amount of travel in the district; and

(c) increase the proportion of travel to work undertaken by public transport.

However, it should be recognised that there is a strong tendency for low density to be associated with higher incomes which, in turn, has implications for car ownership and use.

Population size

The relationship between the size of urban areas and the travel characteristics is an issue of importance in strategic planning, particularly in the context of the allocation of new housing development. A number of conclusions can be drawn:

(a) population decentralisation from the conurbation is associated with an increase in travel demand;

(b) the distance travelled tends to fall as the size of urban areas increases;

(c) there is a sharp rise in the length of work journeys in towns below 50,000 population and, for non-work journeys, of 25,000;

(d) distance travelled by car decreases with increasing urban size;

(e) smaller rural settlements, e.g. below 3,000 population, are especially inefficient;

(f) the most energy efficient urban form is the large town with a high degree of self-containment;

(g) the largest new towns tend to have the highest degree of self-containment.

Urban/regional structure

Studies have shown that:

(a) centralisation has the powerful effect of favouring the use of public transport;

(b) centralisation appears to have some effect in lengthening average journeys;

(c) centralisation tends to reduce the use of the car for work journeys;

(d) poly-centric structures have no major advantages in reducing emissions;

(e) the intermixing of land uses, e.g. employment/residential, within zones does not necessarily reduce travel demand;

(f) decentralisation of workplaces to the suburbs does not automatically lead to a reduction in length or number of work journeys;

(g) concentrating developments in or adjacent to existing centres is likely to be more energy efficient than other alternatives;

(h) green belts may tend to increase travel demand by displacing development to more distant locations.

Sustainability

Sustainable development

Treatment

Treatment involves the physical, chemical or biological processing of wastes to reduce their volume or relative harmfulness.

In relation to waste electrical and electronic equipment, this means any activity after the waste electrical and electronic equipment has been handed over to a facility for depollution, disassembly, shredding, recovery or preparation for disposal and any other operation carried out for the recovery and/or disposal of the waste electrical and electronic equipment.

[Waste Electrical and Electronic Equipment (Waste Management Licensing) (England and Wales) Regulations 2006]

Reduction

Waste

Waste electrical and electronic equipment

Treaty on European Union

The European Economic Community (EEC) was established by the Treaty of Rome in 1957. This has since been amended by the Single European Act 1986, which introduced many significant changes to the original Treaty. This Act established the power of the Community to take action in the field of environmental protection.

The Treaty on European Union actually created the European Union, an institutional framework for political co-operation between the Member States of the Community.

Single European Act 1986

Trespass

Trespass implies the intentional invasion of somebody's person, land or goods. An action for trespass involves a civil claim for damages resulting from false imprisonment, unlawful entry on to the land of another, assault and battery.

Trespass to land is defined as the unjustifiable physical interference with land arising from intentional or negligent entry on to the land. A *continuing trespass* may be caused by continuing entry on to the land or by allowing physical matter to remain on the land.

In order for an action for trespass to land to be brought, three key elements must be present:

(a) that the trespass was direct;

(b) that the act was intentional or negligent; and

(c) a causal link must be proved between the directness of the act and the inevitability of its consequences.

The normal remedies in an action for trespass are an award of damages and/or an injunction.

Damages

Injunction

Negligence

Nuisance

Tort

True Cost of Waste (TCOW)

The cost of waste is always much greater than merely the cost of disposal and can be as much as 5 – 10% of an organisation's turnover. Waste disposal is the obvious visible cost but there are numerous hidden costs.

Waste activity

Waste disposal: hazardous substances

Waste: duty of care

Waste management strategies and policies

Waste minimisation: process or resource efficiency

Waste Minimisation Act 1998

U

Ultra violet light

Ultra violet light occurs naturally from sunlight. It is also manufactured for use in industrial, commercial, public services and medical applications.

Ultra violet light represents a section of the overall electromagnetic spectrum of light extending from the blue end of the visible (400 nm) to the X-ray region (100 nm). It is sub-divided into three distinct wavelength regions described as either UV-A, UV-B or UV-C in increasing order of photon energy.

UV - A 400 nm - 315 nm

This is often referred to as 'black light' and is the longest wavelength region with the lowest energy. It represents the largest portion of natural UV light.

UV - B 315 nm - 280 nm

This is partially blocked by the ozone layer and is the most aggressive component of natural UV light. It is largely responsible for sunburn.

UV - C 280 nm - 100 nm

This is only encountered from artificial light sources since it is totally absorbed by the Earth's atmosphere.

Radiation

Unauthorised or harmful deposits

It is a criminal offence to:

(a) deposit, treat or keep controlled waste, or knowingly permit it to be deposited, treated or kept, without a current Waste Management Licence or in breach of the conditions of a licence (except for domestic household waste dealt with on the premises by the householder); or

(b) treat, keep or dispose of controlled waste in a manner likely to cause pollution of the environment or harm to human health; or

(c) contravene any condition of a Waste Management Licence.

The deposit of waste other than controlled waste can, in certain circumstances, also be a criminal offence.

Statutory nuisances

Waste offences

Urban Regeneration and the Environment (URGENT)

This is a thematic programme of research funded by the Natural Environment Research Council. It aims to stimulate the regeneration of the urban environment through understanding and managing the interaction of natural and man-made processes.

The programme was established to integrate urban ecological and environmental research across the geological, terrestrial, fresh water and atmospheric sciences and works in partnership with city authorities, industry and regulatory bodies.

V

Variation Notice

Where the regulator decides to vary the conditions of a permit, whether on application by the operator or otherwise, it shall serve a Notice on the operator (a Variation Notice) specifying the conditions of the variations of the conditions of the permit and the date or dates on which the variations are to take effect and, unless the Notice is withdrawn, the variations specified in the Notice shall take effect on the date or dates so specified.

[Pollution Prevention and Control (England and Wales) Regulations 2000]

Permit

Regulator

Variation of conditions

A Waste Regulation Authority has the discretion to modify the conditions of a Waste Management Licence:

(a) on its own initiative if the modification is desirable and unlikely to require unreasonable expense on the part of the licence holder; or

(b) on the application of the licence holder.

An application for a modification should be determined within two months or such longer period as may be agreed, failing which there is a deemed refusal.

The Authority has a duty to modify the conditions of a licence:

(a) to the extent necessary to ensure that the licensed activities do not cause pollution of the environment or harm to health, or become seriously detrimental to the amenities of the locality; or

(b) to the extent required by any Regulations in force.

The Secretary of State may further make directions relating to the modification of a licence.

Waste Management Licences

Vehicle emission standards

Vehicle exhaust emission standards are enforced by the Vehicle and Operator Services Agency through roadside checks of vehicles. These standards are specified in the Ministry of Transport test scheme for motor vehicles, including heavy goods vehicles and public service vehicles.

Vehicles: pollution from

Vehicles: pollution from

Exhaust emissions from all classes of vehicle are one of the principal sources of air pollution. It is estimated that 87% of the UK's carbon monoxide emissions come from petrol-engined vehicles. These emissions are further responsible for other pollutants such as 1.3 butadiene which has been shown to be linked with increased risks of lymphoma or leukaemia.

Vehicle pollution is currently regulated by the Road Traffic Act 1988, various EC Directives covering vehicle emissions and UK Regulations made under several statutes covering, for example, the construction and use of vehicles and noise from vehicles.

Vehicle emission standards

Ventilation of buildings

Ventilation is the process of simultaneously removing used or vitiated air from a building and replacing it with fresh air.

Two aspects of ventilation must be considered:

(a) the maintenance of healthy and comfortable conditions; and

(b) the removal of dangerous fumes, gases, dusts and vapours that may be produced during a particular process, e.g. welding.

Ventilation may be provided:

(a) by natural means, ie through open windows and doors;

(b) by mechanical means, ie the use of ducts and fans, air conditioning;

(c) through a combination of the above.

Comfort ventilation

Local exhaust ventilation (LEV) systems

Virgin forest

Forest that has never been subject to timbering processes and in which the dominant old-growth tree species have reached their maximum ages.

W

Warning Notice

Noise Act 1996

Waste

Waste is defined in Section 75 of the EPA as:

(a) any substance which constitutes a scrap material or effluent or other unwanted surplus substance arising from the application of any process; and

(b) any substance and article which requires to be disposed of as being broken, worn out, contaminated, or otherwise spoiled.

Anything which is discarded or otherwise dealt with as if it were waste shall be presumed to be waste unless the contrary is proved.

The question of what constitutes waste has been considered by the European Court of Justice (ECJ) in Vessoso and Zanetti (1990). The ECJ had to consider whether the term 'waste' in the Framework Directive on Waste included substances that could be recycled. The Court was clear in its judgement that waste under the Directive included materials intended for recycling, since it was waste as far as the disposer was concerned, irrespective of the intentions of the recipient. This case is important in view of the fact that the Waste Management Licensing Regulations 1994 incorporated the EC definition of *waste* into national law. National courts interpreting the UK Regulations are required to be consistent with the ECJ's decision in this case.

Waste activity

Waste: duty of care

Waste: environmental consequences

Waste hierarchy

Waste holders' duties

Waste offences

Waste Acceptance Criteria

Under the Landfill (England and Wales) Regulations 2002 – 2005 wastes can only be accepted at a landfill if they meet the relevant Waste Acceptance Criteria for that type of landfill.

There are three different Waste Acceptance Criteria:

(a) inert waste;

(b) non-hazardous waste; and

(c) hazardous waste.

Each criterion might include:

(a) a list of acceptable wastes which do not have to be tested; and/or

(b) leaching limit values for a number of contaminants; and/or

(c) limit values for other parameters.

There are also specific provisions, with related criteria, for the disposal of certain wastes under specific conditions. The provisions cover:

(a) stable non-reactive hazardous waste and non-hazardous waste deposited in the same cell with such waste;

(b) gypsum-based waste and other wastes with high sulphate content; and

(c) asbestos waste.

Hazardous waste

Landfill: disposal of waste

Landfill (England and Wales) Regulations 2002 – 2005

Leaching

Waste

Waste Acceptance Procedures

Waste Acceptance Procedures

Part 2 of Schedule 1 of the Landfill (England and Wales) (Amendment) Regulations 2002 – 2005 sets out the methodology for gathering all relevant information for the safe disposal of waste at landfill sites, the Waste Acceptance Procedures. These procedures comprise three levels of assessment:

(a) *Basic characterisation*: a determination of short-term and long-term leaching behaviour and/or characteristic properties of the waste;

(b) *Compliance testing*: periodic spot tests using simple methods to ensure the waste is still as described by the basic characteristics; and

(c) *On-site verification*: to confirm that the waste is as described in the accompanying characterisation documents.

Basic characterisation is the responsibility of the waste producer. Compliance testing and on-site verification are, on the other hand, the responsibility of the landfill operator.

Wastes that are generated regularly in the same process should require less frequent characterisation but more frequent compliance testing.

Hazardous waste

Landfill: disposal of waste

Landfill (England and Wales) Regulations 2002 – 2005

Waste

Waste Acceptance Criteria

Waste acid tars

Tars which:

(a) contain sulphuric acid;

(b) were produced as a result of the refining of benzole, used lubricants or petroleum; and

(c) are or were stored on land used as a retention basin for the disposal of such tars.

Contaminated land

Contaminated Land (England) Regulations 2000

Remediation Notice

Waste activity

Any activity mentioned in paragraph (a) or (b) of Section 33(1) of the Environmental Protection Act 1990 (deposit, keeping, treatment and disposal of waste) other than:

(a) the incineration of waste falling within Part B of Section 5.1 of Part 1 of this Schedule (disposal of waste by incineration); and

(b) an exempt activity, as defined in Regulation 1(3) and Schedule 3 to the Waste Management Licensing Regulations 1994.

Environmental Protection Act 1990

Exempt activity

Incineration

Waste Management Licensing Regulations 1994 – 2006

Waste management option

Waste offences

Waste planning and recycling

Waste transfer

Waste broker

A person who may exercise control over waste but may not necessarily hold it. For the purposes of the duty of care owed by all waste holders, a waste broker may be considered as sharing responsibility for any transfer of waste that he arranges with the actual parties who effect the transfer.

Controlled waste

Duty of care

Environmental Protection Act 1990

Waste

Waste disposal contractor

Waste Collection Authorities (WCAs)

These are the district councils or London boroughs. Their functions are:

(a) to arrange for the collection of household waste in their area;

(b) to arrange for the collection of commercial or industrial waste on request;

(c) to provide bins/receptacles;

(d) to collect waste and deliver for disposal as directed by the waste disposal authority; and

(e) to investigate and make arrangements for recycling.

Waste

Waste offences

Waste Disposal Authorities (WDAs) and Companies

The WDA is normally the county council in non-metropolitan areas and the district council in metropolitan areas. The functions of the WDA are:

(a) making arrangements for the disposal of controlled wastes collected in the area by the Waste Collection Authorities;

(b) formation of waste disposal companies;

(c) provision of municipal waste sites for household waste to be deposited by residents;

(d) provision of transfer stations; and

(e) waste recycling.

Waste

Waste disposal contractor

Waste: duty of care

Waste disposal contractor

A person who in the course of business collects, keeps, treats or disposes of waste, being either:

(a) a company formed for all or any of these purposes by a waste disposal authority; or

(b) a company, partnership or individual (sole trader).

[Environmental Protection Act]

Waste

Waste Disposal Authorities (WDAs) and Companies

Waste disposal: hazardous substances

Procedures for the safe disposal of hazardous substances should be clearly stated in the supplier's safety data sheet. Much will depend upon the types and quantities to be disposed of, but the waste disposal authority should always be consulted as disposal facilities vary considerably in different areas.

The following points should be considered prior to the disposal of hazardous substances:

(a) only trained and authorised staff should be permitted to dispose of dangerous substances;

(b) where large quantities are concerned, disposal should be undertaken in conjunction with the waste disposal authority;

(c) where contractors provide a service, they should provide the following information:

    (i) the location of the disposal site;

    (ii) the procedure for disposal;

    (iii) whether formal licensing is required for the disposal; and

    (iv) the mode of transport of the dangerous substances from the premises to the disposal site.

The Environmental Protection (Duty of Care) Regulations 1991, made under the EPA, established a system of Transfer Notes and record keeping of waste transfers to help waste holders to comply with their elements of the duty of care.

The Regulations are accompanied by a Code of Practice "*Waste Management – The Duty of Care*" which recommends a series of steps which would normally be sufficient to satisfy the requirements of this duty of care. The Code is admissible in evidence and, if any provision of the Code appears to a court to be relevant to any question arising in proceedings, it shall be taken into account when determining that question.

Duty of care in respect of waste

Environmental Protection (Duty of Care) Regulations 1991

Waste Disposal Authorities (WDAs) and Companies

Waste holders' duties

Waste Management Licences

Waste Management Licensing Regulations 1994 – 2006

Waste offences

Waste Disposal Plans by Waste Regulation Authorities

Waste Regulation Authorities are required to produce a Waste Disposal Plan. This entails consideration of the arrangements required for treating or disposing of controlled waste within their area in order to prevent or minimise pollution of the environment or harm to human health.

A Waste Disposal Plan should specify:

(a) the kinds and quantities of controlled waste the Authority expects to find in its area, or to be transported in or out of the area;

(b) methods of disposal;

(c) licensing policy;

(d) the sites and disposal methods in use and expected to come into use; and

(e) the expected costs,

for the period of the Plan.

The Authority is also required to have regard to the desirability, where reasonably practicable, of giving priority to recycling waste.

In preparation of the Plan, the Waste Regulation Authority must consult the National Rivers Authority, the Waste Collection Authorities in the area, other local authorities affected and representatives of the waste disposal and treatment industries in the area or likely to be in the area.

Controlled waste

Harm

National Rivers Authority

Pollution of the environment

Recycling and disposal of waste

Waste Collection Authorities (WCAs)

Waste Disposal Authorities (WDAs) and Companies

Waste planning and recycling

Waste Recycling Plans

Waste Regulation Authorities (WRAs)

Waste: duty of care

The duty of care in respect of waste applies to any person who imports, produces, carries, keeps, treats or disposes of controlled waste or, as a broker, has control of such waste.

Environmental Protection Act 1990

Environmental Protection (Duty of Care) Regulations 1991

Waste

Waste holders' duties

Waste electrical and electronic equipment

The Waste Electrical and Electronic Equipment (Waste Management Licensing) (England and Wales) Regulations 2006 implemented the Waste Electrical and Electronic Equipment Directive and amended the Waste Management Licensing Regulations 1994.

This Directive aims to minimise the impact of electrical and electronic goods on the environment by increasing re-use and recycling and reducing the amount of such goods going to landfill. It seeks to achieve this by making producers responsible for financing the collection, treatment and recovery of waste electrical and electronic equipment, and by obliging distributors to allow consumers to return their waste equipment free of charge.

The Regulations apply to any organisation which manufactures, imports or re-brands electrical goods and apply to waste electrical and electronic equipment falling within the ten product categories listed in the Directive, namely:

1. Large household appliances
2. Small household appliances
3. IT and telecommunications equipment
4. Consumer equipment
5. Lighting equipment
6. Electrical and electronic tools
7. Toys, leisure and sports equipment
8. Medical devices
9. Monitoring and control instruments
10. Automatic dispensers

The Regulations apply to the following groups:

(a) producers – any business that manufactures, imports or re-brands electrical and electronic products;

(b) retailers and distributors – any business that sells electrical and electronic equipment to end users;

(c) local authorities;

(d) the waste management industry;

(e) exporters and reprocessors; and

(f) business and household users of electrical and electronic equipment.

Waste

Waste: duty of care

Waste: environmental consequences

Waste Management Licensing Regulations 1994

Waste: environmental consequences

The environmental consequences of waste include:

(a) depletion of resources lost in waste;

(b) the waste of energy in avoidable collection, processing, transport and disposal of waste;

(c) the potential for pollution of air, water and land;

(d) loss of habitat; and

(e) the environmental consequences of landfill operations.

Habitat

Landfill (England and Wales) Regulations 2002 – 2005

Release into the air: substances

Release into water: substances

Release to land: substances

Waste

Waste disposal: hazardous substances

Waste: duty of care

Waste offences

Waste hierarchy

The ranking of waste management options in order of sustainability.

Sustainability

Sustainable waste management

Waste holders' duties

Section 34 of the EPA provides that the duty of care applies to any person who imports, produces, carries, keeps, treats or disposes of controlled waste or, as a broker, has control of such waste (waste holders).

Each waste holder is bound by the duty of care to take all such measures applicable to him in that capacity as are reasonable in the circumstances:

(a) to prevent any other person committing the offences in Section 33 (prohibition on unauthorised or harmful deposit, treatment or disposal, etc of waste);

(b) to prevent the escape of the waste from his control or that of any other person;

(c) to ensure that if the waste is transferred, it is transferred only to an authorised person or to a person for authorised transport purposes; and

(d) when waste is transferred, to make sure that it is accompanied by a written description of the waste which will enable other persons to avoid a contravention of Section 33 of the Act and to comply with the duty under Section 34(1) to prevent the escape of waste.

Authorised transport purposes

Environmental Protection Act 1990

Transfer Note

Waste offences

Waste Local Plans

These are plans produced by local authorities for effective disposal of waste by landfill. Such plans are based on:

(a) emphasis on land utilisation policies;

(b) the need for sites and facilities;

(c) the identification of suitable landfill locations; and

(d) identified planning criteria for the development of such sites.

Waste Local Plans must complement the Waste Disposal Plans prepared by the Waste Regulatory Authorities under the EPA.

Waste Disposal Plans by Waste Regulation Authorities

Waste Regulatory Authorities

Waste Management (England and Wales) Regulations 2006

All persons involved with all forms of waste have a duty of care to ensure that it is dealt with correctly and does not pollute the environment.

These Regulations, known as the "Agricultural Waste Regulations", lay down requirements for the effective management of waste by both producers of waste and those who dispose of it or recover it.

Producers of waste have a duty to ensure:

(a) waste contractors have the facilities to deal with waste and are authorised to carry waste;

(b) the waste is transferred to a licensed site; and

(c) the person receiving the waste is issued with a waste Transfer Note which includes a description of the waste and signed by both parties.

Copies of Transfer Notes must be retained for at least two years.

Producers must deal with waste in a number of ways:

Waste storage

Waste can be stored for up to 12 months and must be stored securely to ensure it does not escape from the producer's control or cause pollution. Waste must be stored in appropriate containers.

Waste recovery or disposal

Waste can be removed to a recovery or disposal site by the producer.

Waste transfer

Waste can be transferred to an authorised waste disposal carrier. A Duty of Care Transfer Note must be completed and a copy retained.

Register licence exemptions

In the case of agricultural waste, it may be necessary to register one or more exemptions.

Manage the waste

Where waste producers are considering diversifying into waste management, they must obtain a Waste Management Licence or a Pollution Prevention and Control (PPC) Permit.

Agricultural waste

Environmental Protection (Duty of Care) Regulations 1991

Permit

Pollution Prevention and Control (PPC)

Waste

Waste Management Licences

Waste management facility (licensed site)

Licensed site (waste management facility)

Waste Management Licences

Section 35 of the EPA defines a Waste Management Licence as 'a licence granted by a Waste Regulation Authority (WRA) authorising the treatment, keeping or disposal of any specified description of controlled waste in or on specified land or the treatment or disposal of any specified description of controlled waste by means of a specified mobile plant'.

Where a WRA grants a licence, it will do so subject to any conditions that it deems appropriate. There are two types of Waste Management Licence, namely the site licence, which is granted to the occupier of land, and the mobile plant licence.

An application for a Waste Management Licence must be made to the WRA in writing accompanied by the appropriate fee. No licence can be granted in relation to land unless there is planning permission or an established use certificate which authorises the particular use. A WRA may not reject an application that has been properly made unless:

(a) the applicant is not a fit and proper person;

(b) the rejection is necessary to prevent pollution to the environment, harm to human health or serious detriment to the amenities of the locality.

Waste Management Licensing Regulations 1994 – 2006

These Regulations established a system of waste management licensing and a redefinition of the meaning of 'waste' as previously defined in the EPA.

The Regulations give effect to the definition of 'waste' provided in EC Directive 91/156 which amended the Waste Framework Directive 75/442. As a consequence, waste which is not 'Directive waste' is not household, industrial or commercial waste.

An operator may need a Waste Management Licence if he:

(a) deposits waste;

(b) keeps waste, i.e. stores waste produced by another person;

(c) treats waste, including recycling and the use of mobile plant; or

(d) disposes of waste.

This may be in or on any land or by means of mobile plant, or if the operator knowingly permits any of these activities.

The need for a licence depends on the duration of storage of the waste, the types and quantities of waste to be handled and the activity carried out on site. Where the activity may be exempt from licensing, the operator may still need to register with the local environmental regulator and will be subject to controls to prevent harm to health and pollution of the environment.

Operators who collect, transport, store, handle, process or dispose of animal by-products or catering waste which are not intended for human consumption must meet additional requirements.

To register exemptions with the relevant regulatory authority, an applicant must complete a form provided by the authority and:

(a) provide any plans or other documents that the authority reasonably requests;

(b) state the quantity of waste to be disposed of or recovered; and

(c) pay the relevant fee.

In return, the regulator is expected to enter the particulars in a register or, within 35 days, reject the application, providing written reasons for this rejection. The penalty for failing to register an exemption is set at level 3, currently a maximum of £1000. A renewal application must be made every year.

The Regulations require an establishment to maintain (with certain exceptions) records of the quantity, nature, origin and, where relevant, the destination and treatment method of all waste recovered in the course of that activity. Records, including waste quantities and movements, must be compiled on a monthly basis and maintained for at least two years, and must be available for inspection by the regulator.

Other areas covered by the Regulations include:

(a) land treatment for agricultural use;

(b) reclamation or improvement of land; and

(c) the storage and use of building waste.

Animal by-products

Animal By-Products Regulations 2005

Directive waste

Mobile plant

Regulator

Waste offences

Waste management option

The *Waste Benchmarker* and *Waste Exchange/Materials Calculator* identify the methods of disposal or recovery used for particular waste streams using data from the National Waste Production Survey. Seven different waste management options are used for reporting.

Land disposal

This includes all landfill activities plus lagoon disposal and deep injection to borehole when these are used as disposal methods.

Land recovery

This includes spreading waste on land and surface injection (of organic waste for beneficial treatment of agricultural land), and disposal of inert waste to land under the provisions of waste licensing exemptions.

Re-use

This covers only wastes that are taken off site for re-use. It excludes materials which are re-used on site, i.e. fed back into the manufacturing process.

Recycling

As with re-use, this includes only wastes that are taken off site, and includes materials such as oils and solvents which may be regenerated or refined.

Thermal

This covers incineration with or without energy recovery and the production of waste- derived fuel. It also includes more specialised forms of recovery, such as pyrolysis and gasification.

Treatment

This covers all physico-chemical and biological treatment including anaerobic digestion and composting.

Transfer

Transfer is used for all wastes which do not go directly to final disposal, treatment or recovery. These wastes go through a transfer process and may be bulked up prior to recycling, treatment or disposal.

Disposal

Disposal of waste other than by incineration or landfill

Landfill: disposal of waste

Recovery

Recovery of waste

Re-use

Recycling and disposal of waste

Waste

Waste management strategies and policies

Waste offences

Waste to energy

Waste transfer

Waste management strategies and policies

Recent waste management strategies and polices include:

The European Policy Strategy (1991)

1. Prevention or control at source – use of clean/low waste technology.
2. Reclamation, re-use and recycling as much waste as possible.
3. Disposal of the remaining waste in an environmentally safe manner.

Department of the Environment Policy (1994)

1. Minimise waste production.
2. Make best use of waste that is produced.
3. Minimise pollution from waste.
4. Target 25% of household waste for recycling by the year 2000.

Options (Department of the Environment – 1994)

1. Reduction of waste through improved design and technology.
2. Re-use wherever possible.
3. Recovery through:
   (a) recycling;
   (b) composting; and
   (c) energy recovery.
4. Disposal through:
   (a) incineration; and
   (b) landfill.

Composting

Energy recovery

Household waste

Incineration

Landfill: disposal of waste

Landfill (England and Wales) Regulations 2002 – 2005

Recovery of waste

Recycling and disposal of waste

Reduction

Waste Management (England and Wales) Regulations 2006

Waste minimisation: process or resource efficiency

Waste offences

Waste minimisation: process or resource efficiency

The reduction of waste at source by understanding and changing processes to reduce and prevent waste. Waste minimisation can include the substitution of less environmentally harmful materials in the production process.

Reduction

Waste Minimisation Act 1998

Waste Minimisation Act 1998

This statute gave local authorities new powers to reduce waste at source. Councils may take steps to cut waste, plugging a gap in the powers for Waste Collection Authorities provided by the EPA.

Powers of local authorities

Local authorities may:

(a) include waste minimisation strategies within any waste plan;

(b) give people information about alternatives to wasteful products;

(c) promote waste preventing services;

(d) have reduction targets as well as recycling targets in waste contracts;

(e) promote repair schemes for household appliances; and

(f) attract companies with attractive environmental policies, perhaps by becoming "Waste Prevention Cities".

Recovery and recycling obligations

Reduction

Waste

Waste Collection Authorities (WCAs)

Waste Local Plans

Waste offences

Under Section 33 of the EPA it is an offence to:

(a) deposit controlled waste or knowingly cause or knowingly permit controlled waste to be deposited in or on any land, unless a Waste Management Licence authorising the deposit is in force and the deposit is in accordance with the licence;

(b) treat, keep or dispose of controlled waste, or knowingly cause or knowingly permit controlled waste to be treated kept or disposed of:

(i) in or on any land; or

(ii) by means of any mobile plant;

except under and in accordance with a Waste Management Licence;

(c) treat, keep or dispose of controlled waste in a manner likely to cause pollution of the environment or harm to human health.

In addition to the above offences, there are a number of specific offences under the EPA, namely:

(a) where controlled waste is carried in and deposited from a motor vehicle, the person who controls or is in a position to control the use of the vehicle shall be treated as knowingly causing the waste to be deposited, whether or not he gave any instructions for this to be done (Section 33);

(b) making false statements when applying for a Waste Management Licence (Section 44);

(c) interfering with a waste site and receptacle for waste unless that person has the consent of the relevant authority, contractor or other person (Section 60);

(d) depositing waste other than controlled waste in certain circumstances (Section 63).

Controlled waste

Environmental Protection Act 1990

Unauthorised or harmful deposits

Waste

Waste: duty of care

Waste Management Licences

Waste offences

Waste oil

Any mineral-based lubricating or industrial oil which has become unfit for the use for which it was intended, such as used combustion engine oil, gearbox oil, oil for turbines and hydraulic oil.

[Pollution Prevention and Control (England and Wales) Regulations 2000]

Waste on land

The EPA imposes a duty of care on anyone who imports, carries, keeps, treats or disposes of waste. Such persons must take all reasonable steps to ensure that the waste is collected, transported, treated and disposed of by licensed operators, i.e. those issued with a Waste Management Licence.

Public registers must be maintained by the authorities which detail licence conditions and details of enforcement actions. This Part should be read in conjunction with the system for Integrated Pollution Control (IPC) that is enforced by HMIP on prescribed Category A process industries.

Waste Management Licences

Waste Regulation Authorities (WRAs)

Waste planning and recycling

Section 50 of the EPA requires each Waste Regulation Authority to prepare a Waste Disposal Plan.

The recycling of waste is mainly the responsibility of the Waste Collection Authority. However, the Waste Regulation Authorities and the Waste Disposal Authorities have certain duties and powers in this respect.

The requirements for waste recycling are shown below:

- Waste Collection Authorities have a duty to investigate the arrangements that can practicably be implemented for the recycling of household and commercial waste (Section 49).
- Waste Regulation Authorities are required to consider the desirability of giving priority to waste recycling when drawing up Waste Disposal Plans. However, they need only consider action which is reasonably practicable (Section 50).
- A Waste Collection Authority can require household waste to be placed in separate containers or receptacles if certain wastes are to be recycled (Section 46).

Controlled waste

Directive waste

Environmental Protection Act 1990

Household waste

Recycling and disposal of waste

Waste Collection Authorities (WCAs)

Waste Disposal Authorities (WDAs) and Companies

Waste Disposal Plans by Waste Regulation Authorities

Waste Recycling Plans

Waste Regulation Authorities (WRAs)

Waste Recycling Plans

Every Waste Collection Authority is required to prepare a Waste Recycling Plan under Section 49 of the EPA. In preparation of the Plan, the Authority must consider:

(a) the effect that recycling proposals will have on the amenities in the locality; and

(b) the likely cost or saving to the Authority.

A copy of the Plan must be available for public inspection.

Controlled waste

Recycling and disposal of waste

Waste Collection Authorities (WCAs)

Waste Regulation Authorities (WRAs)

In England, the WRAs function in non-metropolitan counties is given to county councils. In the metropolitan areas, the WRAs are the district councils, with special authorities established for Greater London, Greater Manchester and Merseyside.

The main functions of the WRA are:

(a) preparation of Waste Disposal Plans;

(b) control over the waste management licensing system;

(c) supervision of licensed activities;

(d) inspection of licensed land and landfill sites;

(e) maintaining the public registers; and

(f) reporting to the Secretary of State.

Landfill: disposal of waste

Landfill (England and Wales) Regulations 2002 – 2005

Public registers of information: installations and mobile plant

Public registers of information: waste disposal

Waste Management Licences

Waste Regulatory Authorities

The EPA created three different levels of waste authority, each with a different role in relation to waste management, namely:

(a) Waste Regulation Authorities;

(b) Waste Disposal Authorities; and

(c) Waste Collection Authorities.

Waste Collection Authorities (WCAs)

Waste Disposal Authorities (WDAs) and Companies

Waste Regulation Authorities (WRAs)

Waste strategy

Environment Act 1995

Waste to energy

The practice of incinerating waste products to generate steam, heat or electricity.

Waste transfer

To comply with the duty of care under the EPA, it is essential to ensure that waste is transferred only to authorised persons or to a person for authorised transport purposes.

The following are authorised persons:

- Waste Collection Authority;
- the holder of a Waste Management Licence;
- persons exempted by Regulations made by the Secretary of State under Section 33(3);
- a registered carrier under Section 2 of the Control of Pollution (Amendment) Act 1989;
- any person required not to be registered under the Control of Pollution (Amendment) Act 1989.

Authorised transport purposes

Environmental Protection Act 1990

Waste Collection Authorities (WCAs)

Waste Management Licences

Waste unlawfully deposited

Section 33 of the EPA deals with the unauthorised or harmful deposit, treatment or disposal etc of waste thus:

A person shall not:

(a) deposit controlled waste, or knowingly cause or knowingly permit controlled waste to be deposited in or on any land unless a Waste Management Licence authorising the deposit is in force and the deposit is in accordance with the licence;

(b) treat, keep or dispose of controlled waste, or knowingly cause or knowingly permit controlled waste to be treated, kept or disposed of:

(i) in or on any land; or

(ii) by means of any mobile plant,

except under and in accordance with a Waste Management Licence;

(c) treat, keep or dispose of controlled waste in a manner likely to cause pollution of the environment or harm to human health.

Controlled waste

Environmental Protection Act 1990

Waste

Waste Management Licensing Regulations 1994 – 2006

Waste Management Licences

Waste offences

Water

Water should be taken to include underground and surface waters (both natural and in man-made structures), the latter to include inland waters (i.e. rivers, canals, lakes, estuaries and seas).

[Environmental Information Regulations 1992]

Water abstraction

Water is abstracted from rivers, lakes and watercourses for a variety of domestic, agricultural and industrial purposes. The quality of water abstracted is directly related to the quantity of water available at any time and, where water levels may be low as a result of a drought situation, this may cause a reduction in water quality.

Abstraction licences are issued to the occupier of the land following application to the National Rivers Authority. The occupier must be an occupier of land adjacent to the inland water or an occupier of land above the underground strata from which the water is drawn. Where occupation ceases, a new occupier will need to notify the Authority if he wishes to take over the licence.

The Authority may attach conditions to a licence, for instance requiring the abstractor to return the water to the watercourse after use and monitoring the amounts of water abstracted.

National Rivers Authority

Water Resources Act 1991

Water Act 2003

The four broad aims of this statute are:

(a) the sustainable use of water resources;

(b) strengthening the voice of consumers;

(c) a measured increase in competition; and

(d) the promotion of water conservation.

The Act:

(a) provided the Environment Agency with additional tools for managing water resources and stronger powers to take action against abstractions causing environmental damage;

(b) introduced provisions to increase the scope and public availability of information on water resources which are intended to enable abstractors to plan ahead in an environmentally responsible manner;

(c) introduced provisions to increase the flexibility, accountability and administrative efficiency of the abstraction and impounding licensing system with the intended result of increasing the ease of access to sustainable water resources;

(d) established the Water Services Regulatory Authority along with an independent Consumer Council for Water; and

(e) introduced provisions intended to improve the regulatory regime and to extend the opportunities for competition in the water industry by allowing new entrants to supply non-household customers who use large volumes of water.

Environment Agency

Water abstraction

Water Resources Act 1991

Water classification

This is an important feature for determining the current state of controlled waters and for monitoring improvement or deterioration in standards. The *National Water Council Water Classification System* is generally equated to potential uses of water and provides for the following broad classes.

Good Quality (Class 1a)

Water of high quality suitable for use for potable supply abstractions; game or other high class fisheries; high amenity value.

Good Quality (Class 1b)

Water of less high quality than Class 1a but usable for substantially the same purposes.

Fair Quality (Class 2)

Waters suitable for potable supply after advanced treatment; supporting reasonably good course fisheries; moderate amenity value.

Poor Quality (Class 3)

Waters which are polluted to an extent that fish are absent or only sporadically present; may be used for low grade industrial abstraction purposes; considerable potential for further use if cleaned up.

Bad Quality (Class 4)

Waters which are grossly polluted and are likely to cause nuisance.

Figure 14: WATER CLASSIFICATION

Powers of the Secretary of State

Section 82 of the WRA enables the Secretary of State to make Regulations which classify controlled waters according to certain criteria specified in those Regulations, for instance with regard to bathing waters and the presence of dangerous substances in surface water. The criteria specified in Regulations made under Section 82 in relation to any classification of water must consist of one or more of the following requirements:

(a) general requirements as to the purpose for which the waters to which the classification is applied are to be suitable;

(b) specific requirements as to the substances that are to be present or absent from the water and as to the concentrations of substances which are or can be present in the water;

(c) specific requirements as to other characteristics of these waters.

Authorised discharge consent

Bathing Waters (Classification) Regulations 1991

Coastal waters

Consents: controlled waters

Controlled waters

Ground waters

Inland fresh waters

National Rivers Authority

Permit

Trade effluent consents

Trade effluent

Watercourse

Water classification

Water pollution

Water Protection Zones

Water quality objectives and standards

Water conservation

Environment Act 1995

Watercourse

This includes all rivers, streams, ditches, drains, cuts, culverts, dykes, sluices, sewers and passages through which water flows, except mains and other pipes which belong to the National Rivers Authority or a water undertaker or are used by a water undertaker or any other person for the purpose only of providing a supply of water to any premises.

[Water Resources Act 1991]

Coastal waters

Controlled waters

Fresh water limit

Ground waters

Inland fresh waters

Relevant lake or pond

Relevant river or watercourse

Water Resources Act 1991

Water pollution

Pollution of streams, ground water and other basic water sources, such as wells, implies that the polluting agents could eventually enter the public drinking water supply, unless appropriate purification measures are taken. Water distribution systems may also be a cause of contamination from the actual metal pipes, such as lead and copper pipes. Protection of the public water supply from chemical and bacterial contamination has always been one of the principal areas of public health practice. This entails the regular collection of water samples from a variety of sources and their analysis to detect the presence of these various forms of contamination.

Chemical pollution may be caused by free ammonia and ammonium salts in solution, which are indicators of decomposing organic matter, including faecal matter. Chlorine, present as sodium chloride in natural waters, is introduced by sewage. Nitrogen as nitrites suggests recent sewage pollution undergoing oxidation. Nitrogen as nitrates is an indicator of longstanding pollution from sewage. pH is also a measure of water purity, pure water being neutral with a pH of 7. Acidic waters of pH 5.5 or less may indicate the presence of lead.

The bacterial organisms most commonly used as indicators of faecal pollution are the coliform group as a whole, particularly *Escherichia coli*. High counts of *E.coli* suggest recent pollution. Other intestinal organisms occasionally present in water are *Clostridium perfringens*, which is regularly found in faeces, and faecal *Streptococci*.

Chlorine

Discharge consent

Drinking water

Groundwater pollution

Groundwater Regulations 1998

Ground waters

Heavy metal pollution

Lead and lead poisoning

Lead pollution

Nitrogen oxides

Pollution: definition

Polluter Pays Principle

Watercourse

Water power

The harnessing of the energy derived from water, in the form of motive energy or temperature differences is well established. Water energy can take many forms:

(a) hydroelectric energy produced by hydroelectric dams;

(b) tidal power, which captures energy from tides, and linked with the use of turbines;

(c) wave power, which derives its energy from the force of waves;

(d) ocean thermal energy conversion, a technique which uses the temperature difference between the warmer surface of the ocean and the colder lower levels of same; and

(e) deep lake water cooling, which conserves energy during summer months.

Biofuels

Renewable energy

Solar energy

Wind power

Water Protection Zones

Water Protection Zones may be designated by the Environment Agency with a view to preventing or controlling the entry of poisonous, noxious or polluting matter into controlled waters and to prohibit or restrict the carrying on in a particular area of activities which are considered likely to result in the pollution of any such waters. In a Water Protection Zone the carrying on of certain activities is prohibited.

Controlled waters

Water Resources Act 1991

Water quality

Under the Water Act 1989 water companies are placed under a statutory duty when supplying water to any premises for domestic purposes to supply "only water which is wholesome at the time of supply". The wholesomeness of water supplied for domestic purposes, such as drinking, washing and cooking, is defined in the Water Supply (Water Quality) Regulations 1989.

Drinking Water Inspectorate

Environment Act 1995

Water Act 2003

Water pollution

Water Protection Zones

Water quality objectives and standards

Water quality objectives and standards

Under the Water Act 1989 and the Water Resources Act 1991, the National Rivers Authority (now part of the Environment Agency) was provided with powers to control discharges to watercourses. This includes provision for establishing Statutory Water Quality Objectives for any specific stretch of water. These comprise various quality requirements and the date for compliance with same.

The responsibility for ensuring drinking water is clean and wholesome rests with the suppliers of water, namely the various water companies. Standards for wholesomeness are set out in the Water Supply (Water Quality) Regulations 2000 with respect to water supplied for cooking, drinking, food preparation, washing and other domestic purposes. Water is regarded as wholesome if it contains concentrations or values in respect of a number of properties, elements, organisms and substances that comply with the specified concentrations or values prescribed in the Regulations.

The Regulations establish permitted levels for chemicals, such as lead, mercury and fluorine, together with microbiological contaminants, such as *E. coli* and other coliform bacteria.

Water quality objectives and standards are prescribed according to the potential uses of the water (Use Category), which include:

(a) basic amenity;

(b) general ecosystem;

(c) special ecosystem;

(d) salmonid fishery;

(e) cyprinid fishery;

(f) migratory fishery;

(g) commercial harvesting of marine fish;

(h) commercial harvesting of shellfish;

(i) water contact activity;

(j) abstraction for potable water supply; and

(k) abstraction for industrial and commercial use.

Each Use Category incorporates water quality standards according to the needs of that use.

Ecosystems

Fluorides

National Rivers Authority

Water abstraction

Watercourse

Water Resources Act 1991

Water Resources Act 1991

This Act provides the main body of control relating to the prevention and control of water pollution in England and Wales. The National Rivers Authority (NRA) (now the Environment Agency) is responsible for controlling pollution of *controlled waters* and for achieving the improvements in water quality required in order to meet statutory water quality objectives.

Controlled waters

These are defined in Section 104 as:

(a) *inland fresh waters* – including lakes, ponds, rivers or watercourses above the fresh water limit;

(b) *ground waters* – that is waters contained in the underground strata;

(c) *coastal waters* – including all estuarine waters up to the fresh water limits of rivers and watercourses.

Authorised discharge consents

The control of water pollution is exercised by the NRA through a system of authorised consents. Any discharges made into controlled waters must be authorised by the NRA.

This system of consents enables the NRA to control, by means of *conditions*, the nature and volume of contaminants discharged into water in order to achieve improvements in water quality. Any discharge made without consent, or in breach of the conditions attached to a consent, constitutes a criminal offence.

Consents may be granted to such conditions as the NRA may think fit. Conditions may include matters relating to the nature, origin, composition, temperature, volume and rate of the discharges, and as to the periods during which the discharges may be made. The NRA will also stipulate conditions relating to the monitoring of discharges.

In determining whether to grant a discharge consent or deciding certain conditions to be attached to the consent, the NRA are obliged to take into account a variety of factors, most notably the water quality objectives for the receiving waters. Additionally, the NRA must have regard to its environmental duties. A number of other factors will also be relevant in determining whether to grant a consent and the conditions attached to it. These include:

(a) relevant EU standards in relation either to the substance discharged or the quality of the receiving water;

(b) the impact of the proposed discharge on downstream users and other users of the waters, such as fishing and recreational users; and

(c) any representations made either by interested parties or as a result of consultation.

Once the NRA has determined the conditions that are to be included in a consent it is required to give those persons who made earlier representations 21 days in order to make further representations. The consent cannot be granted until this 21-day period expires.

Provision is made for appeals against the determinations of the NRA to be made to the Secretary of State.

Offences and penalties

Section 85 of the WRA creates the following offences relating to the pollution of controlled waters. A person contravenes this Section if he causes or knowingly permits:

(a) any poisonous, noxious or polluting matter or any solid waste matter to enter any controlled waters or discharges trade or sewage effluent into controlled waters;

(b) any matter, other than trade effluent or sewage effluent, to enter controlled waters by being discharged from a drain or sewer in contravention of a prohibition imposed under Section 86;

(c) any trade effluent or sewage effluent to be discharged into any controlled waters or from land (in England and Wales) through a pipe, into the sea outside the seaward limits of controlled waters;

(d) any trade effluent or sewage effluent to be discharged in contravention of any prohibition imposed under Section 86, from a building or from any fixed plant either onto or into any land or into any waters of a lake or pond that are not inland fresh waters;

(e) any matters whatever to enter any inland fresh waters so as to tend to impede the proper flow of the waters in a manner leading to, or likely to lead to, substantial aggravation of pollution due to other causes or the consequences of such pollution.

Any person who contravenes the provisions of Part III of the WRA, or the conditions of any consent given under the Act, is guilty of a criminal offence and liable:

(a) on summary conviction, to imprisonment for a term not exceeding three months, or to a fine not exceeding £20,000 or to both;

(b) on conviction or indictment, to imprisonment for a term not exceeding two years or to an unlimited fine or to both.

Enforcement

The NRA employs authorised inspectors who have wide-ranging powers, and the authority has the power to prosecute offenders. Inspectors appointed under the Act may:

(a) enter any premises to ascertain whether an offence is or has been committed;

(b) carry out inspections, measurements and tests;

(c) carry out experimental borings; and

(d) install and operate monitoring equipment.

In addition, the NRA has the power to take action to avoid pollution of controlled water, or to take remedial measures after a water pollution incident and recover reasonable costs for such measures from those responsible.

The NRA can serve a Prohibition Notice on a person who discharges into controlled water prohibiting the discharge or prohibiting the continuation of the discharge. Alternatively, the Notice may prohibit the discharge unless certain conditions are observed. It is an offence to discharge in contravention of the terms of a Prohibition Notice.

Wilderness

The wilderness is, fundamentally, a natural environment which has not been modified or affected by human activity.

Ecosystems

Wildlife

This includes all non-domesticated animals, plants and other organisms.

Ecosystems
Wildlife and Countryside Act 1981

Wildlife and Countryside Act 1981

This statute covers the protection of wildlife, nature conservation and public rights of way.

Specific provisions apply in the case of wild birds, animals and plants.

Wildlife

Wild birds

It is an offence to intentionally kill, injure or take any wild bird, their eggs or their nests, disturb specified birds at their nests or their depending young, and to use certain methods of killing, injuring or taking birds.

The Secretary of State may designate Areas of Special Protection to provide further protection to birds. The Act further restricts the sale and possession of captive bred birds and sets standards for keeping birds in captivity.

Wild animals

It is an offence to intentionally kill, injure, take, possess or trade in any specified wild animal. The interference with places used for shelter or protection, or the intentional disturbance of animals occupying such places, is prohibited, together with certain methods of killing, injuring or taking wild animals.

Wild plants

It is an offence to pick, uproot, trade in or possess for the purposes of trade any listed wild plant. The unauthorised intentional uprooting of such plants is prohibited.

Nature Conservation, Countryside and National Parks

This Part provides for:

(a) the notification of Sites of Special and Scientific Interest by the country agencies, together with measures for the protection and management of such sites;

(b) the making of Limestone Pavement Orders which prohibit the disturbance and removal of limestone from such designated areas; and

(c) the designation of Marine Nature Reserves and the bye-laws designed to protect these areas.

The Act prohibits the undertaking of forestry or agricultural operations on land within National Parks which has been either moor or heath land within National Parks.

Public Rights of Way

Surveying authorities must maintain up-to-date definitive maps and statements for the purpose of clarifying public rights of way. The Act also incorporates provisions for traffic Regulation, ploughing, appointing wardens, signposting and the prohibiting of the keeping of bulls on land crossed by public rights of way.

Conservation Area

Endangered species

National Parks

Sites of Special and Scientific Interest

Wilderness

Wildlife

Wind power

Wind power uses kinetic energy in airflows to run wind turbines. A wind turbine is a mechanical device consisting primarily of rotor blades mounted on a tower in order to capture prevailing winds to generate electrical power.

Wind power is increasing in popularity as a renewable energy technology. Due to the variability of wind resources, most turbines produce electricity at an average of 25% of their rated maximum power, but under favourable wind regimes, this can reach 35% or higher.

Wind power is renewable and produces no greenhouse gases during operation. The use of wind turbines is advocated by many organisations and industrialised nations as a means of reducing greenhouse gas emissions.

Greenhouse gases

Renewable energy

Solar energy

Water power

Work environment

The work environment is concerned with the comfort of workers and freedom from environmental stressors whilst at work.

The design and control of the work environment is an important aspect of health and safety in the workplace. Environmental working conditions also have a direct effect on human behaviour at work, the degree of risk of occupational disease and/or injury, and on morale, management/worker relations, labour turnover and profitability.

Fundamentally, three aspects must be considered, namely:

(a) the organisation of the working environment;

(b) the prevention or control of environmental stressors; and

(c) welfare arrangements,

which are dealt with in the Workplace (Health, Safety and Welfare) Regulations 1992 and ACOP to same.

Stress, associated with extremes of temperature, poor standards of lighting and noise is a contributory factor to accidents and occupational ill-health. Many forms of occupational ill-health, e.g. heat stroke, pneumoconiosis and noise-induced hearing loss, are directly associated with a failure to protect people from health risks. Employers need to consider the provision of a healthy working environment in terms of ventilation systems, temperature control, and control over hazardous physical, chemical, biological and work-related agents.

Environmental monitoring in the workplace

Grit, dust and fumes

Isocyanates

Legionnaires' disease

Sick Building Syndrome

Temperature control in the workplace

Ventilation of buildings

Workplace exposure limits (WELs)

Workplace exposure limits (WELs)

HSE Guidance Note EH40 *Workplace exposure limits* gives details of exposure limits that should be used for determining the adequacy of control of exposure of employees by inhalation to substances hazardous to health.

A workplace exposure limit (WEL) is defined as the maximum concentration of an airborne substance, averaged over a reference period, to which employees may be exposed by inhalation. WELs are listed in HSE Guidance Note EH40.

The advice given in Guidance Note EH40 should be taken in the context of the requirements of the Control of Substances Hazardous to Health (COSHH) Regulations, especially:

(a) Regulation 6 (health risk assessment)

(b) Regulation 7 (control of exposure)

(c) Regulations 8 and 9 (use and maintenance of control measures)

(d) Regulation 10 (monitoring of exposure at the workplace)

Virgin forest

Forest that has never been subject to timbering processes and in which the dominant old-growth tree species have reached their maximum ages.

Correct application of the "principles of good practice" outlined in the COSHH Regulations should ensure exposures are controlled below the WEL. Additional guidance may be found in the COSHH General ACOP.

Units of measurement

The list of WELs given in the Guidance Note, unless stated otherwise, relate to personal exposure to substances hazardous to health in the workplace.

Concentrations of gases and vapours in air are usually expressed as parts per million (ppm), a measure of concentration by volume, as well as in milligrams per cubic metre (mg/m^3) of air, a measure of concentration by mass.

Concentrations of airborne particles (fume, dust, etc) are expressed usually in mg/m^3, with the exception of mineral fibres, which are expressed as fibres per millilitre of air.

Control of Substances Hazardous to Health (COSHH) Regulations 2006

Ventilation of buildings

Works Notice

This is a Notice served by the Environment Agency where there may be a potential pollution incident or in the case of an actual pollution incident.

A Works Notice shall:

(a) in the case of a potential pollution incident, describe the nature of the risk to controlled waters, identifying the controlled water which may be affected and the place from which the matter in question is likely to enter those waters;

(b) in the case of an actual pollution incident, describe the nature and extent of the pollution, identifying the controlled waters affected by it;

(c) specify the works of operations required to be carried out by the person on whom the Notice is served, stating his name and address;

(d) give the Agency's reasons for serving the Notice on that person and for requiring those works or operations to be carried out;

(e) inform the person on whom the Notice is served of his right of appeal under Section 161C of the Act (including the time for appealing) and of the requirements imposed by Regulation 3 in relation to its exercise;

(f) state the Agency is entitled (unless the Notice is quashed or withdrawn) to recover from the person on whom the Notice is served its costs or expenses reasonably incurred in carrying out such investigations as are mentioned in Section 161(1) of the Environment Act; and

(g) set out the consequences of Section 161D(1) to (4) of the Act (consequences of not complying with a Works Notice).

Anti-Pollution Works Regulations 1999

Appeals

Controlled waters

Environment Act 1995

Environment Agency

Pollution incidents

Regulator

Other titles from Thorogood

THE A-Z OF HEALTH AND SAFETY

Jeremy Stranks

P/B • 658 pages **£19.99**

ISBN(10): 1 85418 387 7 • (13): 978-185418387-3

R/B • 658 pages **£55.00**

ISBN(10): 1 85418 382 6 • (13): 978-185418382-8

Health and safety law and practice has changed considerably in recent years and all organisations must be fully up to speed with best practice. In accessible A-Z format, this book is a major new reference work by an acknowledged expert in an area of crucial importance to every organisation, large and small, private and public.

THE A-Z OF FOOD SAFETY

Jeremy Stranks

P/B • 520 pages **£19.99**

ISBN(10): 1 85418 379 6 • (13): 978-185418379-8

R/B • 520 pages **£55.00**

ISBN(10): 1 85418 384 2 • (13): 978-185418384-2

A detailed and comprehensive guide to the legal and practical risks associated with food safety, including all the latest developments in UK and European legislation – in accessible A-Z format. A timely and valuable source of reference and guidance in an increasingly litigious society for everyone working in environmental health, food production and sales and catering.

THE A-Z OF EMPLOYMENT PRACTICE

David Martin

P/B • 712 pages • 2nd edition **£19.99**

ISBN(10): 1 85418 327 3 • (13): 978-185418327-9

R/B • 712 pages • 2nd edition **£55.00**

ISBN(10): 1 85418 322 2 • (13): 978-185418322-4

This book comes at a time when managers are faced with still more new legislation, obligations and potential penalties. It explains what the law is and then what to do, providing expert advice on every aspect of employment practice from recruitment, pay and incentives to maternity/paternity leave, personnel records, contracts and holidays.

"This book covers everything you need to know about good employment practice... This is a really useful book. Every manager should have one."

PROFESSIONAL MANAGER

"This book will be of value to all businesses, particularly perhaps smaller businesses where the director/owner needs to be his or her own personnel or HR manager... a valuable guide for every manager and would-be leader."

JOHN SUNDERLAND. CHAIRMAN, CADBURY SCHWEPPES PLC

THE A-Z OF FACILITIES AND PROPERTY MANAGEMENT

David Martin

P/B • 416 pages **£19.99**

ISBN(10): 1 85418 313 3 • (13): 978-185418313-2

R/B • 416 pages **£55.00**

ISBN(10): 1 85418 3184 • (13): 978-185418318-7

A major new reference work, in an easy-to-use A-Z format, covering all aspects of facilities and property management, strategy, administration and control, backed up by a wealth of practical suggestions. Covers all the latest legislation on waste, energy consumption and environmental issues and offers valuable insights into the management of property assets.

THE A-Z OF MANAGEMENT CONCEPTS AND MODELS

Bengt Karlof and Fredrik Lövingsson

P/B • 440 pages **£18.99**
ISBN(10): 1 85418 390 7 • 13): 978-185418390-3

H/B • 440 pages **£35.00**
ISBN(10): 1 85418 385 0 • (13): 978-185418385-9

An A-Z of all the essential concepts and models applied in business and management. A superb and comprehensive source of reference for professionals and students, with 124 detailed entries from Balanced scorecard to Zero-based planning.

MANAGE TO WIN

Norton Paley

P/B • 448 pages **£15.99**
ISBN(10): 1 85418 395 8 • (13): 978-185418395-8

H/B • 448 pages **£29.99**
ISBN(10): 185418 301 X • (13): 978-185418301-9

Learn how to reshape and reposition your company to meet tougher challenges and competitors, when to confront and when to retreat, how to assess risk and opportunity and how to move to seize opportunities and knock out the competition.

"This book is a 'must have' for any manager intent on success."
EDWARD J. FRED, CEO & PRESIDENT, CPI AEROSTRUCTURES, INC.

MANAGING PEOPLE FOR THE FIRST TIME

Julie Lewthwaite

P/B • 352 pages **£12.99**
ISBN(10): 1 85418 332 X • (13): 978-185418332-3

"The value of this book is that it makes a worthwhile attempt to help the first-time manager. Combining training material with a storyline involving real people makes it a lot more digestible than a textbook."
PEOPLE MANAGEMENT

"There are books on managing people by the truckload, but little specifically for the first time manager. The whole range of management knowledge, theory and practice is contained in this easily absorbed text." BUSINESS EXECUTIVE

MASTERING PEOPLE MANAGEMENT

Mark Thomas

P/B • 232 pages • 2nd edition **£14.99**

ISBN(10): 1 85418 328 1 • (13):978-185418328-6

How to build and develop a successful team by motivating, empowering and leading people. Based on in-depth experience of developing people and initiating change within many organisations, Mark Thomas provides a shrewd, practical guide to mastering the essential techniques of people management.

MASTERING LEADERSHIP

Michael Williams

P/B • 288 pages • 2nd edition **£14.99**

ISBN(10):1 85418 308 7 • (13):978-185418308-8

Without a grasp of what true leadership implies you cannot hope to develop a really effective team. With telling insight, Michael Williams shows what distinguishes truly high-achieving teams from the rest of the pack.

"A must-read for anyone who wants to become a better leader. Easy to read and packed full of practical advice about how to make things happen. A complete course on business leadership and personal development."

DR PATRICK DIXON, CHAIRMAN, GLOBAL CHALLENGE LTD AND FELLOW, LONDON BUSINESS SCHOOL

falconbury
BUSINESS SEMINARS

Focused on developing your potential

Falconbury, the sister company to Thorogood publishing, brings together the leading experts from all areas of management and strategic development to provide you with a comprehensive portfolio of action-centred training and learning.

We understand everything managers and leaders need to be, know and do to succeed in today's commercial environment. Each product addresses a different technical or personal development need that will encourage growth and increase your potential for success.

- Practical public training programmes
- Tailored in-company training
- Coaching
- Mentoring
- Topical business seminars
- Trainer bureau/bank
- Adair Leadership Foundation

The most valuable resource in any organization is its people; it is essential that you invest in the development of your management and leadership skills to ensure your team fulfil their potential. Investment into both personal and professional development has been proven to provide an outstanding ROI through increased productivity in both you and your team. Ultimately leading to a dramatic impact on the bottom line.

With this in mind Falconbury have developed a comprehensive portfolio of training programmes to enable managers of all levels to develop their skills in leadership, communications, finance, people management, change management and all areas vital to achieving success in today's commercial environment.

What Falconbury can offer you?

- Practical applied methodology with a proven results
- Extensive bank of experienced trainers
- Limited attendees to ensure one-to-one guidance
- Up to the minute thinking on management and leadership techniques
- Interactive training

- Balanced mix of theoretical and practical learning
- Learner-centred training
- Excellent cost/quality ratio

Falconbury In-Company Training

Falconbury are aware that a public programme may not be the solution to leadership and management issues arising in your firm. Involving only attendees from your organization and tailoring the programme to focus on the current challenges you face individually and as a business may be more appropriate. With this in mind we have brought together our most motivated and forward thinking trainers to deliver tailored in-company programmes developed specifically around the needs within your organization.

All our trainers have a practical commercial background and highly refined people skills. During the course of the programme they act as facilitator, trainer and mentor, adapting their style to ensure that each individual benefits equally from their knowledge to develop new skills.

Falconbury works with each organization to develop a programme of training that fits your needs.

Mentoring and coaching

Developing and achieving your personal objectives in the workplace is becoming increasingly difficult in today's constantly changing environment. Additionally, as a manager or leader, you are responsible for guiding colleagues towards the realization of their goals. Sometimes it is easy to lose focus on your short and long-term aims.

Falconbury's one-to-one coaching draws out individual potential by raising self-awareness and understanding, facilitating the learning and performance development that creates excellent managers and leaders. It builds renewed self-confidence and a strong sense of 'can-do' competence, contributing significant benefit to the organization. Enabling you to focus your energy on developing your potential and that of your colleagues.

Mentoring involves formulating winning strategies, setting goals, monitoring achievements and motivating the whole team whilst achieving a much improved work life balance.

falconbury
BUSINESS LAW SEMINARS

Falconbury – Business Legal Seminars

Falconbury Business Legal Seminars specialises in the provision of high quality training for legal professionals from both in-house and private practice internationally.

The focus of these events is to provide comprehensive and practical training on current international legal thinking and practice in a clear and informative format.

Event subjects include, drafting commercial agreements, employment law, competition law, intellectual property, managing an in-house legal department and international acquisitions.

For more information on all our services please contact: Falconbury on: Telephone +44 (0)20 7729 6677 or visit the website at: www.falconbury.co.uk.